Science Discovers God

Also by Ariel A. Roth: *Origins: Linking Science and Scripture.*

To order, call 1-800-765-6955.

Visit us at www.reviewandherald.com for information on other Review and Herald® products.

Science Discovers God

Seven Convincing Lines of Evidence for His Existence

Autumn House® Publishing
www.autumnhousepublishing.com
A Division of **REVIEW AND HERALD® PUBLISHING**
Since 1861

Published by Autumn House® Publishing, a division of Review & Herald® Publishing, Hagerstown, MD 21741-1119

Autumn House® titles may be purchased in bulk for educational, business, fund-raising, or sales promotional use. For information, please e-mail SpecialMarkets@reviewandherald.com.

This book was
Edited by Gerald Wheeler
Copyedited by James Cavil
Cover design by Trent Truman
Cover art: Close-up of Eye: ©Péter Gudella/123rf.com, Space scene: ©Spectral/123rf.com
Interior design by Tina M. Ivany
Typeset: Bembo 11/14

PRINTED IN U.S.A.

12 11 10 09 08   5 4 3 2 1

Library of Congress Cataloging-in-Publication Data
Roth, Ariel Adrean, 1927-   .
Science discovers God: seven convincing lines of evidence for his existence / Ariel A. Roth.
   p. cm.
Includes index.
1. Religion and science. 2. God—Proof. I. Title.
215-dc22
                              2007004908

ISBN 978-0-8127-0448-8

Dedication

To my very patient wife, Lenore.

She, more than most, realizes that when one writes a book, almost everyone within the sphere of influence of the author also suffers!

Acknowledgments

I am indebted to so very many with whom I have had extensive and most fruitful conversations. My students, and especially my graduate ones, have been a persistent and refreshing source of new ideas and challenges.

I am grateful for the editorial skills of Gerald Wheeler who does marvels as he converts my clumsy wordings into easily understandable expositions. His knowledge, interest, and insights into this convoluted conflict have been especially helpful.

A number of my colleagues with special qualifications and expertise have given extremely helpful and wise suggestions for the manuscript or parts thereof. I am especially indebted to Mark de Groot, James Gibson, Paul Giem, Edwin A. Karlow, Marcus Ross, Larry Roth, William Shea, and Tim Standish for their knowledgeable and wise counsel. However, they bear no responsibility for any of the errors that may have crept into the final copy, nor for my views and prejudices, for which I take full responsibility.

Contents

Preface

Is there any meaning or purpose to human lives? Does God exist? If He does, why does He permit so much suffering? And do we have to believe in Him? After all, hasn't science been able to explain most things without having to invoke God? Our deepest thoughts struggle with such questions as we search for answers about our origin, our purpose for being, and our ultimate destiny. Few are able to ignore these perplexing enigmas as we contemplate the mysteries of our being and the universe we live in. The issue of whether God exists or not is one that simply will not go away.

Fortunately, when it comes to ultimate questions about origins, all is not conjecture. In recent years scientists have made a number of remarkable discoveries that reveal such precision and complexity in the universe around us that it is becoming very difficult to suggest that everything resulted just from chance. It looks as if a very perceptive God had to be involved in designing the marvelous intricacies that we find everywhere in the universe.

Some scientists will immediately insist that science cannot consider God, because it and God represent separate realms of thought. Unfortunately, such a view imposes a narrow outlook on science that limits its ability to find all truth. Science cannot discover God and His role as long as it excludes Him from its explanatory menu. If science hopes to provide meaningful and truthful answers to our deepest questions, it needs to get out of the prison of secularism in which it has now trapped itself. Science should be open to the possibility that God exists and not exclude Him as belonging only to another realm of inquiry. *This book approaches the question of God's existence from the perspective that science is—or at least should be—an open search for truth, and that we will allow the data of nature to direct us wherever it may lead.* Frequently science itself indulges in various speculations and hypotheses, such as the existence of other universes beyond ours or of life originating all by itself. To be consistent, science should also be willing to consider the possibility that there is a God. Such open-mindedness could be important in case God does exist.

It is interesting that the pioneers of modern science, such as Kepler, Galileo, Boyle, Pascal, Linné, and Newton, all included the concept of God in their scientific outlook. They often spoke of Him, and they considered their scientific investigations as the continuing discovery of the laws that He had created. Those intellectual giants demonstrated how science and an awareness of God can work together as we study nature. Since that time science and God have gone separate ways, and at present science essentially ignores the concept of a deity. Furthermore, some scientists are deeply concerned that a religious takeover of society would seriously hamper science. On the other hand, we find suggestions of a renewed interest in God on the part of some scientists and other academicians. This has resulted in part because of recent significant discoveries such as the very exact values necessary for the basic forces of physics, and the extremely complex biochemical pathways of living organisms. Such findings raise grave doubts about any suggestion that they just happened to have come about by chance, and it is becoming more reasonable to believe in the existence of a God behind the origin of the universe than in the extreme improbabilities we have to postulate for a universe that came into being on its own.

This book follows the broad approach that I believe is essential to provide the comprehensive view that the question of God's existence deserves. Because the most significant challenges to His existence have come from science, the discussion focuses essentially on scientifically related topics. In order to help the general reader evaluate the findings and conclusions of science, I have included a number of accounts of how scientists make their discoveries, especially those details that seem to touch on the question of God's existence.

This book starts with a brief historical review that leads us to the surprising fact that four out of 10 scientists in the United States believe in a personal God who answers their prayers. The paradox is that very few, if any, of those same scientists will discuss God in scientific journals and textbooks. What many scientists believe in and what they publish about when they take a scientific stance, can be quite different things. The book then discusses a number of key issues related to God's existence. These include the intricate organization of the matter of the universe and the precision of the forces of physics. Then a number of biological topics will follow, including the origin of life, the genetic code, and such complexities as the eye and the brain. Next we will consider the problem that time poses for evolution when we analyze the fossil record. It turns out that the suggested geologic eons are totally inadequate for the various explanations postulated.

The last third of the book addresses the intriguing question of why, in the context of so much data that seems to require a God in order to explain what we see, scientists still remain silent about Him. We will broach that question from the perspective of both the sociological strength of dominant ideas, such as evolution, and the exclusiveness and elitism of a highly successful scientific enterprise. The conclusion of the book is that science is providing abundant evidence that there is a God. The hope is that scientists are going to allow Him back into the scientific perspective, as once was the case for the pioneers of modern science.

This book deals mainly with two strongly contrasting worldviews. On the one hand, we find those who limit reality only to what they can simply observe in nature. For them, that is essentially all there is. This fits closely with the current scientific mindset or ethos that excludes God. Others believe there exists a transcendent reality above the currently observable. Such a view would mean that our existence does have ultimate meaning. The Being who designed us has endowed us with such attributes as consciousness, understanding, concern for others, and a sense of justice. In other words, there is more to reality than simple observable matter, and our existence has purpose to it. Whichever of these two approaches we adopt has a profound effect on our worldview and personal philosophy. This treatise proposes that the current separation between these two contrasting worldviews is not valid. The data of science itself is essentially forcing us to conclude that something unusual is going on, and that it looks as if a knowledgeable and transcendent God was involved in creating the complexities that scientific observation keeps uncovering.

Is this book objective? Is it free of bias? Unfortunately the answer in both cases is no. Who can claim complete objectivity? On the other hand, I have made every effort to be fair to the data and have paid special attention to the best data. I then invite readers to draw their conclusions on the basis of the data and not just generally accepted inferences. This book is not simply a survey of prevailing interpretations. Some conclusions are not mainline. If we are going to improve on accepted views, we have to be willing to escape from them.

Several terms in the text, such as "truth," "science," "religion," "God," "evolution," and "creation," are vital to the dialogue, but have varied use and meaning. I invite the reader to use the glossary at the end of this book to clarify their meaning as used in this discussion. In some cases I have identified special use in the text.

Having spent more than 50 years dealing with the controversy between science and religion, I very much realize how emotionally laden the worldview issues that delineate one's personal philosophy can become. I am also fully aware that some will find my approach unpleasant. For this I am sorry. We all have much to learn from each other, and I would urge those with different views to keep communicating and contributing to humanity's total fund of knowledge.

Ariel A. Roth
Loma Linda, California

A Note About Large Numbers

I realize that some readers have an aversion to numbers. While I am fascinated with them, I have tried to keep them to a minimum. Occasionally I have had to use extremely large numbers. For quick general comparison, instead of writing out such long numbers, I simply use the common convention of using a superscript number after the ordinary number 10 to indicate the number of zeros present (powers of 10). The following examples illustrate the system.

$$10^1 = 10$$
$$10^2 = 100$$
$$10^3 = 1,000 = \text{a thousand}$$
$$10^4 = 10,000$$
$$10^5 = 100,000$$
$$10^6 = 1,000,000 = \text{a million}$$
$$10^7 = 10,000,000$$
$$10^8 = 100,000,000$$
$$10^9 = 1,000,000,000 = \text{a billion}$$
$$10^{10} = 10,000,000,000$$

Etc.

The little superscript number simply gives the number of times the number 10 is multiplied by itself, and is the same as the number of zeros if I had written the number out the ordinary way. This saves the reader from having to count all the zeros in large numbers, and makes for easier comparisons. For instance, you can easily see that 10^{19} has two more zeros than 10^{17} without having to count all the zeros had they been written out.

In this system the reader needs *especially* to keep in mind that each zero multiplies the number by 10—hence 10^3 (1,000) is 10 times larger than 10^2 (100); and similarly, 10^7 (10,000,000) is 1,000 times smaller than 10^{10} (10,000,000,000).

Chapter One

Can a Scientist Dare to Believe in God?

Science without religion is lame, religion without science is blind.[1]

—*Albert Einstein*

NEVER AT REST

Deeply committed to religion, he wrote extensively about the biblical prophecies of Daniel and the Apocalypse. A member of a commission to build 50 new churches around London, he helped in the distribution of the Bible to the poor.[2] Was he a pastor, a theologian, or an evangelist? No, he was none of them. Instead, he was the individual that many consider to be the greatest scientist of all time. Sir Isaac Newton stood head and shoulders above the other minds of his time as he helped lay down the firm foundations of modern science. Both a profound reverence for God along with a relentless devotion to thorough scientific investigation distinguished his life.

Isaac Newton (Figure 1.1) came into the world as a Christmas Day present in 1642, but unfortunately his father had died three months earlier. He was apparently premature at birth and so small that he could fit in a quart pot. Paradoxically, his meager beginnings from an uneducated and undistinguished family background produced the dean of philosophers of his time. His father, though no pauper, reportedly could not sign his own name. Isaac's childhood was a mosaic of experiences characterized by his insatiable desire to calculate the best design for all kinds of devices such as kites and sundials. Because he loved books and had few friends, preferring study to socializing, people did not always understand or appreciate him. When he left home to become a student at Cambridge University, the servants rejoiced at his departure, commenting wryly that he was fit for nothing but the university.[3] Described as being "never at rest,"[4] he tended to work alone and in-

Figure 1.1 *Sir Isaac Newton. From a painting by Sir Godfrey Kneller around 1689.*
By kind permission of the trustees of the Portsmouth Estates.

tensely on his various projects, sometimes forgetting to eat or sleep.

At Cambridge Newton immediately distinguished himself, and soon became a renowned member of the faculty. He sent to the Royal Society in London a novel kind of reflecting telescope that he had made (Figure 1.2). It caused a great sensation, generating considerable enthusiasm, and soon caught the attention of the leading astronomers of Europe. Shortly thereafter Newton gave the Royal Society thoroughly prepared documents about the properties of light and color that received much appreciation. Because he was reticent about presenting new ideas, years would often pass between the start of a project and when he would let others know about it. He released only a little of his work, "but each portion was an imperishable monument to his genius."[5]

It was probably inevitable that a highly successful but young scientist should draw some criticism from the old guard, and in Newton's case that did not take long. Several controversies developed, and historians have made much of them. Newton could be a formidable foe. After he had spent years on his discoveries, he sometimes found it difficult to be patient with those who had hardly thought at all about his new ideas or did not understand them but instead chose to oppose them.

A famous and prolonged conflict developed between Newton and Robert Hooke, the curator of experiments at the Royal Society. Hooke was no ordinary scientist, bordering on the genius level himself. Furthermore, he had written the treatise *Micrographia,* which also dealt with light and optical topics. Hooke considered himself the final authority on many things and had the obnoxious habit of claiming that he had made most discoveries himself. When the Royal Society in London discussed Newton's ideas and discoveries, Hooke quickly asserted that most of Newton's ideas had already appeared in his *Micrographia.* Newton, who was not there but in Cambridge, eventually pointed out that most of Hooke's concepts about light came from the famous French scientist and philosopher René Descartes! With all the tact of an uncoordinated walrus, Hooke patronizingly suggested to Newton that, as a novice, he should continue to work on telescopes, and leave the field of experimental light to those who had already developed satisfactory concepts.[6]

A severe controversy began brewing. In London secret meetings of the nation's leading intellectuals convened at a popular coffeehouse. They met to discuss Newton's ideas, with Hooke concluding, as expected, that the younger man had adopted some of Hooke's own ideas.[7] The participants also disputed the nature of light, an issue that remains somewhat unsolved to this day. Also they considered the question of what causes different colors of light. Newton, who had performed a multitude of experiments on the topic, briefly

Figure 1.2 *The reflecting telescope that Sir Isaac Newton built and gave to the Royal Society in 1671. By kind permission of the Royal Society. © The Royal Society.*

dismissed Hooke's arguments as invalid. The controversy continued for years until Hooke's death. "To Hooke," one historian summarizes, "Newton was a fearsome rival; to Newton, Hooke was nothing more than an intolerable nuisance, a skulking jackal unfit to feed among the lions."[8]

Others, besides Hooke, also challenged Newton's light concepts. On the main European continent an elderly Jesuit teacher at Liège in Belgium, who called himself Linus, took issue with Newton's ideas about colored light. He had experimented with prisms, as Newton had, and held that clouds in the sky caused the various colors of light. When Linus communicated his views to the Royal Society, Newton replied with instructions on how to conduct a crucial experiment that would settle the dispute, and he urged that the Royal Society try it. Further correspondence from Liège indicated that Linus had died, but that his very loyal pupil, John Gascoines, was ready to take up the battle against Newton. Suggestions that Newton had performed his experiment only once reflect on both a pathetic ignorance of the scientist's thoroughness and the superficiality of the comments from Liège. The Royal Society, with Robert Hooke present, finally performed the crucial experiment that Newton had suggested, and we can surmise that Hooke was not enthusiastic about the outcome.[9] The results were exactly as Newton had predicted. One would think that this would have quieted the objections from Liège, but it didn't. Another professor, Anthony Lucas, took up the battle against Newton, but it soon became obvious that Lucas and Newton operated at two widely different levels of objectivity. Finally Newton requested that letters from Lucas no longer be passed on to him.

Even more famous is the battle between Isaac Newton and Gottfried Wilhelm Leibniz. It involved the issue of which of them had first discovered the complex mathematical procedures of calculus. Soon the disagreement reached international proportions. Leibniz in Germany had a retinue of supporters, mostly on the main European continent, while in England the Royal Society served as a loyal base, endorsing Newton as the inventor. Both scientists had been accused of stealing calculus from the other. The enigma, which historians have investigated ever since, still lacks a few factual details that would permit final resolution. In general, scholars agree that most likely both invented calculus independently,[10] Newton before Leibniz, but Leibniz being the first to publish his findings (the calculus symbols that he developed are still the ones taught today). As the conflict intensified, Newton's camp claimed that Leibniz refused to acknowledge an early letter he had received from Newton that suggested calculus. On the other hand, some have claimed that Newton influenced in his favor the reports from the Royal Society that indicated that he had invented calculus long before Leibniz. Newton was president of that prestigious organization during the last 24 years of his life as the feud continued. As for Leibniz's calculus, Newton was of the opinion that second inventors count for nothing.

One can rightly accuse Newton of being a recluse, especially during his earlier years, and although he shied away from confrontations, he did not hesitate to use the force of his intellect and position to minimize the work of those who opposed him. Yet he also had a kindly side to him. When his half brother became ill with a malignant fever, his mother nursed him to health, but she eventually came down with the fever herself. When he learned what had happened, Isaac left Cambridge and hurried to her home to take personal charge of her care. One of his relatives reports that Newton stayed up whole nights with her, giving her physical treatments, dressing her blisters with his own hands, thus using that manual dexterity for which he was so famous, to lessen the pain.[11] But all his efforts could not stop the devastating disease, and she eventually died. While his mother's second marriage and the fact that she did not bring him up had strained family relationships, he still proved to be a loyal and dutiful son. As executor of her will, he saw to it that she was buried next to his own father whom he had never seen.

Newton, who was reticent to publish anything, eventually published the results of many years of study in his *Principia*[12] which has been hailed as "perhaps the greatest event in the history of science—certainly the greatest till recent years."[13] Furthermore, "no living persons could challenge its originality or power. Newton had become the admitted dictator of scientific thought, and there was no one able to cross swords with him."[14] The importance of the three-volume *Principia* is that it introduced an unprecedented and very high level of observational and mathematical rigor to science, thus dramatically improving respect for such studies. Newton placed the discipline on a much firmer foundation than it had had in the past. *Principia* is full of mathematical deductions, covering topics such as gravity, celestial mechanics, comets, the moon, tides, the motion of fluids, and the laws governing them. His studies dealt a deathblow to the popular grand cosmological system developed by the great French mathematician and philosopher René Descartes, who is renowned for the famous saying, "I think, therefore I am." Descartes proposed that the planets move by the action of rotating vortices in an ether, or medium, that extends throughout the whole universe. Newton's elegant calculations, showing how gravity explained many details of the precise rotation patterns of planets, eliminated any need for Descartes' ideas. At the end of the second edition of *Principia* Newton added some concluding remarks under the title *General Scholium*. Here some of his religious fervor also comes to light as he gives credit to God as Creator, commenting that "this most beautiful system of the sun, planets, and comets could only proceed from the counsel and dominion of an intelligent and powerful Being."[15]

Newton also eventually published the result of his many investigations on light and optics. It appears that he had much of it prepared when one day upon returning from chapel at Cambridge he found that a candle had started a fire that had burned his manuscript and other very valuable documents. The loss so disturbed him that it is reported that he was not himself for a month. Some have described it as a mental breakdown, while others totally disagree.[16] All the details of this genius' life have been the subject of extreme scrutiny and speculation.[17] More than a decade after the fire he finally published his studies on light under the title of *Opticks*. The historian of science Sir William Dampier comments that "Newton's work on optics, even if it stood alone, would have placed him in the front rank of men of science."[18] *Opticks* merited three English editions as well as two French and two Latin ones.

Newton received many honors. At Cambridge his mathematical prowess won him the position of Lucasian professor of mathematics. After he moved to London, the government appointed him master of the mint and he became involved in many civic concerns. The Académie des sciences in France elected him as a foreign associate. Queen Anne bestowed the coveted knighthood on him, and he became Sir Isaac Newton. Voltaire, one of the great French leaders in the burgeoning free thought and reasoning movement of that time, was personally acquainted with Newton. He lauded the scientist, commenting that "if all the geniuses of the universe were assembled, he should lead the band."[19] More than a century later famed French mathematician and cosmologist Joseph Lagrange suggested that Newton's seminal *Principia* was assured for all time "a preeminence above all other productions of the human intellect."[20] Recently, in discussing the most important individuals of the past millennium, *Time* selected Newton as the most influential person of the seventeenth century.[21] Without doubt he possessed one of the greatest minds of all time.

Newton, along with all his superlative scientific understanding, had a profound devotion to God, and this has significant implications when we consider the relationship of religion to science. He did not approve of disbelief in God, stating that "atheism is so senseless and odious to mankind that it never had many professors,"[22] and he did not condone any levity about religious matters. Whenever it happened in his presence, he severely criticized it.[23] While most scientists of his time believed in God and commonly referred to Him in scholarly writings, Newton distinguished himself by his extensive studies of religious topics. Isaac left to posterity a prodigious number of writings. At least one third involve religious topics.

Especially interested in biblical prophecies, he studied everything he could on the topic, whether written in Greek, Aramaic, Latin, or Hebrew. He compiled long lists of the various interpretations. The relationship between biblical prophecies and history was of special concern to him, and before his death he had prepared a manuscript dealing with the interpretation of historical dates. Theologians and commentators needed them to establish correct reference points for biblical prophecies. His manuscript was published after his death under the title *Chronologies of Ancient Kingdoms Amended*. The two primarily prophetic books of the Bible, namely Daniel and the Apocalypse (Revelation), especially interested him. Studying them he used the same analytical approach that he employed when examining nature. Developing a series of 15 "rules for interpreting the words and language in Scripture,"[24] he regarded the prophecies in the two different books as a foretelling of world history. Many current interpretations of these biblical books still echo those of Newton's. Several years after his death his studies in this area were published as *Observations Upon the Prophecies of Daniel and the Apocalypse of St. John*.[25] Also he wrote on the life of Christ and other religious subjects, sometimes showing great independence in his theological thinking, such as rejecting the traditional Christian doctrine of the trinity for the Godhead. Newton believed, as the Bible indicates, that all nations came from Noah, and that God created all things, as He states He did in the Ten Commandments.[26] To him both the study of God's nature and that of God's sacred Scripture were all part of his overwhelming desire to know Him more fully.

In addition, Newton studied and wrote extensively about alchemy. Thoroughly familiar with the alchemical literature of his day, he approached the subject with the same analytical attitude that he applied to other topics. Some charlatans had given alchemy a bad name as they attempted to fake the transformation of base elements into gold, but in Newton's time, in part because of the careful work of Robert Boyle, alchemy was beginning to emancipate itself from a mystical cloak on its way to becoming respectable chemistry. Some have tried to imply a mystical personality to Newton because of his alchemical writings, but this seems to belie his thoroughly rational (i.e., based on reason) approach to physics, mathematics, and the Bible. While some of the implications of alchemy may have been of interest to his metaphysical questions, he still sought experimental verification just as he did in physics.[27]

The aura of religious fervor that developed around Newton brought him many admirers. A renowned Frenchman tried to establish a new Religion of Newton church. Another Frenchman severely criticized England for not giving due respect to Newton's divinity. Furthermore, he suggested, the calendar should be revised, starting with the date of Newton's birth, and a church should be built at Newton's birthplace.[28] The Swiss-born mathematician Fatio de Duillier was a good friend of Newton's, and a letter from him reflects Newton's spiritual depth and influence. Fatio became ill and did not expect to live. Writing to Newton what he thought might be his final letter, he said, "I thank God my soul is extremely quiet, in which you have had the chief hand."[29]

Newton found his final resting place among England's greatest in the revered Westminster Abbey. Paradoxically, about a century and a half later Charles Darwin, who had very different ideas about God, was also buried in Westminster Abbey, just a few feet away from Newton's tomb. When I visited the graves of these two gigantic scientific icons, I could not refrain from musing about the contrasting legacies about God that they had bequeathed to the world. That difference is the basis of much of the discussion in the chapters ahead.

To Newton, God was not an ordinary concept. He had a deep reverence for Him, commenting that "this Being governs all things, not as the soul of the world, but as Lord over all.... The supreme God is a Being eternal, infinite, absolutely perfect."[30] To him God was also an intensely personal being who loves us and whom we should love and respect. We hear a ring of sincerity as he urges that "we must believe that there is *one God* or supreme Monarch that we may fear and obey him and keep his laws and give him honour and glory. We must believe that he is the father of whom are all things, and that he loves his people as his children that they may mutually love him and obey him as their father."[31]

Probably more than any other person, Isaac Newton helped establish science on a firm foundation. He did this by applying rigorous standards to his investigations and publications. To some it may seem paradoxical that one of the world's top scientists was such an intensely religious person. But Newton's life clearly illustrates how excellent science and a strong belief in God can work together.

NEWTON WAS NOT ALONE

Newton lived at a critical moment in the history of science. It was the time when modern science was extricating itself from the tight grip of centuries of tradition. Observation, experimentation, and mathematical analysis had begun to replace the philosophical dogma of the Middle Ages. The ensuing Renaissance, also known as the "the revival of learning," created an atmosphere of intellectual turmoil. The leading scientists around that time became the pioneers of modern science; and like Newton, they strongly endorsed God as the creator of all. The principles of modern science emerged within an intellectual matrix in which God was the dominant figure.

Johannes Kepler (1571-1630), who worked in Prague, ranks among the leading scientists of all time. He showed that the planets move around the sun in an oval pattern instead of a circular one. Very adept at mathematics, he developed three principles, known as Kepler's laws, that describe planetary motion. They have survived almost intact to this day. Like the famous Italian astronomer Galileo (1564-1642), Kepler saw a rigorous relationship between God and the mathematics of nature. Kepler's motivation for his investigation was to find the "mathematical harmonies in the mind of the Creator."[32] Like Newton, he also wrote about the life of Christ.[33]

The versatile Frenchman Blaise Pascal (1623-1662), was another brilliant mind of the era. Skilled in theology and fluid dynamics, he laid the foundation of mathematical probability theory. The principles he established serve as the basis for our present method of studying many problems in physics, biology, and sociology. Pascal was a devout and profoundly religious man. We see his implicit commitment to God when he comments that "the whole course of things must have for its object the establishment and the greatness of religion."[34]

Many historians of science consider the pioneer English scientist Robert Boyle (1627-1691) to be the father of chemistry. One of his major contributions was to overthrow the classic idea of only four basic elements: fire, air, earth, and water. Chemistry students know him especially for Boyle's law, which explains the inverse relationship of pressure and volume in gases. Boyle believed that one glorifies God by explaining His creation, and that God created the world and was continually needed to keep it going.[35] Historian Frank Manuel comments that "the traditional use of science as a form of praise to the Father [God] assumed new dimensions under the tutelage of Robert Boyle."[36] Boyle gave large portions of his wealth to religious causes in Ireland and New England.

One of the leading biologists of this time was Swedish Carl von Linné (1707-1778). The foremost faculty member at Uppsala University, his fame for classifying almost everything attracted scholars from all over the world. He helped establish the currently used binomial system of naming organisms using genus and species terms. Again he, like many other scientists of his time, believed that "nature is created by God to His honour and for the blessing of mankind, and everything that happens happens at His command and under His guidance."[37]

Not all of the scientists of this period took the Bible so implicitly. In France the naturalist Buffon proposed nonbiblical views that minimized God's importance in nature, but he was part of a small minority.

NOW: A CONFRONTATION OF VIEWS

Thousands were attending a meeting of the Geological Society of America in New Orleans. The chair of one session pointed out that "creation is scientific prostitution" and added that creationists are "as crooked as a $3 bill" (the United States has no such currency). Another speaker claimed that "biblical catastrophism," namely geological interpretations based on the worldwide flood described in the Bible, is "dishonest" and "nasty." Someone else declared that one "should not let science fall to the fraud of creationists." These were just a few of the comments I heard.[38] While the speakers presented some valid evidence to support their allegations, it was no ordinary scientific discussion. Gone was the image of the calm, cautious, white-coat-clad scientist. The severe reaction had been stimulated in part by a Gallup Poll of adults in the United States that indicated that not many of the general public were following science. A total of 44 percent of those surveyed felt that God had created humanity within the past 10,000 years. Another 38 percent believed that God guided in the development of the human race during millions of years. Only 9 percent accepted the scientific model that humanity had evolved for millions of years and that God was not involved in the process. A few had no opinion. The Gallup organization has repeated the same poll at least five more times with essentially the same results.[39] It appears that most find it difficult to think that humanity's existence has no meaning or purpose, and that we just happen to be here by accident.

The critical comments against the concept of Creation quoted above illustrate how the present climate of opinion of many scientists toward the Bible is quite different than it was for the pioneers of modern science. Those early scientists fervently believed the Bible to be the Word of God—that it was truth. Now scientists often speak of the Bible as essentially invalid mythology. However, this does not mean that scientists no longer believe in God. A few years ago I attended an international geological congress in Paris. A pipe organ concert in the great cathedral of Notre Dame was scheduled as a special cultural event. To my pleasant surprise I noted that many of the geologists prayerfully knelt down in respect as they entered the cathedral. One would have to surmise that most of them believed in God. The picture can be complicated by different meanings of God and religion. Some scientists sometimes freely express their belief in some kind of religion, but not in God. Others draw a sharp line between religion and science.[40] One can define religion in many ways, such as moral rectitude, etc., but the usual understanding of the word "religion" is that of worship of one or more gods. We will proceed with that understanding in mind.

How many scientists believe in God? While one can get all kinds of figures about this in various publications as well as uncontrolled opinions on the Internet, two surveys published in the prestigious journal *Nature* seem to be valid. One randomly picked 1,000 individuals from the listing of scientists in *American Men and Women of Science* and queried their beliefs in God. But what do we mean by God? Again the word "God" can mean many different things. Is God a personal being, is He a principle, or as one of my zoology professors told me, is God nature? To most God is the Supreme Being, the creator and sustainer of nature. This survey used a very narrow interpretation of God, one that would not encourage a positive response. Those scientists who believed in God had to affirm that "I believe in a God in intellectual and affective communication with humankind, i.e., a God to whom one may pray in expectation of receiving an answer. By 'answer' I mean more than the subjective, psychological effect of prayer." The scientists could also indicate that they did not believe in such a kind of God, or that they did not know. About 40 percent said they believed in the type of God that answers their prayers; 45 percent did not; and 15 percent had no definite belief. Probably more than 40 percent believe in God, but not the kind of deity portrayed by the narrow definition in the questionnaire. One scientist wrote in the margin of his questionnaire, "I believe in God, but I don't believe that one can expect an answer to prayer." [41] Interestingly this survey conducted in 1996 was the same as one done 80 years earlier with essentially the same results. Soon after the 1996 survey, members of the prestigious National Academy of Sciences were also queried about their beliefs in God using the same questions. There only 7 percent said they believed in the kind of God who answers prayers as defined in the survey question. [42]

Why should such a small proportion of academy members believe in God? Several factors seem to be involved. [43] One might expect that the greater degree of specialization in science that the academy members have would tend to limit their outlook. Specialization can easily restrict one's view, especially if one neglects to look beyond one's own discipline. Furthermore, the elitism associated with being a member of the academy can reflect an attitude of superiority and pride easily engendered by the success of science. Such pride can contrast sharply with the humility and worshipful attitude encouraged by a belief in God. Some have seriously suggested that more members of the National Academy of Sciences believe in God than will admit it, and that various sociological factors play a significant complicating role. [44] A longstanding attitude holds that to be scientific, one must remain free from religion. At the time of the survey, the academy was preparing one booklet and revising another one, both encouraging the teaching of evolution in public schools while opposing the presentation of creation. Such activities and outlook would not encourage advocating belief in God. In contrast, one member of the academy recently dared to criticize evolution in the press, pointing out that it is too supple and often used to explain such opposing concepts as aggressive and altruistic behavior. Furthermore, he argued that evolution contributes little to experimental biology.[45]

We need to keep in perspective that the academy represents less than 2 percent of the scientists listed in *American Men and Women of Science.* As such, it obviously does not represent the opinion of the scientific community as a whole, in which 40 percent believe in a God that answers their prayers. But why are science textbooks, articles, and media presentations essentially barren of references to God? The incongruity no doubt reflects the aversion that the present scientific ethos seems to have toward religion, but does not reflect the true beliefs of many scientists. Attitudinal and sociological factors that we will consider later can probably best explain the disparity.[46]

On the other hand, scientists and other authorities from the Discovery Institute have been making a very significant impact through books,[47] lectures, and the Web. They have been promoting the idea that some kind of intelligent design has to exist for nature, and that idea is receiving widespread consideration as the "intelligent design" (or "ID") movement gains popularity. But leading scientists strongly oppose even this slight suggestion of some kind of God. An evolutionist in a recent issue of the *American Scientist* reports that "the success of the ID movement to date is terrifying. In at least 40 states, ID is being considered as an addition to the required science curriculum in public schools."[48] One gets a little of the "flavor" of the controversy from a briefing on intelligent design held for the United States Congress. Presenters from the Discovery Institute emphasized that they were there "only to open minds which had been kept closed by an elite scientific priesthood."[49]

An incident in Kansas further reflects on both the growing importance of the intelligent design concept and the threat it poses to evolution. In order to evaluate what should be included in the public school curriculum, the state board of education called for several days of discussion between proponents of intelligent design and of evolution. Unfortunately the evolutionists did not show up at the meetings to confront the intelligent design advocates. But they did feel free to express their views at news conferences outside the meetings. The American Association for the Advancement of Science, the largest general science organization in the world and the publisher of the prestigious journal *Science*, guided the boycott. The reasons the evolutionists gave for boycotting the session included the possibility of rigged hearings, a desire to avoid confusing the general public, and that it would be better to discuss the matter at a later time. However, such mundane excuses leave the evolutionists vulnerable to serious criticism. One board of education member commented that she was "profoundly disappointed that they've chosen to present their case in the shadows" and that she "would have enjoyed hearing what they have to say in a professional, ethical manner."[50] When something really challenges the dominant secularism of science, evolutionists can understandably feel uncomfortable.[51]

A number of modern scientists still accept the concept of a six-day creation by God as depicted in the Bible. A recent book titled *In Six Days: Why 50 Scientists Choose to Believe in Creation*,[52] presents essays by 50 scientists with doctoral level degrees, explaining why they believe the biblical account of creation. The commitment of the pioneers of modern science to the Bible and its creation account is still alive now in spite of a great deal of contention and strident criticism from leading scientists. Referring to the book mentioned above, evolutionist Richard Dawkins of Oxford University in England comments that he "would not have believed such wishful thinking and self-deception possible."[53] On the other side of the Atlantic, Harvard's late Stephen Gould also derided the discussion about creation. In his opinion science has provided very adequate answers without invoking God. He characterizes evolution as "as well documented as any phenomenon in science," and "one of the greatest triumphs of human discovery."[54] The battle trenches are being dug deeper and deeper.

Some wonder why, in this age of science, so many in the United States believe that God created human beings. One contributing factor is "the surprisingly high percentage of biology teachers who endorse creationism."[55] This statement by the editor of the journal *The American Biology Teacher* under the rubric "educational malpractice" reports on a number of surveys of secondary level biology teachers in various states. The results show that between 29 and

69 percent think that "creationism should be taught in science classes in public schools," and between 16 and 30 percent actually do present it. In contrast, the National Association of Biology Teachers issued a statement in 1995 declaring evolution to be "an unsupervised, impersonal, unpredictable and natural process."[56] Using the words "unsupervised" and "impersonal" suggested to many that the association was adopting an atheistic stance, and indeed was making the *theological* statement that no God exists at all. After extended disputations, the NABT removed the offending words from the statement. Some reporters from the public press then accused the scientists of capitulating to the creationists. Complicating the equation is the subtle fact that the question of God's existence is so emotionally laden that many scientists and other scholars just keep quiet about it. Scientists differ widely in opinion about *the God question*. We will use the expression "the God question" from time to time to refer to the specific issue of *whether or not God exists*.

SURGING INTEREST IN THE GOD QUESTION

During the past decade several important conferences dealing with the question of the existence of a designer or God have convened. Especially noteworthy are the Cosmos and Creation conference at Cambridge University (1994); Mere Creation conference at Biola University (1996); Science and the Spiritual Quest conference at the Berkeley campus of the University of California (1998); Nature of Nature conference at Baylor University (2000); and God, Nature, and Design conference at Oxford University (2008). These meetings have first-class scientists as presenters and a few Nobel laureates occasionally participate. Numerous other conferences on this topic have occurred in many corners of the world. Many ideas are under consideration. When it comes to the dominant question about the origin of life, the salient concepts being evaluated include: (a) life evolved by itself and no God was involved *(naturalistic evolution)*; (b) there is some kind of designer *(intelligent design)*; (c) God used the process of evolution *(theistic evolution)*; (d) God created various forms of life during billions of years *(progressive creation)*; (e) God created the various forms of life a few thousand years ago as implied in the Bible *(recent creation)*.

Evidence of burgeoning interest in the God question abounds. The number of courses dealing with the relation of science to religion has increased dramatically. While one could hardly find any such courses a few decades ago in American institutions of higher learning, many hundreds enrich present curricula.[57] Incentives from the John Templeton Foundation have no doubt contributed to this. The anthology *Cosmos, Bios, Theos*[58] presents contributions from many distinguished scientists, including more than 20 Nobel laureates, discussing science, religion, and the existence of God. The journal *Science*, arguably the world's most prestigious scientific journal, presented in 1997 a discussion under the title "Science and God: A Warming Trend?"[59] The news and letters sections of some scientific journals occasionally reflect the issue. The American Association of Petroleum Geologists' *Explorer* for January 2000 had an editorial-discussion article suggesting that geologists stay out of creation debates because of the politics involved and because " '...a scientist who goes and debates with these folks is going to get chewed up.'... 'They've got all sorts of buzzwords and keywords that they can trip you up with, if you aren't familiar with their tactics.' "[60] The response from the readers of the editorial was overwhelmingly against it, indicating that science should be more open to various ideas about creation or God.[61]

Space exploration also raises the question of God's existence. When the famous Russian cosmonaut Gherman Titov returned from space he reportedly declared that he could not find any gods and that he had looked for angels and could not find them. He had been only 137 miles (221 kilometers) above the surface of the earth. Later, however, earthlings watched as Apollo astronauts 240,000 miles (386,000 kilometers) away circled the moon and read to an admiring public the first words in the Bible: "In the beginning God created the heaven and the earth."

The public press often joins the discussion. An issue of *Newsweek* for 1998 splashed the words "Science Finds God" across its cover, and in 2006 one could read "God vs. Science" as the headline on the cover of *Time* magazine. Journals such as *Christianity Today, New Scientist, Skeptic,* and *Skeptical Inquirer* quite often discuss the connection between science and religion, sometimes devoting most of an issue to the topic.

Some scientists dare to believe in God. Occasionally leading scientists have written extensively about the relation of science to God. Paul Davies, professor of theoretical physics at the University of Newcastle upon Tyne in England, has written a popular book, *God and the New Physics*. He ventures that "science offers a surer path to God than religion."[62] Davies tends to be cautious about identifying too narrowly the kind of God he has in mind. In a later book he comments about the "powerful evidence that there is 'something going on' behind it all. The impression of design is overwhelming."[63] In addition, he supports the thesis that scientists can be religious: "Following the publication of *God and the New Physics*, I was astonished to discover how many of my close scientific colleagues practice a conventional religion."[64] John Polkinghorne has spent more than 25 years working as a theoretical-particle physicist at Cambridge University. Then he redirected his orientation and became an Anglican clergyman and later a college administrator at Cambridge. Devoting himself to the study of the relationship of science to theology, he has published a number of books on the topic. He believes that God upholds and is active in the universe, and that furthermore He facilitates our freedom of choice.[65] Many other scientists have expressed their belief in God, and several collections of such comments have gone to press.[66]

SCIENCE AND THE RATIONAL GOD OF THE BIBLE

A fascinating idea promoted for more than a half century challenges the contrasts suggested between science and God. The concept is that science developed in the Western world especially because of its Judeo-Christian background. In other words, instead of science and God being worlds apart, science owes its origin to the kind of deity described in the Bible. An impressive number of scholars support the thesis.[67]

The world-renowned philosopher Alfred North Whitehead, who taught at both Cambridge and Harvard universities, proposes that the ideas of modern science developed as "an unconscious derivative from medieval theology."[68] The concept of an orderly world as inferred from the single, rational, and consistent God of the Bible (monotheism) provided the basis for belief in the cause-and-effect concept of science. The many unpredictable pagan gods of other cultures were capricious, and thus did not fit with the consistency that makes science possible. R. G. Collingwood, who was the Waynflete professor of metaphysical philosophy at Oxford University, points out that the belief that God is all-powerful facilitated the change of view of nature from imprecision to precision,[69] and precision fits well with the exactitude obtainable in science. In the Netherlands the late Reijer Hooykaas,

professor of the history of science at the University of Utrecht, also emphasizes that the biblical worldview contributed to the development of modern
science. Of special importance was the relative anti-authoritarianism nur-
tured by the Bible as compared to restricted Middle Ages practices. It helped
to free science from the dominance of theologians.[70] One of the leading
scholars in this area is Stanley L. Jaki, who, with doctorates in physics and theology, has been honored as distinguished professor at Seton Hall University
in New Jersey. Jaki astutely points out that Hindu, Chinese, Mayan, Egypt-
ian, Babylonian, and Greek cultures all had, in varying degrees, starts in science that, however, ended in stillbirths. He attributes this to a lack of belief
in the rationality of the universe pervading such cultures. The Judeo-Christian tradition of the Bible provided the rational kind of God necessary for
the establishment of science.[71] It is paradoxical that the God who may be the
very cause for the establishment of modern science now finds Himself thoroughly rejected by the current secular stance of science.

We cannot say that the broadly accepted concept of a causal relationship
between the God of the Judeo-Christian tradition and modern science is
an unquestionable fact—it is just that the acceptance of this idea suggests
that there is not a strong dichotomy between science and the kind of God
described in the Bible. That God is a deity of cause and effect and is consistent, and that fits well with science.

CONCLUDING COMMENTS

The pioneers of modern science, such as Kepler, Boyle, and Newton,
were devout believers in God and the Bible. They saw no conflict between
Him and science because He had created the principles of science. Obviously
great scientists can believe in a God who is active in nature. Since that time,
there has been a parting of the ways. Science has gone off on its own, iso-
lating itself from religion and trying to answer many things, including the
profound questions of our origin and purpose, without referring to God at
all. While many scientists believe in Him, at present He is essentially excluded from all scientific interpretations. Contemporary leading scientists
have especially set the tone for a science separate from God.

A redefinition of the practice of science has emerged over time, and that is an important point to keep in mind. In general, most consider science to be the

study of facts and explanations about nature, but details of definitions can vary dramatically. When scholars began to lay down the foundations of modern science, those who studied nature (scientists) were called natural historians or natural philosophers and such individuals glorified in their writings the God they considered to be active in nature. Often they referred to Him as the creator of all. Since He had established the laws of nature, He was thus a part of the scientific interpretation. God's importance in science gradually decreased, especially in the late nineteenth century. Now we observe a strong trend in the practice of science to ignore God, and if you do try to include Him, you will be considered unscientific. God is excluded simply by definition. This view closes the door to science discovering Him. In this mode, science is no longer an open search for truth, and it can lead to error, especially in case God does exist!

In this book we propose that a scientist should be open to the possibility that God exists, and that science should follow the data of nature wherever it may lead. *Our concern is to find truth*, not to fit our conclusions within a narrow definition of science. In the pages ahead we will generally consider science to be, as mentioned above, the study of facts and interpretations about nature. A basic question we will discuss in the final chapter is why science now chooses to exclude God from its explanatory menu.

The past few decades have seen a moderate warming trend toward religion and God in science, and the God question is being seriously addressed, reflecting some of the ways science and God have worked together in the past. Furthermore, the deity described in the Bible is a consistent, rational Being that fits well with the cause-and-effect principles of science. Actually, in terms of fundamental rational approaches, God and science are not that different, and the rift that has developed between them deserves to be erased.

[1] Einstein A. 1950. Out of my later years. New York: Philosophical Library, p. 26.

[2] Manuel FE. 1974. The religion of Isaac Newton. Oxford: Oxford University Press, p. 6.

[3] Westfall RS. 1993. The life of Isaac Newton. Cambridge: Cambridge University Press, p. 18.

[4] Westfall RS. 1980. Never at rest: a biography of Isaac Newton. Cambridge: Cambridge University Press.

[5] More LT. 1934. Isaac Newton: a biography. New York: Dover Publications, Inc., p. 97.

[6] *Ibid.,* p. 106.

[7] Christianson GE. 1984. In the presence of the Creator: Isaac Newton and his times. New York: Macmillan, Inc., p. 193.

[8] *Ibid.,* p. 194.

[9] *Ibid.,* p. 197.

[10] Dampier WC. 1949. A history of science: and its relations with philosophy and religion, 4th ed. New York: Macmillan Co., p. 159; Westfall. The life of Isaac Newton, pp. 276-286. [For publishing information, see note 3, above.]

[11] Westfall, The life of Isaac Newton, p. 134. [See note 3.]

[12] The full title of the treatise is: Philosophiae naturalis principia mathematica.

[13] Dampier, p. 154. [See note 10.]

[14] More, p. 287. [See note 5.]

[15] Newton I. 1686, 1934. Mathematical principles of natural philosophy and his system of the world. Translated into English by Andrew Motte in 1729, revised translation by Florian Cajori. Los Angeles: University of California Press, p. 544.

[16] More, pp. 390, 391. [See note 5.]

[17] For instance, see some of the suggestions in: Manuel FE. 1968. A portrait of Isaac Newton. Cambridge: Harvard University Press.

[18] Dampier, p. 160. [See note 10.]

[19] As quoted in: Miller DC. 1928. Newton and optics. In: The History of Science Society: Sir Isaac Newton, 1727-1927: a bicentenary evaluation of his work. Baltimore: Williams and Wilkins Co., p. 15.

[20] *Ibid.*

[21] Gray P. 1999. The most important people of the millennium. Time 154(27):139-195.

[22] Brewster D. 1885. Memoirs of the life, writings, and discoveries of Sir Isaac Newton, volume 2. Reprinted (1965) from the Edinburgh edition. New York: Johnson Reprint Corp., p. 347.

[23] Christianson, p. 355. [See note 7.] Manuel, The religion of Isaac Newton, pp. 6, 61. [See note 2.]

[24] Manuel, The Religion of Isaac Newton, pp. 116-125. [See note 2.]

[25] Newton I. 1733. Observations upon the prophecies of Daniel and the apocalypse of St. John. London: printed by J. Darby and T. Browne.

[26] Westfall, The life of Isaac Newton, pp. 301, 303. [See note 3.]

[27] Christianson, p. 225. [See note 7.]

[28] Manuel, The religion of Isaac Newton, p. 53. [See note 2.]

[29] Turnbull WH, ed. 1961. The correspondence of Isaac Newton, Volume III, 1688-1694. Cambridge: Cambridge University Press, pp. 229, 230.

[30] Newton, Mathematical principles of natural philosophy and his system of the world, p. 544. [See note 15.]

[31] As quoted in: Manuel, The religion of Isaac Newton, p. 104 [see note 2]; from Yahuda MS. 15. 3, fol. 46^{r}.

[32] Dampier, p. 127. [See note 10.]

[33] Manuel, The religion of Isaac Newton, p. 61. [See note 2.]

[34] Pascal B. 1952. Pensées. In: Pascal B. The provincial letters; Pensées; scientific treatises. Trotter WF, trans. Great Books of the Western World Series. London: Encyclopedia Britannica, p. 270.

[35] Dampier, p. 140. [See note 10.]

[36] Manuel, The religion of Isaac Newton, p. 33. [See note 2.]

[37] Nordenskiöld E. 1928, 1942. The history of biology: a survey. Eyre LB, trans. New York: Tudor Pub. Co., pp. 206, 207.

[38] For further comments, see: Roth AA. 1983. Where has the science gone? Origins 10:48, 49.

[39] See: http://www.gallup.com/poll/content/default.aspx?ci=1942. Viewed June 2005.

[40] Gould SJ. 1999. Rocks of ages: science and religion in the fullness of life. New York: Ballantine Books.

[41] Larson EJ, Witham L. 1997. Scientists are still keeping the faith. Nature 386:435, 436.

[42] Larson EJ, Witham L. 1998. Leading scientists still reject God. Nature 394:313.

[43] For a general review of some factors related to this issue, see: Pearcey NR. 2004. Total truth: liberating Christianity from its cultural captivity. Wheaton, Ill.: Crossway Books, pp. 97-121.

[44] For further discussion, see: Larson EJ, Witham L. 1999. Scientists and religion in America. Scientific American 281(3):88-93.

[45] Skell PS. 2005. Why do we invoke Darwin? The Scientist 19(16):10.

[46] See chapters 7, 8.

[47] Some significant publications, among many, are: Behe MJ. 1996. Darwin's black box: the biochemical challenge to evolution. New York: Touchstone; Dembski WA. 2004. The design revolution: answering the toughest questions about intelligent design. Downers Grove, Ill.: InterVarsity Press; Dembski WA. 1999. Intelligent design: the bridge between science and theology. Downers Grove, Ill.: InterVarsity Press; Johnson PE. 2000. The wedge of truth: splitting the foundations of naturalism. Downers Grove, Ill.: InterVarsity Press; Johnson PE. 1991. Darwin on trial. Downers Grove, Ill.: InterVarsity Press; Wells J. 2000. Icons of evolution: science or myth? Why much of what we teach about evolution is wrong. Washington, D.C.: Regnery Publishing, Inc.

[48] Shipman P. 2005. Being stalked by intelligent design. American Scientist 93:500-502.

[49] See: http://www.atheists.org/flash.line/evol10.htm. Viewed June 2005.

[50] Associated Press release, Topeka, Kans., May 9, 2005. See: http://www.cbsnews.com/stories/2005/05/09/national/main693896.shtml. Viewed June 2005.

[51] For a comprehensive review of some of the argumentation, see: Dembski. The design revolution: answering the toughest questions about intelligent design. [See note 47.]

[52] Ashton JF, ed. 1999. In six days: why 50 scientists choose to believe in creation. Sydney: New Holland Publishers (Australia) Pty, Ltd.

[53] Dawkins R. 2000. Sadly, an honest creationist. Free Inquiry 21(4):7, 8.

[54] Gould SJ. 1999. Dorothy, it's really Oz. Time 154(8):59.

[55] Moore R. 2001. Educational malpractice: why do so many biology teachers endorse creationism? Skeptical Inquirer 25(6):38-43.

[56] Larson, Witham. Scientists and religion in America. [See note 44.]

[57] Ibid.

[58] Margenau H, Varghese RA, eds. 1992. Cosmos, bios, theos: scientists reflect on science, God, and the origins of the universe, life, and Homo sapiens. La Salle, Ill.: Open Court Pub. Co.

[59] Easterbrook G. 1997. Science and God: a warming trend? Science 277:890-893.

[60] Brown D. 2000. Quiet agenda puts science on defense: creation debate evolves into politics. American Association of Petroleum Geologists Explorer 21(1):20-22.

33

[61] See 10 letters in: Readers' Forum. 2000. American Association of Petroleum Geologists Explorer 21(3):32-37.

[62] Davies P. 1983. God and the new physics. New York: Simon and Schuster, p. ix.

[63] Davies P. 1989. The cosmic blueprint: new discoveries in nature's creative ability to order the universe. New York: Touchstone, p. 203.

[64] Davies P. 1992. The mind of God: the scientific basis for a rational world. New York: Simon & Schuster, p. 15.

[65] Giberson KW. 2002. Bottom-up apologist: John Polkinghorne—particle physicist, Gifford lecturer, Templeton Prize winner, and parish priest. Christianity Today 46(6):64, 65; Polkinghorne J. 1990. God's action in the world. CTNS Bulletin 10(2):1-7. See also: Polkinghorne J. 1986. One world: the interaction of science and theology. London: SPCK; Polkinghorne J. 1988. Science and creation: the search for understanding. Boston: New Science Library; Polkinghorne J. 1989. Science and providence: God's interaction with the world. Boston: New Science Library.

[66] Some examples are: Ashton JF, ed. 2001. The God factor: 50 scientists and academics explain why they believe in God. Sydney: Thorsons, Harper Collins Publishers, Australia; Ashton. In six days: why 50 scientists choose to believe in creation (note 52); Barrett EC, Fisher D, eds. 1984. Scientists who believe: 21 tell their own stories. Chicago: Moody Press; Clayton P, Schall J, eds. 2007. Practicing science, living faith: interviews with 12 leading scientists. New York: Columbia University Press; Mott N, ed. 1991. Can scientists believe? Some examples of the attitude of scientists to religion. London: James & James; Richardson WM et al., eds. 2002. Science and the spiritual quest: new essays by leading scientists. London: Routledge.

[67] For a recent review see: Stark R. 2003. For the glory of God: how monotheism led to reformations, science, witch hunts, and the end of slavery. Princeton, N.J.: Princeton University Press, pp. 147-157.

[68] Whitehead AN. 1925. Science and the modern world. New York: Macmillan Co., p. 19.

[69] Collingwood RG. 1940. An essay on metaphysics. Oxford: Clarendon Press, pp. 253-255.

[70] Hooykaas R. 1972. Religion and the rise of modern science. Grand Rapids: William B. Eerdmans Pub. Co., pp. 98-162.

[71] Jaki SL. 1974. Science and creation: from eternal cycles to an oscillating universe. New York: Science History Publications; Jaki SL. 1978. The road of science and the ways to God: the Gifford lectures 1974-1975 and 1975-1976. Chicago: University of Chicago Press; Jaki SL. 2000. The savior of science. Grand Rapids: William B. Eerdmans Pub. Co., pp. 9-48.

Chapter Two

The Very Fine-tuned Universe

So then gravity may put ye [the] planets in motion but without ye [the] divine power it could never put them into such a circulating motion as they have about ye [the] sun, and therefore for this as well as other reasons I am compelled to ascribe ye [the] frame of this system to an intelligent agent.[1]

—*Sir Isaac Newton*

WHAT IS OUT THERE?

Few awe-inspiring vistas can surpass the myriads of glistening stars visible on a clear night. Unfortunately, today only those who live away from large cities get to see them. Streetlights and smog obliterate the magnificent pageant of various shades of blue, yellow, and red stars. Most are privileged to see only a few bright stars or a pale moon struggling through the haze of civilization. However, the universe that we are discovering beyond our earth is much grander than just what we can see on a clear night.

Armed with powerful telescopes and other sophisticated instruments, scientists have been making amazing discoveries. Specialists calling themselves cosmologists, physicists, philosophers, theologians, astrophysicists, and astronomers all lay claim to interpreting what is being discovered. This is one of the most exciting areas of research, and one with profound philosophical implications. We are finding that the universe appears to be very precisely adjusted so as to permit both it and us to exist. Before considering that, we will look at what scientists have encountered so that we will sense some of the reasons they believe the universe to be finely tuned.

One of the striking features of the clear night sky is a long irregular "cloud" of stars across the heavens, popularly known as the Milky Way. We are actually part of that cloud, which is a gigantic disk-shaped mass of stars (Figure 2.1). When we look toward the edges of the disk, i.e., at the Milky Way, we see many more stars than we do toward the flat surfaces of the disk, which is most of the rest of the sky. It is a bit like being in a crowd—you see

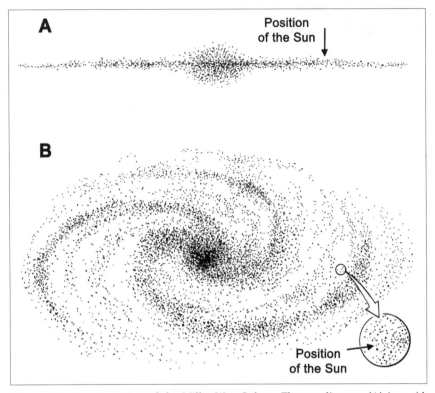

Figure 2.1 *Representation of the Milky Way Galaxy. The top diagram (A) is a side view, looking at the edge and showing the thick bulge in the center. The lower diagram (B) is a nearly planar view revealing the spiral arms and the approximate position of our sun.*

many more people if you look out around you than if you gaze down at the ground or up at the sky. Astronomers call such a disk of stars an island universe or a *galaxy*. Ours, the Milky Way Galaxy, harbors some 100 billion stars somewhat similar to our own sun. Our sun has a yellowish color. Some stars are cooler and appear more reddish, while others are hotter and bluish. The four blue Trapezium stars in the Orion constellation have 10 times the *mass* (quantity of matter) of our sun and shine thousands of times more brightly.[2] Stars sometimes seem to be influenced by gravity in a way that suggests that a lot of extra matter exists somewhere out there. Physicists refer to it as *dark matter,* because it does not emit light, as stars do. Apparently the universe has much more dark matter than stars, but science has many unanswered questions about it. In fact, we are not sure what dark matter is, or if it really exists, and there are more questions about dark energy. Such enigmas are only a small part of the many mysteries we are constantly discovering about our universe.

The stars in our galaxy disk are not evenly distributed. They tend to concentrate in elongated arms that spiral out gently from the center (Figure 2.1). We live on the edge of one of those arms, out about two thirds of the distance from the center of our galaxy. The center of our galaxy has a bulge where the disk is thicker. One or more of those infamous black holes may lurk there. Black holes have such an extreme pull of gravity that not even light can escape, so they appear dark. If you ventured too close to one of them, you would also be trapped.

Our whole galaxy appears to be rotating magnificently in space. Our sun would take about 250 million years for a complete rotation around our galaxy.[3] While that may not seem very fast, the distances are so vast that our sun must travel at 504,000 miles per hour (225 kilometers per second) to do a complete circuit in this length of time.

Most of the stars you see in the night sky are other suns in our Milky Way Galaxy. However, if you look carefully at the Andromeda constellation, even without the use of a telescope, you can faintly see the Andromeda Galaxy that lies far beyond ours. It has about as many stars as our own galaxy, and close by are smaller satellite galaxies consisting of several billion stars. The gravitational attraction of the Andromeda galaxy holds them in a cluster. The Milky Way and Andromeda galaxies are what we call spiral galaxies because of the open spirallike arrangement of their stars, but most galaxies are different. A common type is elliptical, some are more spherical, and others are irregular in shape.

Our galaxy forms part of a "Local Group" of some 34 galaxies that lie on the edge of the much larger Virgo Cluster of galaxies. Astronomers have also discovered a sheetlike array of galaxies known as the "Great Wall."[4] The number of galaxies we have discovered using telescopes both on earth and in space is almost beyond belief. Our known universe has about 100 billion galaxies, each with an average of 100 billion stars.[5] Are there other galaxies or universes beyond what we can see? We don't know. Any such suggestions must remain highly speculative.

We all have exciting events in our lives that we never forget. One of mine took place in 1987 while traveling in Australia. I glanced up at the night sky and saw an extremely bright star where before there had been only a very faint one. How could that be? What I was viewing was a rare event—the explosion of a supernova—and that was one of the greatest explosions ever seen. Ancient history records a few of them, but this was the best one to be observed in modern times. What is believed to have happened is that a faint star, which had about 10 times the matter of our sun, eventually collapsed because of the effect of gravity on such a tremendous mass. The collapse caused an explosion that produced an extremely bright star in just a few hours. It remained conspicuously visible for several weeks. The supernova probably produced a neutron star, and the matter of such an object is extremely dense and can eventually collapse farther into a black hole. It is estimated that on earth just a teaspoon of matter from that collapsed star would weigh some 500 million tons. Such things may seem more plausible if we realize that ordinary "solid" matter is almost all empty space anyway. The reason X-rays can easily pass through our bodies is that we are mostly empty space, and that includes our brains also! If you get rid of the empty space between and within atoms you have very heavy matter. An atom is very empty, thousands of times emptier than represented in our traditional illustrations of atoms (see Figure 2.2, p. 42). The outside diameter of an atom is estimated at about 10,000 times that of its central nucleus, while almost all of the matter is concentrated in the nucleus. So there is lots of empty space in an atom to collapse into. If all of humanity were compressed down to the density of a neutron star, all of us together would be only the size of a pea.[6]

An exploding supernova is just one example of our dynamic universe. We also see quasars that, though much smaller than galaxies, can be 1,000 times brighter. They may also harbor some of those intriguing black holes. Then there is the suggestion that some galaxies might be cannibalizing other galaxies. Our universe appears highly active.

Fortunately things are more placid around our solar system, in which we have eight planets, including our own earth, revolving in orderly fashion around our beneficent sun, which provides us with a steady source of energy. Some astronomers have dethroned Pluto as an official planet, but it is still there with its "moon." The planets, which on first appearance in the night sky resemble slowly moving stars, do not emit light, but merely reflect it from the sun. Together they possess at least 60 moons,[7] and that includes the lonely one encircling our earth that gives us something to sing and write poems about. The four inner planets, which include the earth, have a solid surface. Mars is the most like our earth. Venus, orbiting closer to the sun than the earth, oddly spins backwards compared to its neighboring planets. This complicates any idea of a simple model for the formation of planets by a single event. The outer planets have much more mass, but are mostly gaseous with small rocky cores. Pluto, that is farther out than the planets, is different and consists in part of some methane ice and, like Venus, spins the opposite direction from most of the other planets. Saturn, noted for its many astonishing rings, is so light that it would actually float on water, if you could find a pond of water that large. The largest planet, Jupiter (also gaseous), has a moon, Io, that is intensely volcanic. Between Mars and Jupiter is a ring of many thousands of small irregular rocky bodies called asteroids. Some of them occasionally make a fiery entry into our atmosphere, producing streaks of light called meteors. Jupiter is so massive that it attracts a lot of debris that would otherwise hit the earth. Astronomers estimate that if it were not there the earth would be struck "about a thousand times more frequently than it is already by comets and comet debris."[8] Icy comets with long tails that travel around our solar system in predictable paths also add to the intrigue of our complicated solar system. Recently we have been discovering a number of planets around other suns.

THE EXTREME IMMENSITY OF THE UNIVERSE

From our tiny earth it is not easy to comprehend how far away other parts of the universe are. Our sun may seem to be just a little way out there, but it is nearly 93 million miles (150 million kilometers) away. We have trouble conceptualizing such figures. It may help if you realize that if you should journey from the earth to the sun at the speed of a commercial jetliner, it would take you 19 years of continuous travel to get there. A voyage to Pluto at jetliner speed would require 741 years. Proportionately, if the sun were about the size of a room (three meters across), the earth would be about the size of an apricot, circling one-quarter mile (one-third kilometer) away, and Pluto would be the size of a pea, eight miles (13 kilometers) out.

Compared to the universe, our solar system is extremely small. In order to talk about the rest of the universe it is easier to use a much larger unit of measure than kilometers so that we don't have to fill too many pages with zeros. Astronomers employ another unit called the *light-year*, and that is the distance that light travels in a year. It is equal to about 5,879,000,000,000 miles (9,461,000,000,000 kilometers).

Light from the sun requires eight minutes to reach the earth, so when you see a large solar flare on the sun flashing out some 60,000 miles (95,000 kilometers) from the sun's surface, it actually occurred eight minutes earlier. The closest star (sun) beyond our solar system is Alpha Centauri, and light from there spends four years reaching earth, so we say it is four light-years away. Our Milky Way Galaxy is around 100,000 light-years from edge to edge, and astronomers estimate the Andromeda galaxy to be 2 million light years from us. As a result, it would take a long time to travel there. What we see now going on there is not up-to-date. The more distant galaxies of the universe are estimated at billions of light-years away. Since it takes so long for the light from these more distant stars to reach us, astronomers interpret what they see now from distant stars as representing what happened a very long time ago.

While the visible universe has an estimated 70 sextillion (7 followed by 22 zeros) stars, space is astoundingly empty because of the tremendous distances between stars, galaxies, and clusters of galaxies. If all the atoms of all the matter in the universe were evenly distributed throughout the volume of the universe we would have only one atom for every five cubic meters of space.[9] This means that a volume equivalent to an ordinary house room would contain only about six atoms. On a larger scale, we find that galaxies are millions of light-years away from each other. It may be a good thing that matter is so sparsely distributed in our universe. Physicist Freeman Dyson[10] estimates that if the distance between stars had been 10 times closer than it is, there is a high probability that some other star would have gotten close enough to our solar system to disrupt the orbits of the planets, something that would be disastrous for life on earth.

WHAT IS THE UNIVERSE MADE OF?

Our immense universe consists of tiny ordinary atoms that scientists once thought to be the smallest thing that could exist and thus could not be subdivided into smaller parts. However, about a century ago, researchers discovered parts of atoms called electrons. Very tiny, they have a negative electric charge. Before long physicists encountered much larger parts of atoms they named protons that have a positive charge, and then equally large particles they labeled as neutrons that had no charge. A proton has a mass (quantity of matter) that is 1,836 times that of an electron. Would these parts be the smallest elementary parts of matter? A few decades ago we found that if you smashed fast-moving protons into each other they apparently broke up into smaller units now called quarks. And that was just the beginning of the discoveries made in this intriguing area of science. Physicists have described at least 58 kinds of subatomic particles.[11] Most particles have a corresponding antiparticle that has an opposite charge, and when the two collide they annihilate each other. Then we have the question of whether some of these are really particles. Many aspects of this area of study we don't fully understand.

Our simplified concept of atoms is that they consist of a central nucleus composed of protons and neutrons, while electrons orbit on the outside (See Figure 2.2, p. 42). The nucleus of our lightest element, hydrogen, has only one proton and one electron on the outside. Helium has two protons, two neutrons, and two electrons. Carbon and oxygen, the elements so essential for life, usually have six and eight of each of these basic components respectively. Heavier elements have many more as well as more complicated relationships between the various parts.

When you look at ordinary white light, what you may not realize is that what you see is actually a mixture of all kinds of colors. The white light on a television or computer screen is actually a combination of red, green, and blue light, as a good magnifying lens will easily show you. You become more aware of this when you see white sunlight separated into the different colors of a rainbow by raindrops. Science uses that phenomenon to discover a lot about the chemical composition of the universe. By passing a narrow bundle of light from a star through a glass prism, astronomers can view the different kinds of colors produced by the stars, and they have learned a great deal from what they have seen. The very active atoms in the stars produce this light as the electrons around the nuclei of the atoms release some of their energy when they jump from one orbit to the next. Each kind of atom produces a

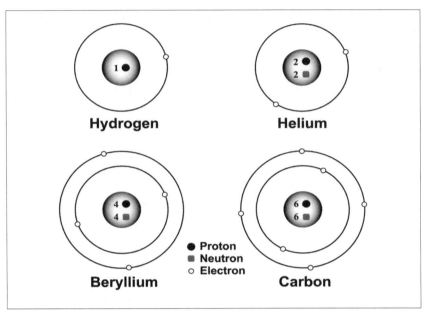

Figure 2.2 *Traditional representation of some simple atoms. The nucleus is the gray sphere in the center of each kind of atom. Electrons are on the outside. The beryllium atom shown is beryllium-8, which is somewhat unstable. The usual form of beryllium is beryllium-9, which has an extra neutron in its nucleus.*

different color pattern. For instance, if you see certain specific kinds of red, blue, violet, and deep-violet color, you know that you have hydrogen atoms. By studying the light from many stars in the universe, astronomers have found that they have the same kind of elements that we find on earth, but the proportions are quite different. We have an abundance of heavier elements, such as oxygen, silicon, and aluminum, that form 82 percent of the crust of the earth, while 97 percent of the universe appears to consist of the two lightest elements we know of, namely hydrogen and helium.

IDEAS ABOUT THE UNIVERSE

Some assume the universe has always been here, in which case the question of how it began is meaningless. Christian, Jewish, and Islamic believers think that God created the universe. Eastern religions such as Hinduism and Buddhism have a variety of ideas and suggestions of repeated cycles of change over time. A few centuries ago humanity had all kinds of speculations about the nature of the universe. Back then a number of intellectual giants appeared, including Sir Isaac Newton, who described laws of gravity and motion that explained the paths of the stars. His work had a profound impact on the thinking of his time. Scientists had begun to show that the universe was explainable and predictable. As a result some saw less need for God. Since so many things were increasingly being explained, some even suggested that the work of physicists might be over. But quantum theory and relativity changed all that. We will briefly look into the development of these ideas because it provides helpful insights into how science works.

Serious trouble started about a century ago, not in the realm of the stars but with the tiny submicroscopic world of their atoms and the energy they emit. The area of study known as quantum theory deals with concepts that are sometimes frankly spooky when contrasted with our normal cause-and-effect universe that we intuitively take for granted. Introduced by Max Planck (1858-1947), quantum theory proposed that certain physical quantities could assume certain defined values, but not ones in between. Furthermore, electrons could behave in some respects as waves do, but in other cases act as particles. Some investigative results were predictable, but only on a statistical level and only when the researchers considered many events together. On an individual basis, however, valid predictions were not possible. One of the great concepts to come out of these studies was Werner Heisenberg's uncertainty principle. It states that you cannot precisely know both the position and momentum (velocity multiplied by mass) of a particle. All of this has been fruitful fodder for philosophical speculation, including such concepts that there is no real quantum reality, or that the unpredictability we encounter in quantum theory is the basis of our freedom of choice. A cautious conclusion is that we still have much more to learn about the weird world of quantum theory. Anyone who claims to fully understand quantum theory simply doesn't! Nevertheless, the concept has been quite fruitful in the development of such exotic devices as lasers and superconducting magnets, and cosmologists have used it extensively in theoretical models of the developing universe. One of the best results has been a broadening of humanity's philosophical outlook. It has helped us realize that reality is not just the simple ideas we understand—that we need to take into account the uncertain and the unpredictable.

Equally baffling to the way we usually see things is the theory of relativity. Introduced by Albert Einstein (1879-1955), one of the greatest geniuses of our time, the theory has proved to be remarkably useful. Einstein, born in Germany and educated in Switzerland, firmly believed in God, but not the kind of God Christians usually think about, one who acts as a Creator and involves Himself in our personal lives. To Einstein the consistency, order, and harmony of the universe represented God. His famous comment "God does not play dice" reflects this. He made that statement as an objection to some of the uncertainties of quantum theory.

In relativity theory you cannot go faster than the speed of light, and the speed of light in a vacuum is always the same regardless of the movement or direction of either the source or the observer. The picture may be more complicated, however. For example, a few recent findings suggest that there may have been some variation in the speed of light or closely related factors.[12] In relativity theory many other physical factors can change dramatically, but we usually do not notice them because within our normal realm of observations the changes are so minute. But if you studied something traveling near the speed of light, you would notice that clocks slow down, lengths get shorter, and mass increases. At the speed of light, mass should theoretically become infinite, which puts limits on how fast anything can travel. Relativity theory declares that space can become curved, and mass can be changed into energy and energy into mass (as depicted by the well-known expression $E=mc^2$).

Many observations confirm the validity of relativity. Time should appear to run slower near massive bodies, and it does. Very accurate clocks run faster at the top of a water tower than at its base, where they are closer to the mass of the earth. Our marvelous global positioning systems can take such differences into account to enhance their accuracy.[13] Research has found that large masses such as our sun bend light, something also predicted by relativity. Using atomic clocks placed on airliners, it is possible to detect minute effects of relativity even though the airliners fly at only one millionth the speed of light.[14] The faster you go in space, the slower you should age. As a result, you could travel very rapidly in space for a few weeks and return to earth and find that many years had passed by and your friends and family would be aged or dead.[15]

Does relativity overthrow Newton and his carefully worked-out formulas of celestial mechanics? No, but it adds a new dimension to Newton's work and especially applies to more extreme conditions. Newton's concepts still work at our ordinary level of experience and for the motion of the solar system, except for a minor problem with the planet Mercury, which relativity can explain better.

While even more advanced concepts may supplant relativity in the future, the concept does explain many things, and it has been remarkably well confirmed through the years. The fact that time can be modified is stunning. Some researchers even suggest that time does not really exist—that it is only something we imagine. But it is still a useful concept, at least for our world, and we had better get to work on time!

THE EXPANDING UNIVERSE AND THE BIG BANG

At the beginning of the past century the American astronomer Vesto Slipher, studying the light coming from galaxies, noted evidence that indicated that some galaxies were moving away from us at the incredible rate of 600 miles (1,000 kilometers) per second. One of the ways we calculate how fast a galaxy is retreating is to note how much its light spectrum has shifted from its normal pattern. The greater the shift, the faster the galaxy is moving, a conclusion based on the common Doppler effect we often note when an ambulance with a blaring siren travels at first toward and then away from us. The pitch of the siren drops dramatically after the ambulance passes us, and the faster the ambulance goes, the greater the change in pitch or frequency of the sound waves. When the ambulance rushes toward us, the sound waves are relatively "compressed," and the pitch of the sound is higher. But when moving away they "stretch" and the sound is lower.

Light waves from stars behave in some respects like sound waves from an ambulance. The faster the stars advance toward or away from us, the greater the increase or decrease in frequency noted as the light waves are compressed or stretched out from their source. Now, the frequency of the light waves is what determines the color of the light. For instance, we find that blue light has a higher (faster) wave frequency than red light. Hence, if the normal pattern of lines in the spectrum of light from a star gets shifted toward the red side (lower frequency) of the spectrum, this means that the star is moving away from us. But if it has shifted toward the blue side (higher frequency), the star is heading toward us.

It turns out that light from distant galaxies has a reddish characteristic, a trait astronomers call the redshift. They interpret this as meaning that the stars are moving away from us, some at 100 million miles per hour (50 thousand kilometers per second). Such analysis is much more complicated than just a simple redshift. Some very good evidence does not agree with the redshift. As a result, some speak of light getting tired over great distances, and others have suggested alternative explanations,[16] but prevailing opinion now favors excluding such concepts.

In the 1920s the famous astronomer Edwin Hubble was studying galaxies using the then-new 100-inch telescope on Mount Wilson, in California. He found that the farther away a galaxy was, the faster it was receding. His observation has become known as Hubble's law and has added more intrigue to the question of what is going on out there. Hubble estimated distances on the basis of how bright certain standard astronomical features were, somewhat the same as determining how far away a candle is by its brightness. The method has not proved to be very accurate, because not all stars shine equally brightly. Astronomers now measure stellar distance by the brightness of what they call Cepheid variable stars. They have found that some stars of a specific brightness will dim and brighten over a regular period. By measuring how long the variable period of such a star is, they learn how bright the star normally is and can then estimate the distance of the galaxy containing the star.

Scientists have attempted to determine the exact age of the universe by assuming that it started very small and then calculating how long it would take to expand to its present size. Recent estimates place the age of the universe in the region of 10 to 15 billion years.

The idea that the universe is expanding at a rapid rate posed a serious challenge to traditional views of the early twentieth century. If it is actually growing, this means that in the past it was smaller and before that smaller yet and eventually you come to a point at which you start thinking about when, how, and why the universe ever got started in the first place. The implication of all this is that the universe has not always been here. It opens the door for wondering how things got started, and whether some mastermind such as that of God could have started things, and if not God, how then did anything get started? However, the idea of God doing things in nature is now a rather unpopular view in science. The noted astronomer Robert Jastrow comments that "when a scientist writes about God, his colleagues assume he is either over the hill or going bonkers."[17] Nevertheless, suggesting that the universe suddenly sprang into existence sounds close to the biblical account of God beginning things.

Einstein found the idea that the universe had any beginning both senseless and irritating.[18] Surprisingly, his relativity equations did indicate an expanding universe that would have a beginning, a fact pointed out to him by the Dutch astronomer Willem de Sitter and the Russian mathematician Alexander Friedman (who also found an error in Einstein's calculations). Einstein attempted to solve the problem of expansion by proposing a new unknown force in nature. He added a hypothetical cosmological constant, which would perfectly cancel out the concept of expansion, thus providing a static universe. However, Hubble's redshift data was quite convincing, and Einstein finally admitted that proposing an unknown force was the greatest blunder of his life. Paradoxically, physicists are again returning to variations of Einstein's cosmological constant to explain recent data suggesting that the universe is not only expanding but is accelerating the rate. Other ideas, such as the universe repeatedly expanding and then contracting in a so-called oscillating universe, and that of a steady-state universe, in which new matter is continuously being created, avoid the issue of how to begin a universe, but such concepts no longer receive much acceptance.

If the universe had a beginning, what happened at that momentous moment? We don't know, but theoreticians have offered some interesting ideas. The presently accepted model is called the big bang. That name came from the famous British cosmologist Sir Fred Hoyle, who has been one of the theory's most vocal critics. He introduced the name big bang as a derogatory designation, but the dramatic and descriptive term stuck. In general it postulates that about 12 billion years ago all of the matter of the universe was in a particle smaller than the nucleus of an atom. It was so tiny that it would take 10^{32} such particles laid side by side to make a millimeter.[19] However, the particle would have been extremely heavy and hot, having near infinite density and temperature. During the first period of time for the universe, estimated at one 10^{43} part of a second, we have what scientists refer to as a singularity. During this time conditions were so different that our laws of physics break down and do not apply. Any details are highly speculative. The universe proceeded to expand as it cooled down. An especially rapid period of the expansion called inflation is assumed to have occurred between one part out of 10^{35} to one part out of 10^{33} of the first second. Quarks formed, and protons and neutrons emerged next as expansion continued. By the time the universe was seconds old the nuclei of some simple atoms started to appear. Expansion continued on and on, and stars and galaxies developed when the universe was around 1 billion years old. Galaxies kept forming, and our heavier elements came into existence as stars collapsed. Newer stars and solar systems appropriated these heavier elements as a more mature kind of universe took shape. What happens at the end of all this? Cosmologists have offered various ideas. In the future the universe may slow down and collapse into a huge catastrophic universal big crunch, or it may keep on expanding into an eventually featureless void.

Is this story really true, or is it fantasy resulting from an overdose of science fiction? Are we just dealing with a game of big numbers touted by a few dominating personalities, or are we approaching much-wanted truth? The big bang requires so many fortunate circumstances that some call it the ultimate free lunch, and it indeed challenges our normal concepts of reality. But then so does the universe itself. Some noted astronomers, such as Robert Jastrow,[20] who claims to be an agnostic, and Hugh Ross,[21] who is a Christian believer, see the big bang as evidence for God starting things in the beginning. Besides that, it is not hard to read something of a similar process when the Bible itself speaks of God "stretching out the heavens" in at least five passages.[22] Could God have used a process similar to the big bang in creating the universe? We don't know. One does not have to depend upon the big bang as evidence to believe in God. As we will see below, the matter of the universe is organized in such precise and versatile ways that, regardless of the big bang, a designer God seems to be necessary.

The English astronomer royal, Sir Martin Rees, perceptively points out that "the Big Bang theory has lived dangerously for more than thirty years."[23] Part of the reason it survives is simply that scientists have not proposed anything better, and part is that some impressive data does support it, but still other data challenges it. Points favoring the big bang include: (a) the evidence that the universe is expanding; (b) the proportion of hydrogen to helium that is close to what one would expect from the big bang; (c) an impressive microwave background radiation found all over the universe that has a pattern similar to what the big bang theory suggests. Some minute variations that certain scientists interpret as being responsible for the formation of galaxies have been found in this radiation.

The big bang concept also has serious problems, especially when one assumes that the process occurred without some kind of designer: 1. How could the precision needed for what we see just happen? We will consider some of the details below. 2. We have the baffling problem of the mysterious nature of dark matter that has the potential to change a lot of ideas. 3. Also significant is the problem of the singularity during the first few moments of the big bang that admittedly excludes the laws of science as we know them.

The famous cosmologist Stephen Hawking, especially known because he has been so productive in spite of having Lou Gehrig's disease (amyotrophic lateral sclerosis, or ALS) and being confined to a wheelchair, has attempted to get around the problems of a singularity and of a beginning for the universe. He has combined two great pillars of cosmology, namely, relativity and quantum theory, and added concepts of string theory and branes[24] that deal with dimensions beyond our normal four (three space dimensions and one for time). Also he includes mathematical concepts of imaginary time and imaginary numbers,[25] and suggests a universe with no boundaries in space and time and no need for a beginning or end.[26] As a result, he seems to favor a universe that "would simply be." "What place, then, for a creator?" he has questioned.[27] His views have not met wide acceptance. Hawking occasionally refers to God, but usually in an evaluating and not an accepting context. According to some he may be a deist.[28] A deist believes in some kind of God who started things a long time ago, but is not presently active in nature. In Hawking's recent book *The Universe in a Nutshell* he proposes a purely mechanistic approach.[29] Many cosmologists admit they don't know how the big bang started, while others see that mystery as possible evidence for God.

SOME EXAMPLES OF FINE-TUNING IN THE UNIVERSE

During the past quarter century a firm and important trend has developed within the cosmological community.[30] It recognizes that many facts point to a "just right" kind of universe that alone enables the existence of life, at least on the earth. Few deny the extremely unusual nature of these physical parameters, which are difficult to explain as having come about just by chance. Table 2.1 summarizes some of the findings. One has to imagine the wildest of coincidences to think that these factors, and sometimes their extremely precise interrelationships, happened just by luck. Many see in the evidences of fine-tuning in the universe the imprint of highly intelligent design. Others, of course, don't know, but very few will not acknowledge that something most unusual is going on.

Some of the factors involved are best understood in terms of probabilities. Probability figures sometimes get abused, especially by those who misrepresent what they mean, but when used properly, they can give us quite accurate representations of the chances involved in a situation. It does not take a professional gambler to realize that if you flip a coin, you have one chance out of two for it to land "heads up," or that a dice (die) has one chance out of six of landing with the number 5 on top. If you have one yellow marble and 99 blue marbles in a bag, you have only one chance out of 100 that you will pick out the yellow marble from the bag on the first try without looking.

Probability, which is the chance of a specific outcome occurring, decreases dramatically when you consider several improbable events happening together. To be mathematically correct when you combine improbable events, you have to multiply the improbability of one by the improbability of another, etc.[31] As an example, the chance of getting a number 5 from rolling a dice once is one out of six. The chance of getting a 5 on each of two dice is only one out of 36 ($1/6 \times 1/6$); for a 5 on each of three dice it is one out of 216 ($1/6 \times 1/6 \times 1/6$); and for a 5 on each of four dice in one throw, it is one chance out of 1,296 ($1/6 \times 1/6 \times 1/6 \times 1/6$). In other words, if you keep on throwing four dice again and again, all four will end up with a 5, on an average, only once out of every 1,296 throws. The combined improbabilities we find for the universe are unimaginably smaller and more unlikely. A few examples of improbabilities in our universe follow.

TABLE 2.1

THE FINE-TUNED UNIVERSE

FACTOR	DESCRIPTION
MATTER	Matter is highly organized into more than 100 kinds of elements that interact to form anything from the minerals of planets to highly complex molecules of organisms. The atoms of these elements are composed of subatomic particles that have to have precise characteristics. **For instance, if the mass of the proton were different by just one part in a thousand, there would be no atoms or elements.**
CARBON	The element carbon, which is so essential for life, has a resonance level that greatly favors its occurrence. **If that resonance level had been 4 percent lower or if that of oxygen had been just 1 percent higher, there would be virtually no carbon.**
SUN	The sun faithfully keeps on providing us with just the right amount of light and heat necessary for life on earth. **If the sun were just 5 percent closer or 1 percent farther from the earth, it would rid our planet of all life.**
STRONG NUCLEAR FORCE	The strong nuclear force binds together the parts of the nucleus of atoms. **If that force were 2 percent stronger, we would have no hydrogen and consequently no sun, no water, and no life. If it were 5 percent weaker, we would have only hydrogen and nothing else.**
WEAK NUCLEAR FORCE	The weak nuclear force controls some of the radioactive decay of atoms. In the sun it regulates the fusion of hydrogen into helium. **If that force were slightly stronger, helium would not form, and if it were slightly weaker, no hydrogen would remain.**
ELECTRO-MAGNETIC FORCE	This force deals with charged particles such as electrons, and thus controls chemical changes between atoms. It is a very important component of light. **If it were slightly stronger, such stars as our sun would be red stars and much cooler. If slightly weaker, stars would be extremely short-lived hot blue stars.**
GRAVITY	Gravity keeps galaxies, suns, and our earth together. The precise relation of its strength to that of the strength of the electromagnetic force is extremely critical. **If either of these forces varied by only the minutest amount, this would be disastrous for such stars as our sun.**

The sun. Life would not be possible without the sun, because the earth would be excruciatingly cold. We take the sun for granted, seldom appreciating its consistency in providing us with warmth and light. Sunlight through the process of photosynthesis in plants gives us our necessary food. The orbit of the earth seems to be in just the right place to give us the temperature that our carbon-based life requires. If it were closer or farther away, we would soon experience intolerable temperatures. The surface temperature of the planet Venus, closer to the sun, is about 860° F (460° C), while that of Mars, farther out than the earth, is 9.4° F (-23° C). It has been estimated that if earth were only 5 percent closer or 1 percent farther from the sun, it would rid our planet of all life.[32]

The sun produces its energy by combining (fusing) hydrogen to form helium (Figure 2.2). Such fusion converts about 0.7 percent of the mass of the hydrogen to energy.[33] It is the same kind of process that takes place when a hydrogen bomb explodes, and we can think of our sun as a controlled hydrogen bomb. Solar fusion has been providing us with the right amount of heat and light for a very long time, and estimates suggest that it can keep going for another 5 billion years. The sun is very hot on its surface, and mathematical models of what is going on inside indicate that it is even hotter there. Dramatic planet-size sunspots and flares keep appearing on its surface, indicating its violent activity. The sun appears to be in a balance between the force of gravity pulling its cooler surface inward and the outward pressure from nuclear activity inside. These forces, specifically their basic constant values, as we will discuss below, appear to be at highly critical levels.

Origin of carbon. Carbon is an extremely versatile element that forms the chemical backbone of life on earth, specifically the organic molecules that we find in living organisms including proteins, carbohydrates, fats, and DNA. It turns out that a remarkably fortuitous set of circumstances favors the existence of this essential element. When cosmologists first studied the formation of elements by fusion in stars, they noted that the reactions would favor only the minutest trace of carbon, but carbon is the fourth most common element in the universe. The famous British scientist Sir Fred Hoyle proposed that carbon must have a particular energy resonance level that would facilitate its formation from the combining of nuclei of helium and beryllium atoms. Resonance is agreement between different factors (energy levels and targets) that permit certain things to happen. It is a bit like having the right swing of the bat for the ball being pitched—if all is correct, you get a home run. Likewise the proper resonance level helps in the formation of new atoms. Such resonance greatly enhances the chance that a beryllium nucleus, which results from the fusion of two helium nuclei, will combine with another helium nucleus to form a carbon atom (Figure 2.2). Without this resonance the helium and beryllium would just go on and behave ordinarily, as though nothing mattered. When Hoyle's colleagues at the California Institute of Technology looked for the resonance level of carbon, they found it at just about the value that Hoyle had predicted. One of them, Willy Fowler, later received a Nobel Prize for his studies in this area. The next element in this proposed synthesis series would be oxygen, which would result from adding a helium nucleus to a carbon nucleus (Figure 2.2). It turns out that oxygen has a resonance level just below what is produced so that little of the carbon gets changed to oxygen, thus preserving the needed carbon. John Barrow of the Astronomy Center of the University of Sussex calls this "well-nigh miraculous."[34] Scientists have calculated that if the resonance level of carbon had been 4 percent lower, or if that of oxygen had been 1 percent higher, there would be virtually no carbon.[35] To some, it seems as if God must have loved the carbon atom!

Hoyle's remarkable prediction and the experimental demonstration that it was true is a landmark event in cosmology, and one that according to some, "cannot be overemphasized."[36] Such events illustrate how science can predict. It is science at its best, and scientists tend to make sure that such events do not get overlooked. Hoyle himself, who rejects the idea of a God and Christianity,[37] was also somewhat overwhelmed by the results. He stated that "a commonsense interpretation of the facts suggests that a superintellect has monkeyed with physics, as well as with chemistry and biology, and that there are no blind forces worth speaking about in nature. The numbers one calculates from the facts seem to me so overwhelming as to put this conclusion almost beyond question."[38] Cosmologists John Gribbin and Martin Rees, who, like Hoyle, entertain other views than creation by God for the origin of the universe, are also impressed, stating, "There is no better evidence to support the argument that the Universe has been designed for our benefit—tailor-made for man."[39] Whether one thinks that carbon formed in the stars, as many cosmologists believe, or by some other process, it is hard to escape the suggestion that special factors are related to its crucial role in living organisms.

Strong nuclear force. Physics has four known basic forces. The strengths of their basic constants are remarkably suited to their functions. The most powerful is the strong nuclear force that binds quarks together into protons and neutrons, and then into the nuclei of atoms. Fortunately the force works only over very short distances within the nucleus of atoms; otherwise, the universe might be just one blob held together by the strong nuclear force, and there would be no individual atoms, stars, or galaxies. It appears that the strong nuclear force has to be within close limits to function properly. If it were 2 percent stronger we would have no hydrogen,[40] and without hydrogen no sun for heat, no water essential for life, and no living organisms (whose organic compounds have an abundance of hydrogen). But were the strong nuclear force just 5 percent weaker, we would have only hydrogen in the universe,[41] and all things would be very simple.

Weak nuclear force. Thousands of times fainter than the strong nuclear force, it acts on certain particles within the nucleus of atoms and controls some forms of the radioactive decay of atoms. The weak nuclear force helps regulate the fusion of hydrogen in the sun so that it can keep going for billions of years instead of blowing up like a bomb. If it were slightly stronger, helium, the product of fusion in the sun, would not form, and if it were slightly weaker, no hydrogen would remain in the sun.[42]

Electromagnetic force. This force operates beyond the nucleus of atoms and interacts with electrically charged particles. Having a lot to do with the principles that govern chemical changes, it functions to guide electrons as they orbit the nucleus of atoms. When the electrons change orbits, they can release part of their energy in the form of visible light. If the force were slightly stronger, stars such as our sun would be red ones and too cold to give us the warmth we need. But if slightly weaker, stars would be short-lived, extremely hot blue stars,[43] and we would have way too much heat, but only for a short time.

Gravity. In contrast to the other three forces we have mentioned, gravity is extremely weak. The strong nuclear force is an astounding 10^{39} times greater than gravity. However, in contrast to the strong nuclear force, whose range is within the nucleus of atoms, gravity is extremely far-reaching, exerting its attractive force even between galaxies. Gravity keeps galaxies together, guides the stars in their orbits, and holds the matter of stars together. It is an extremely important force that has to be tuned to a very precise value to give us a balanced universe.

Physicists have attempted to establish a relationship between the four basic forces mentioned above into what they call a grand unified theory, but thus far a causal association between gravity and the other forces has eluded them. In these four forces we find that each seems to be at the proper level for the specific function it performs and for its relationship to the operation of the other forces.

One of the delicate balances that science has noted is the precise relationship that exists between gravity and electromagnetism. Physicist Paul Davies comments, "Calculations show that changes in the strength of either force by only one part in 10^{40} would spell catastrophe for stars like the sun."[44] Under such conditions we would not have our benevolent sun there to warm us up. One part out of 10^{40} is such a minute value that it is difficult to imagine. A hypothetical example may help. Suppose that you had a spherical pile of wooden matchsticks much larger than the entire volume of the earth. The pile is not only a million times the volume of the earth—it is more than a million times a million times the volume of our planet. Such a pile would barely fit between the earth and the sun. Now only one matchstick in the whole pile has a head on it and the rest are bare, headless matchsticks. Since you are extremely cold, you need that one match with a head to start a fire. Your chance of picking the matchstick with a head out of the pile, on the first try, without looking, is greater than one out of 10^{40}. Thus there is a greater probability that you would have found the right matchstick than for gravity to have the right value.

How reliable are such figures? Physicists sometimes talk about even lower probabilities for other relationships in the universe such as one chance out of 10^{50}, 10^{60}, or 10^{100}. A few years ago such kinds of figures helped establish the concept that the universe is really fine-tuned, and science now generally accepts such figures. But one also needs to keep in mind that these deductions are based on extremely complicated data and interpretations, and that the conclusions are sometimes disputed. Even slight changes in these forces or related factors could profoundly alter inferences. On the other hand we are dealing with so many extremely precise relationships that it is difficult not to conclude that the universe does have significant fine-tuning. How could the four forces already discussed select their just right values through the incredible range of 10^{39} times that they have from weakest to strongest, and then have the proper realms of function in which they work, all just by chance, to produce a universe that seems so well suited to support life? Famed theoretical physicist Freeman Dyson comments that "as we look into the Universe and identify the many accidents of physics and astronomy that have worked together to our benefit, it almost seems as if the Universe must in some sense have known that we were coming."[45] The universe seems precisely configured to support life.

Mass of subatomic particles. We mentioned earlier that in an atom, a proton has a mass that is 1,836 times that of an electron, and a neutron weighs very slightly more than a proton. The precision of that slight difference is crucial. Stephen Hawking points out that if that difference "were not about twice the mass of the electron, one would not obtain the couple of hundred or so stable nucleides [elements and their isotopes] that make up the elements and are the basis of chemistry and biology."[46] In other words, just a slight change in the mass of a proton or neutron, and we would have no chemical elements, no chemical changes, no chemists, or any larger things, such as planets, suns, and galaxies. The mass of a proton cannot vary by even one part in 1,000.[47]

Three-dimensional space. We take many things for granted, including the number of dimensions that space has. Why just three? We can think of no dimensions as a dot. One dimension gives us a line, two a surface, and three solid objects. Then we speak of time as a fourth dimension, but that is not a dimension of space. String theory postulates up to 11 dimensions, but curls many of them up into invisibility and/or unimportance. However, string theory is not completely consistent and essentially lacks direct experimental authentication.[48]

Again, why does space have only three dimensions? In the original configuration of the universe, why did we not end up with two or four or many more? A two-dimensional universe would be extremely bizarre. A two-dimensional cat would fall apart (Figure 2.3), and a two-dimensional chicken would not hold together either, let alone provide two-dimensional eggs for two-dimensional omelets that would be extremely flat. Intelligent life with any degree of complexity could not exist in two dimensions—it needs a three-dimensional universe. And it turns out that four dimensions of space (not including time) would also be disastrous. The pull of gravity keeps our earth in its orbit around the sun instead of going straight out into space, as would be expected. In a four-dimensional universe, an "orbiting planet that was slowed down—even slightly—would then plunge ever-faster into the sun, rather than merely shift into a slightly smaller orbit, . . . conversely, an orbiting planet that was slightly speeded up would quickly spiral outwards into darkness."[49] Scholars have noted this relationship for a long time. The famous theologian William Paley pointed to this special evidence of design by God two centuries ago. A four-dimensional universe would have the same problem even on the atomic level, because we would have no stable orbits for electrons around the nucleus, and thus we "could not have atoms as we know them."[50]

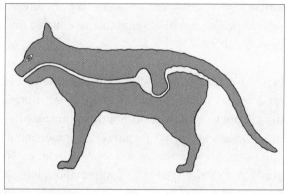

Figure 2.3 *A two-dimensional cat. Note that the digestive tract completely separates the top portion from the lower one, and that the unfortunate animal cannot hold itself together.*

Where did the laws of nature come from? Most scientists have a profound respect for the laws of nature. Such laws make science possible, intelligible, logical, and extremely fascinating. For instance, gravity and electromagnetic forces follow what we call the inverse square law. They decrease in strength in proportion to the square of the distance from the source. If you double the distance, their force is only one fourth of what it was originally, which explains why the light from a candle gets dim so fast as you move away from it. Many other laws exhibit equally complicated mathematical relationships. How could such precision arise? Where did the laws of nature, which often represent specific values and complicated interconnections, come from? In a naturalistic context, in which there is no God, one has to postulate a tremendous lot of fortuitous and precise happenstances.

One might suggest that the laws just came out of the necessity for existence, but this is speculation on a grand scale. Why not have just disorganized blobs of degenerate amorphous goo for a universe? That is what you would expect from random activity, but it is not what we find. Instead, we are discovering quarks and all kinds of other subatomic particles that interact with each other to form more than 100 highly organized kinds of elements that can interact with each other in vital ways. Such interactions sometimes release energy, as is the case with the sun, or they result in the kinds of chemical changes required for life, such as in the production of hormones. These intricate atoms form things smaller than water molecules, and as large as suns, galaxies, and the whole universe itself. The organization of matter is highly intricate, coordinated, and extremely versatile.

How could an organized universe spring out of nothing and just happen to have the laws necessary for its existence? It all seems contrary to the tendency toward disorganization that we normally see in nature. Active things tend to get mixed up, not more organized. When rain splashes on dust, or a tornado blows houses around, it increasingly disorganizes things. They don't organize themselves any more than an explosion in a printing factory produces a dictionary. Such examples illustrate some of the consequences of the second law of thermodynamics and remind us that changes in nature tend toward disorganization, toward mixing things up, and the more time you have, the more things will get chaotic. Scientists call such disorganization entropy. The more things get scrambled, the greater the entropy, and conversely, the more organized, the less entropy. I often notice an increase in entropy on my desk as books, articles, snail mail, e-mail, CDs, and faxes keep pouring in and get jumbled up with each other. According to the second law of thermodynamics, the universe is headed toward maximum disorganization, or entropy, and that indicates that it must have been more organized in the beginning than it is now. Whether you believe that the universe began by the big bang or any other model, the second law of thermodynamics *implies that the universe has both a beginning and an organizer.* If it had existed "forever," we should expect that it would be highly disorganized by now, but it is still highly organized, suggesting a fairly recent origin.

Science has estimated the probability that the organization of the universe could just happen by chance, and it turns out to be way smaller than any normal understandings of plausible possibilities. The Oxford University physicist-mathematician Roger Penrose, in the context of probabilities, remarks: "How big was the original phase-space volume . . . that the Creator had to aim for in order to provide a universe compatible with the second law of thermodynamics and with what we now observe? . . . The Creator's aim must have been: namely [precise] to an accuracy of one part in $10^{10(123)}$. "[51] This is an incredibly small probability. Such figures imply that without a Creator, the kind of organized universe that we have, represents one chance out of the number 1 followed by 10^{123} zeros.[52] If you should try to write that number out by placing a zero on each atom in the known universe, you would run out of atoms long before you would zeros. The universe has only about 10^{78} atoms. Such improbabilities should encourage anyone to look for other alternatives than just chance for the origin of the universe. Many scientists recognize these improbabilities but have not provided any realistic alternatives that fit within the confines of materialistic interpretations that exclude the existence of a God.

RESPONSES TO THE EVIDENCE FOR FINE-TUNING

Few deny the unusual nature of the data indicating a finely-tuned universe, although some minimize it. The list of unusual features is much longer than the few cited above. Cosmologist Hugh Ross lists some 74 examples as well as a number of other parameters necessary for the existence of life.[53] The reader may want to consult more of the literature covering this topic, which in the past two decades has exploded.[54] Does fine-tuning mean that there is a God who is the intelligent Creator of the universe? Not necessarily, according to some authorities in the field, but their argumentation is patently unimpressive. The responses to the data have been varied, fascinating, and instructive. We will discuss the main ones under three subheadings.

The anthropic cosmological principle. You can spend many hours reading the scientific literature trying to figure out what the anthropic principle (anthropic cosmological principle) is, but don't expect any final answers. The philosopher John Leslie generalizes it as: "Any intelligent living beings that there are can find themselves only where intelligent life is possible."[55] This is obviously self-evident statement, it hardly answers the question of how the universe came to be so fine-tuned. Two specialists on this topic, John Barrow and Frank Tipler, in referring to the anthropic principle, suggest that "astronomers seem to like to leave a little flexibility in its formulation perhaps in the hope that its significance may thereby more readily emerge in the future."[56] The concept is ill-defined, different authors interpreting it in various ways, and the leading architect of the concept, Brandon Carter,[57] wishes he had not used the word "anthropic," which refers to human beings, in its designation.[58] The anthropic principle sometimes gets confused with "anthropic balances" and "anthropic coincidences" that refer especially to the fine-tuned universe data.

The anthropic principle, as commonly understood, has at least four forms: weak, strong, participatory, and final. While the four forms are difficult to define, in general the weak form focuses on the fact that observers must be in life-permitting conditions. The strong form stresses that the universe must have the right conditions for life to develop at some stage. The participatory form derives some ideas from quantum theory and suggests the peculiar proposition that observer participation is a moving force in the cosmos. The final anthropic principle looks to the future, proposing that information processing will advance in the universe to the point that even our consciousness will be preserved, thus achieving some kind of immortality.

Scientists sometimes employ the anthropic principle to emphasize our special privileged position in the universe. A universe without life will not be observed—hence, our situation is unusual, and we are looking at things from a selected, although limited, observer perspective. To that extent the principle may have some validity, but our unusual observer privilege can also mean special design by God, which is not at all the usual interpretation of the principle. Occasionally some answer the question of the fine-tuned universe by pointing out that if it weren't so, we simply wouldn't be here.[59] We have here a non sequitur—that is, the answer does not apply to the question. It is similar to being out in a desert and asking about where the water in an oasis comes from, only to be told that if it were not present, trees would not grow there.

While the literature discussing the anthropic cosmological principle is extensive,[60] understandably it is a controversial concept. Some scientists and philosophers have bequeathed to it, or its various aspects, some derogatory comments such as: "devoid of any physical significance,"[61] "have turned the original argument on its head,"[62] "offers no explanation at all,"[63] and "anthropic principles serve only to obfuscate."[64] Clearly the anthropic principle is not objective science.

The many universes explanation. Could there be other universes that we don't know about? Could there be different and numerous kinds of universes? By using the sheer force of numbers we could suggest that there are zillions of universes, and ours just happens by chance to have all the right characteristics for life. This idea has received serious consideration as an explanation of the fine-tuned universe we find ourselves in. We just happen to be in the right universe among many others. But such a suggestion lacks support. Because you can explain almost anything you want to by this kind of argument, it is essentially a useless one. No matter what you find, you just say that it just happened that way in one of a large number of universes. The real problem is Where are those other universes? Where do we find any scientific evidence that they exist? There seems to be none whatsoever.

Leading cosmologists such as Martin Rees and Stephen Hawking sometimes cautiously endorse the idea of many universes. Some associate this idea with interpretations of the strong anthropic principle, while others completely disagree. It is not an area in which you will find any consensus. The idea of many universes has been fruitful turf for lots of musings about our existence, life, and the cosmos. It is not hard to wander off into such imaginary realms, especially when you can mix a modicum of reality with them so they seem more plausible.[65] The humorist Mark Twain comments that "there is something fascinating about science. One gets such wholesale returns of conjecture out of such a trifling investment of fact."[66] He may not have been so far off the mark. There is an element of caution that one should sometimes heed in the aphorism that "cosmologists are often in error but seldom in doubt."

Some have speculated about other universes or even places in our own universe that might have life forms based not on carbon, as for life on earth, but on solid hydrogen or liquid sulfur. The elements silicon and boron are favorite candidates for non-carbon organisms. Others have suggested that life might not be based on atoms but on the nuclear strong force or gravity.

Such life might have created civilizations in neutron stars. There may be universes out there whose nature totally escapes us, or our solar system may be the equivalent of an atom in a much grander scheme of things. Philosopher John Leslie comments: "These are speculations such as make the God hypothesis appear tame indeed."[67]

One can argue that there is always the possibility that all kinds of other universes do exist out there, offering all kinds of ingenious contrivances, but this is not science—it is just imagination. Referring to the concept of an infinite number of universes, Hugh Ross appropriately comments: "This suggestion is a flagrant abuse of probability theory. It assumes the benefits of an infinite sample size without any evidence that the sample size exceeds one."[68] The only sample we know of is our own universe, and there does not seem to be any other. One has to postulate a very huge number of universes to try to reduce all the many improbabilities noted for the fine-tuned universe we live in. Such a suggestion deliberately ignores the scientific principle known as Ockham's razor (also known as the Principle of Parsimony). The principle urges that explanations be kept as few and as simple as possible. Postulating many universes is rampant speculation, not careful reasoning based on known facts.

The fine-tuned universe indicates design. Not all the evidences of fine-tuning of the universe may be correct, and it is expected that some of our scientific interpretations regarding them will change over time. However, the large number of examples and the incredible precision of many of them make it extremely difficult to think that it is all a case of just instances of good luck after more good luck. Furthermore, these values are usually intimately interrelated. Leslie rightly comments, "A trifling change, and the cosmos collapses in a thousandth of a second or flies to pieces so quickly that there is soon nothing but gas too dilute to become gravitationally bound."[69] Also we need to keep in mind, as we illustrated with the dice examples earlier, that the correct mathematical expression in combining several improbabilities is obtained by multiplying these values. This makes the total improbability for a fine-tuned universe much larger than any of the separate improbabilities by themselves.

Could this all happen by chance? How many of these fine-tuned values can we explain away and still feel comfortable about our objectivity? For instance, one can fantasize that all the particles in the universe just acciden-tally sprang into existence 10 seconds ago, and just happened to produce the configuration we observe in nature. However, rationality and an eagerness to really find what is true would dictate that we look for more reasonable al-ternatives. The reality we see about us is not that capricious. The evidence we have is overwhelmingly in favor of some kind of design for our fine-tuned universe.

Several leading astronomers, such as Robert Jastrow, founder of NASA's Goddard Institute for Space Studies, and Owen Gingerich of the Smithson-ian Astrophysical Observatory of Harvard, favor the design interpretation. The astronomer George Greenstein at Amherst College comments: "As we survey all the evidence, the thought insistently arises that some supernatural agency—or, rather, Agency—must be involved. Is it possible that suddenly, without intending to, we have stumbled upon scientific proof of the exis-tence of a Supreme Being? Was it God who stepped in and so providentially crafted the cosmos for our benefit?"[70] Part of the impetus for such conclu-sions comes from the belief that a beneficent Creator has revealed Himself in the sacred Scriptures called the Bible. This raises the specter of religion, and some scientists are uncomfortable mixing science and religion regardless of rather overwhelming evidence in favor of a Creator. However, if we are hop-ing to find truth, we may need to eliminate our prejudices, approach the data with an open mind, and follow the evidence wherever it leads.

CONCLUDING COMMENTS

While the universe is huge, we also find it is all composed of minute sub-atomic particles. All of these parts are related by physical laws and a variety of other factors that make possible the existence of a universe that can sustain life. The precision we see strongly indicates a designer behind the universe (Table 2.1). Some scientists accept this conclusion; others do not.

A number of the latter have often tried to attribute the existence of these precise factors to a vague non sequitur type of anthropic principle, and others to a multiplicity of imaginary universes. But how many coincidences of precise fine-tuning can one face before having to recognize that they re-ally need explaining? If one wants to avoid the conclusion that there is a de-signer, one can resort to the alternatives given above. However, they are essentially distractions from the rather overwhelming scientific data indicating that some intelligence must have fine-tuned the matter and the forces of the universe so that it would be suitable for life. Any such Designer would obviously surpass the universe He created.

---

[1] Newton I. 1692. Second letter to Bentley. In: Turnbull HW, ed. The correspondence of Isaac Newton, Volume III, 1688-1694. Cambridge: Cambridge University Press, p. 240.

[2] Rees M. 2000. Just six numbers: The deep forces that shape the universe. New York: Basic Books, p. 42.

[3] Jastrow R. 1992. God and the astronomers, 2nd ed. New York: W. W. Norton and Co., Inc., p. 11.

[4] Wilkinson D. 2001. God, time and Stephen Hawking. London: Monarch Books, p. 35.

[5] Hawking SW. 1996. A brief history of time: the updated and expanded tenth anniversary edition. New York: Bantam Books, p. 38.

[6] De Pree C, Axelrod A. 2001. The complete idiot's guide to astronomy. Indianapolis.: Alpha Books, p. 277.

[7] The past few years have revealed about as many other small orbiting "moons," especially around the outer planets. See: Cowen R. 2003. Moonopolies: The solar system's outer planets host a multitude of irregular satellites. Science News 164:328, 329.

[8] Ross H. 1995. The Creator and the cosmos: how the greatest scientific discoveries of the century reveal God, 2nd ed. Colorado Springs: NavPress, p. 137; see also: The editors. 1993. Our friend Jove. Discover 14(7):15.

[9] Rees, p. 73. [For publishing information, see note 2, above.]

[10] Dyson F. 1979. Disturbing the universe. New York: Harper & Row Pub., Inc., p. 251.

[11] Ross H. 1996. Beyond the cosmos. Colorado Springs: NavPress, p. 30.

[12] Webb JK et al. 2001. Further evidence for cosmological evolution of the fine structure constant. Physical Review Letters 87(9):091301-1-4.

[13] Hawking. A brief history of time, pp. 33, 34. [See note 5.]

[14] Rees, p. 33. [See note 2.]

[15] Wilkinson, p. 111. [See note 4.]

[16] For discussions and evaluations, see: Arp H. 1998. Seeing red: redshifts, cosmology and academic science. Montreal: Apeiron; de Groot M. 1992. Cosmology and Genesis: the road to harmony and the need for cosmological alternatives. Origins 19:8-32; Hoyle F, Burbidge G, Narlikar JV. 2000. A different approach to cosmology: from a static universe through the big bang towards reality. Cambridge: Cambridge University Press; Narlikar JV. 1989. Noncosmological redshifts. Space Science Reviews 50:523-614.

[17] Jastrow, p. 9. [See note 3.]

[18] As reported in Jastrow, p. 21. [See note 3.]

[19] Based on the 10^{-33} centimeters suggested in Wilkinson, p. 47. [See note 4.]

[20] Jastrow. [See note 3.]

[21] Ross. The Creator and the cosmos. [See note 8.]

[22] Job 9:8; Psalm 104:2; Isaiah 40:22; Jeremiah 10:12; Zechariah 12:1.

[23] Rees, p. 117. [See note 2.]

[24] Hawking SW. 2001. The universe in a nutshell, New York: Bantam Books.

[25] *Ibid.*, pp. 82, 83; Overman DL. 1997. A case against accident and self-organization. Lanham, Md.: Rowman and Littlefield Pub., Inc., p. 161.

[26] Hawking. The universe in a nutshell, pp. 82, 83. [See note 24.]

[27] Hawking. A brief history of time, p. 146. [See note 5.]

[28] Ross. The Creator and the cosmos, p. 91. [See note 8.]

[29] See: also Wilkinson, pp. 70, 71. [See note 4.]

[30] For further discussion, see: Strobel L. 2004. The case for a creator: a journalist investigates scientific evidence that points toward God. Grand Rapids: Zondervan, pp. 93-192.

[31] This assumes that the various probabilities are independent of each other.

[32] Hart MH. 1979. Habitable zones about main sequence stars. Icarus 37:351-357.

[33] Rees, p. 47. [See note 2.]

[34] Barrow JD. 1991. Theories of everything: the quest for ultimate explanations. Oxford: Clarendon Press, p. 95.

[35] Gribbin J, Rees M. 1989. Cosmic coincidences: dark matter, mankind, and anthropic cosmology. New York: Bantam Books, p. 246.

[36] *Ibid.*

[37] Ross, The Creator and the cosmos, p. 113. [See note 8.]

[38] Hoyle F. 1981. The universe: past and present reflections. Engineering and Science 45(2):8-12.

[39] Gribbin, Rees, p. 247. [See note 35.]

[40] Leslie J. 1989. Universes. London: Routledge, p. 35.

[41] *Ibid.*, p. 36.

[42] Overman, pp. 140, 141. [See note 25.]

[43] Leslie, p. 4. [See note 40.]

[44] Davies P. 1984. Superforce: the search for a grand unified theory of nature. New York: Simon and Schuster, p. 242.

[45] As quoted in: Barrow JD, Tipler FJ. 1986. The anthropic cosmological principle. Oxford: Oxford University Press, p. 318.

[46] Hawking SW. 1980. Is the end in sight for theoretical physics? Physics Bulletin 32:15-17.

[47] Barrow, Tipler, p. 400. [See note 45.]; Leslie, p. 5. [See note 40.] Ross. The Creator and the cosmos, p. 114. [See note 8.]

[48] Woit P. 2002. Is string theory even wrong? American Scientist 90(2):110-112.

[49] Rees, p. 135. [See note 2.]

[50] Hawking. A brief history of time, p. 181. [See note 5.]

[51] Penrose R. 1989. The emperor's new mind: concerning computers, minds, and the laws of physics. Oxford: Oxford University Press, p. 344. See also: Dembski WA. Intelligent

design, pp. 265, 266; Leslie, p. 28 [see note 40]; Overman, pp. 138-140 [see note 25].

[52] Such figures are based on assumptions that can be debated. For instance, Penrose assumes the big bang and that the universe is a thermodynamically closed system. The figures do serve to illustrate how highly organized the universe is.

[53] Ross H. 1998. Big bang model refined by fire. In: Dembski WA, ed. Mere creation: science, faith and intelligent design. Downers Grove, Ill.: InterVarsity Press, pp. 363-384.

[54] A sampling of some significant references are: Barrow, Tipler. [See note 45]; Carr BJ, Rees MJ. 1979. The anthropic principle and the structure of the physical world. Nature 278:605-612; Carter B. 1974. Large number coincidences and the anthropic principle in cosmology. Reprinted in Leslie J, ed. 1998. Modern cosmology and philosophy, 2nd ed. Amherst, N.Y.: Prometheus Books, pp. 131-139; Davies P. 1992. The mind of God the scientific basis for a rational world. New York: Simon and Schuster; Davies PCW. 1982. The accidental universe. Cambridge: Cambridge University Press; Gonzales, G, Richards JW. 2004. The privileged planet: how our place in the cosmos is designed for discovery. Washington, D.C.: Regnery Pub., Inc.; Greenstein G. 1988. The symbiotic universe: life and mind in the cosmos. New York: William Morrow and Co., Inc.; Gribbin, Rees [see note 35.]; Leslie. universe [see note 40]; Overman [see note 25]; Rees [see note 2]; Ross. The Creator and the cosmos [see note 8]; Ward PD, Brownlee D. 2000. Rare earth: why complex life is uncommon in the universe. New York: Copernicus; Wilkinson [see note 4].

[55] Leslie, Universes, p. 128. [See note 40.]

[56] Barrow, Tipler, p. 15. [See note 45.]

[57] Carter, pp. 131-139. [See note 54.]

[58] Leslie., Modern cosmology and philosophy, pp. 1-34. [See note 54.]

[59] For example, Heeren F. 2000. Show me God: what the message from space is telling us about God, revised ed. Wheeling, Ill.: Day Star Publications, p. 234.

[60] See the references in note 54 and also the extensive list on pages 23-26 in Barrow, Tipler. [See note 45.]

[61] Silk J. 1994, 1997. A short history of the universe. New York: Scientific American Library, p. 9.

[62] Gingerich O. 1994. Dare a scientist believe in design? In: Templeton J, ed. Evidence of purpose. New York: Continuum, pp. 21-32.

[63] Boslough J. 1985. Stephen Hawking's universe. New York: William Morrow and Co., p. 124.

[64] Swinburne R. 1989, 1998. Argument from the fine-tuning of the universe. In: Leslie Modern cosmology and philosophy, pp. 160-179. [See note 54.]

[65] For complications when you exclude a designer, see: Strobel, pp. 138-152. [See note 30.]

[66] As quoted in: Fripp J, Fripp M, Fripp D. 2000. Speaking of science: Notable quotes on science, engineering, and the environment. Eagle Rock, Va.: LLH Technology Pub., p. 56.

[67] Leslie. Universes, p. 53. [See note 40.]

[68] Ross The Creator and the cosmos, p. 99. [See note 8.]

[69] Leslie. Universes, p. 53. [See note 40.]

[70] Greenstein. The symbiotic universe, p. 27. [See note 54.]

Chapter Three

How Did Life Get Started?

The origin of life appears to me as incomprehensible as ever,
a matter for wonder but not for explication.[1]

—*Franklin M. Harold, biochemist*

MICROBES

The woman would soon give birth to her baby, and she was crying. The hospital had assigned her to its First Clinic, and that was the one place in which she did not want to be. Instead, she begged to go to the Second Clinic. She explained to Dr. Ignaz Semmelweis that mothers were more likely to die in the First Clinic than in the Second. The comment greatly troubled Semmelweis, who was a young attending physician in the First Clinic. Was the woman right? He decided to investigate. When he did, he found the statistics appalling. Looking at the hospital records he found that in six years nearly 2,000 women had died in the First Clinic, and less than 700 in the Second.[2] This incident took place in the Vienna General Hospital of Austria a century and a half ago, when epidemics of the dreaded childbed fever (puerperal fever) were not that uncommon. Too often, about four days after giving birth, a new mother would become feverish and nearly always die within a week. Medical science of the time thought the disease resulted from some kind of noxious vapor in the air or from problems with the mother's milk. Sometimes physicians would employ fresh air as a control measure. All of this did not explain why the death rate in the First Clinic was almost three times as high as in the Second.

Physicians who, as part of their training and research studied the bodies of the dead, ran the First Clinic. Midwives who did not participate in such research operated the Second Clinic. Could this have something to do with the dramatic difference in death rates? A breakthrough came when one of

Semmelweis's colleagues cut himself while performing an autopsy. He developed fever on the fourth day and died soon thereafter. A review of his autopsy showed the same kind of findings as the ones that had been identified with the women who had succumbed to childbed fever. Here was a man who had perished from childbed fever, but it was supposed to be a woman's disease! Could it be that by cutting himself, the colleague had gotten too closely associated with the body of one who had died of the dread disease? Semmelweis introduced strict procedures, using chlorine to clean hands so as to prevent the transfer of what he called "cadaveric poison" from the bodies of the dead to the patients in the First Clinic. The results were dramatic: death rates dropped from 12 percent to around 1 percent. What had caused so many deaths was that the physicians would perform autopsies on those who had died of childbed fever and then attend to mothers giving birth without washing their hands, passing on the deadly disease.

One would think that public opinion would have hailed Semmelweis's success as a great breakthrough, but too often humanity does not follow the data where it leads. While some accepted Semmelweis's conclusions, the medical establishment did not. Jealousy lurked in the hospital, and to concede that physicians might have caused so many deaths was a difficult thing to face. Besides that, hospitals that did not perform any autopsies still had mortality rates as high as 26 percent. Many ridiculed the idea of cleaning one's hands with chlorine. Semmelweis's chief in Vienna did not renew his contract. Many petitions resulted only in an offer of an inferior position. A discouraged and despondent Semmelweis quietly left Vienna, returning to his native Hungary without even contacting his friends.

In 1861 Semmelweis published the results of his study on how to prevent childbed fever. When he sent it to many physicians in Europe, they did not receive it well. The professional community believed that his idea had been discredited. Becoming more and more concerned about all the dying young mothers, he sent out accusatory pamphlets denouncing those spreading the disease. As his depression deepened, his wife finally agreed to have him interned in an insane asylum, where he died two weeks later, joining thousands of mothers who were also martyrs to closed minds and prejudice. Resistance to truth can be formidable. Fortunately, a few years later medical science recognized that Semmelweis was right, and he is now given the respect due for having been a leader in the victory over the very deadly childbed fever.

What Semmelweis and others of his time did not know is that a tiny live microbe, related to the ones that cause "strep" throat and scarlet fever, causes childbed fever. A few scientists had begun discovering a world of tiny organisms, but no one had yet established a solid connection between microbes and contagious diseases. Now, because of dramatic advances in science, we know which microbe (germ) causes which disease, and researchers can often write many books about a single microbe.

Microbes are extremely complicated. One of the best-studied examples is *Escherichia coli,* found in the digestive tract of humans and animals as well as in soil. While it is usually a harmless microbe, a few are fearsome germs. It is tiny rod-shaped organism that is so small that it would take 500, placed end to end, to equal a millimeter (12,800 for an inch). Although it is microscopic, we have discovered that it is extremely complicated. On the outside, each microbe has four to 10 elongated spiral filaments (flagella) protruding from the body that rotate to propel the organism along. Researchers have thoroughly studied the motor at the base of the flagella,[3] and it is a good example of the "irreducible complexity" that we will consider later. On the inside, about two thirds of the microbe consists of some 40 billion molecules of water. Beyond these simple water molecules the composition of the organic molecules is of staggering complexity. By complexity we refer to elements that must depend on each other in order to function properly,[4] and not just a lot of unrelated parts.

The DNA (deoxyribonucleic acid) of a cell is the information center that directs the cell's activities, providing the genetic formula that in the case of *Escherichia coli* codes for more than 4,000 different kinds of protein molecules. The DNA is a fine threadlike loop of nucleic acid that is so long it has to be scrunched up many times to fit in the microbe. In fact, it is 800 times longer than the microbe itself! How the organism manages to access all its genetic information boggles our imagination. Table 3.1 gives some details of the composition of one *Escherichia coli* organism. Protein, carbohydrate (polysaccharide), lipid (fatlike substances), and other special molecules comprise some 5,000 different kinds of molecules, most of which are replicated many times, for a total of several hundred million special molecules in a sin-

TABLE 3.1

ESTIMATED COMPOSITION OF A SINGLE ESCHERICHIA COLI CELL*

COMPONENT	NUMBER OF MOLECULES	NUMBER OF KINDS OF MOLECULES
Protein	2,400,000	4288
Ribosomes	(20,000)	(1)
DNA	2	1
RNA	255,480	663
Polysaccharides	1,400,000	3
Lipids	22,000,000	50
Small metabolites and ions	280,000,000	800
Water	40,000,000,000	1

Based on information from: Blattner FR, et al. 1997. The complete genome sequence of Escherichia coli *K-12. Science 277:1453-1474; Harold FM. 2001. The way of the cell: molecules, organisms and the order of life. Oxford: Oxford University Press, p. 68; Javor GT. 1998. Life: an evidence for creation. Origins 25:2-48; Neidhardt FC, ed. 1996. Escherichia coli and* Salmonella: *cellular and molecular biology, 2nd ed. Washington, D.C.: ASM Press, CD version, section 3.*

gle microscopic microbe. Just because something is small does not mean that it is simple. What people once assumed to be simple life forms have turned out to be unbelievably complex. The baffling question is how did such intricacy ever get organized in the first place?

Warning: the next four paragraphs are not easy reading, but you should get their meaning even if you don't remember all the details. DNA itself is a complex molecule shaped somewhat like a twisted ladder. Details of a small portion appear in Figure 3.1. The molecule consists of basic units called nucleotides that incorporate a sugar, a phosphate, and the all-important bases that make up the genetic information needed to run a cell such as *Escherichia coli.* Four kinds of bases comprise DNA: adenine, thymine, guanine, and cytosine (abbreviated as A, T, G, and C). RNA (ribonucleic acid), similar to DNA and important in communicating information within the cell, replaces thymine (T) with uracil (U). The DNA of *Escherichia coli* consists of 4,639,221 individual bases.[5]

Proteins are versatile molecules acting as both chemical factories and structural parts of cells. They are built of anywhere from dozens to many hundreds of simpler molecules or building blocks called amino acids. Living organisms usually have 20 different kinds of amino acids. In a protein the amino acids are attached end to end, like links on a chain or beads on a string (Figure 3.2). The chain is then folded many times, commonly helped by special large protein molecules, appropriately called chaperones. The position of the various kinds of amino acids along the chain determines the final shape of the molecule. The shape of a protein is extremely important to its function, and only minor variations in the amino acid order are possible if the protein is going to work properly on the right kind of molecule.

When the cell needs a particular protein, a portion of the appropriate DNA is copied to messenger RNA molecules. They in turn are read by

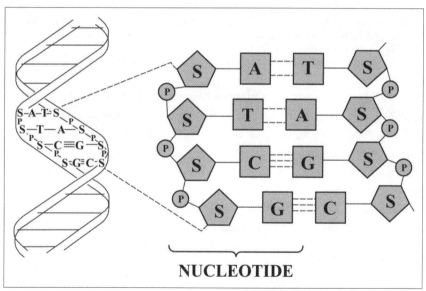

Figure 3.1 *Representation of the structure of DNA. The double coil is illustrated at the left, and a portion expanded at the right. A, T, G, and C represent the bases: adenine, thymine, guanine, and cytosine, respectively. S represents a sugar, and P is the phosphate. A nucleotide consists of P, S, and one of A, T, G, or C. The dashed lines toward the right side represent the hydrogen bonding between bases that unites the two DNA strands.*
After Figure 3 in Evard R, Schrodetzki D. 1976. Chemical evolution. Origins 3:9-37.

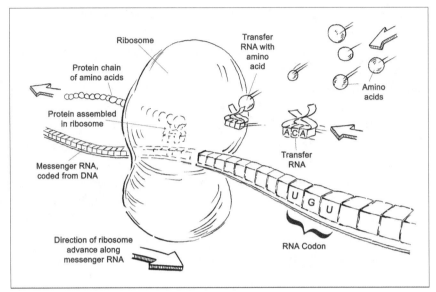

Figure 3.2 *Ribosome activity. The ribosome moves to the right as the code on the messenger RNA is matched by the code on the transfer RNA that has the proper amino acid for that code. The amino acids join together in the ribosome and come out as a protein molecule chain illustrated at the left.*
Based on Figure 4.6 in Harold FM. 2001. The way of the cell. Oxford: Oxford University Press.

transfer RNA, that in combination with special molecules called aminoacyl-tRNA synthetase, which are specific for each kind of amino acid, place the correct amino acids where they are needed in the protein being assembled. This occurs in highly specialized structures called ribosomes (Figure 3.2), which add amino acids at the rate of three to five per second. Ribosomes themselves are complex, formed of some 50 different protein molecules and lots of RNA. One *Escherichia coli* organism will harbor 20,000 of them.

How does the cell select the proper amino acid when making a protein molecule? This is done through the all-important genetic code formed by the A, T, C, and G bases of the DNA, and the A, U, C, and G bases of RNA. Computers work using only two kinds of basic symbols while by contrast, living organisms employ four bases. It takes three bases to code for one amino acid. For instance, in RNA, GAU codes for the amino acid glycine, and CGC codes for the amino acid arginine. The triplet, or unit, of bases coding for an amino acid is called a codon. The codons for the 20 different kinds of amino

TABLE 3.2

THE GENETIC CODE

FIRST LETTER	SECOND LETTER				THIRD LETTER
	U	C	A	G	
U	phenylalanine phenylalanine leucine leucine	serine serine serine serine	tyrosine tyrosine stop stop	cysteine cysteine stop tryptophan	U C A G
C	leucine leucine leucine leucine	proline proline proline proline	histidine histidine glutamine glutamine	arginine arginine arginine arginine	U C A G
A	isoleucine isoleucine isoleucine start, methionine	threonine threonine threonine threonine	asparagine asparagine lysine lysine	serine serine arginine arginine	U C A G
G	valine valine valine valine	alanine alanine alanine alanine	aspartate aspartate glutamate glutamate	glycine glycine glycine glycine	U C A G

To find the code (codon) of an amino acid, look up its name in the table and follow the respective columns and rows for the first, second, and third letters. For instance, the codes for glutamine are CAA and CAG.

acids appear in Table 3.2. Other codons start and stop the assembly line process that makes proteins. Since there are 64 possible codons and only 20 kinds of amino acids in living organisms, several different codons formulate for the same amino acid. Living organisms employ all possible codons.

Enough of overwhelming detail. We could go on and on, page after page, describing many more cellular systems similar to the protein production mechanism. By now you should be getting the idea that a microbe is a precise and extremely complicated thing. As long as *Escherichia coli* is alive, it carries on thousands of chemical changes that we collectively refer to as metabolism, and it also reproduces more microbes like itself.

Organisms such as *Escherichia coli* are among the simplest living forms that exist. Viruses, which are much smaller, do not qualify as living organisms. Consisting of only a lifeless combination of DNA or RNA and proteins, they cannot reproduce by themselves, and thus could not represent the first forms of life on earth. Once one came into being, that would be the end. They get duplicated only by the complex systems of the living cells that they happen to be visiting. A few microbes (mycoplasma) whose dimensions are about one tenth those of *Escherichia coli* probably represent the smallest forms of independent life so far discovered.[6] While science has not studied them as thoroughly, we do know that some have more than a half million bases in their DNA, together coding for nearly 500 different kinds of proteins that perform a multitude of specific functions. If life on earth arose by itself, how did all the right parts ever come together by chance so as to produce the first living thing?

THE BATTLE OVER SPONTANEOUS GENERATION

The pioneer chemist Jan Baptist van Helmont (1577-1644) provided a formula for making mice. If you would hide dirty rags with grain and cheese in an attic, you would soon find mice there! The experiment still works now, but we no longer believe that the mice can just arise spontaneously. From the days of antiquity until quite recently it was commonly held that simple organisms emerged from nonliving matter. Simple observation demonstrated the process, commonly called spontaneous generation. To deny it was to ignore reality. Worms just appeared in apples, and in the springtime frogs showed up in mud. Furthermore, consider the existence of such nasty organisms as tapeworms. Because many argued that God would not have created them, they must have arisen spontaneously in people's bodies. Few held the current view that such parasites represent degenerate forms of originally free living organisms. People assumed that simpler organisms just developed all by themselves wherever they showed up. Now we know that all living things have to come from other living things. The battle to settle the issue was one of the most contentious in science and lasted for two centuries.

One of the early pioneers in this combat was the Italian physician Francesco Redi (1626-1697). People had long observed that maggots, the larval stage of flies, develop in decaying meat (it was before we had refrigeration). But where did the maggots come from? Redi decided to try producing maggots in the remains of several different kinds of animals, including snakes, pigeons, fish, sheep, frogs, deer, dogs, lambs, rabbits, goats, ducks, geese, hens, swallows, lions, tigers, and buffalo. It amazed him to see that regardless of what type of animal remains he used, he always found the same kind of maggots and flies. He also knew that in the summer, hunters would wrap cloth around their meat to preserve it. Could it be that the maggots came from flies and did not appear spontaneously in the meat? To test the idea, he allowed meat to decay in open jars and also in jars covered with gauze that excluded the flies. Because no maggots formed on the meat protected from flies, he concluded that they did not arise spontaneously, but rather came from flies.

Still it did not resolve the issue. Some ideas can take a long time to die. After Redi's time other scientists became involved. As the controversy raged, experiments that involved heating various kinds of organic broths at various temperatures in open and sealed containers gave conflicting results. Sometimes organisms appeared, and sometimes they did not. The question of whether life had to have access to air became an important issue. Strangely, the idea that life could arise spontaneously was even more accepted in the nineteenth century than in Redi's time.[7] Truth was retrogressing.

Then, from the hand of Louis Pasteur (1822-1895), one of the best scientists of all time, came what many consider to be the deathblow to the idea of spontaneous generation. The extremely competent and productive Pasteur worked on a great variety of science projects. He saved the wine industry of his native France by first demonstrating that microbes caused the wines to spoil, then devising a method of preserving the wines by using only moderate heat, which killed off the offending microbes but preserved the flavor.

We now use the same process for milk and call it pasteurization. He developed methods of vaccination against anthrax and rabies, and got involved in the spontaneous generation battle. Using cleverly designed experiments, he was able to answer the various arguments of those who defended spontaneous generation. By using flasks with convoluted access tubes, he was able to demonstrate that broth properly heated would not generate life even though it had open access to air. In his usual exuberant style Pasteur proclaimed: "Never will the doctrine of spontaneous generation recover from the mortal blow of this simple experiment."[8]

But Pasteur was wrong! While his experiments clearly demonstrated that life can come only from other life, and both microbiologists and the medical profession increasingly confirmed that view, other ideas were lurking on the horizon. In England Charles Darwin had just come out with his famous 1859 book *The Origin of Species*. It advocated that advanced organisms had gradually evolved from simpler ones by a process of natural selection, in which the fittest organisms survived over the less fit. Eventually the concept muddied the issue of spontaneous generation. Darwin did not advocate spontaneous generation in *The Origin of Species*. In fact, in later editions he spoke of life "having been originally breathed by the Creator."[9] However, his approach reopened the spontaneous generation door, for if advanced organisms could develop from simple ones all by themselves, why could life not also originate by itself? Later Darwin expressed interest in spontaneous generation, suggesting that "in some warm little pond" proteins might form, "ready to undergo still more complex changes."[10] His later view fit well with a growing interest in naturalistic (mechanistic) explanations. Such concepts sought to eliminate any need for God in nature.

None of the scientists of that time, including Semmelweis, Pasteur, or Darwin, had any idea how complex the smallest kinds of organisms were. If science had known that, one can wonder if evolution would have ever gained the acceptance that it did. The French offered little support for Darwin's secular ideas. Nationalistic interests helped the French Academy of Sciences align firmly on the side of Pasteur. *The scientific community would eventually follow the peculiar pathway of rejecting spontaneous generation for organisms that are now living, but accepting it for the first organism that appeared on earth billions of years ago.* We call that process chemical evolution.

CHEMICAL EVOLUTION

At the beginning of the past century, as evolution began to gain acceptance, interest also focused on how life originated all by itself. Without question, it is the most baffling problem that biological evolution faces, and trying to answer it has become a minor scientific enterprise. By 1924 the famous Russian biochemist A. I. Oparin proposed a scenario whereby simple inorganic and organic substances might assemble into more complex organic compounds, and they in turn could form simple organisms. In England the brilliant population geneticist and biochemist J. B. S. Haldane worked on some of the same ideas. Others added details, and the concept that life originated long ago all by itself in what many often refer to as a "warm organic soup" became a topic of serious consideration.

In 1953 Stanley Miller, working in Nobel Laureate Harold Urey's laboratory at the University of Chicago, reported on a landmark experiment that has become an icon for advocates of spontaneous generation. The experiment sought to simulate the kinds of conditions on earth that might have existed before life originated and that might have given rise to living organisms. Using a closed chemical apparatus that excluded oxygen, Miller exposed a mixture of the gases methane, hydrogen, ammonia, and water vapor to electrical sparks. The apparatus had a trap to collect the delicate organic molecules that might get produced. After many days he discovered that many different kinds of organic molecules had formed, including a few of the amino acids occurring in living organisms. Researchers have repeated and improved on the experiment many times, and it appears that it can create the different kinds of amino acids found in proteins, four of the five bases in nucleic acids,[11] and some sugars. Biology teachers have taught millions of students about the experiment, and scientists and teachers have hailed it around the world as evidence of how life could have originated by itself. For a half century discussion has fermented about the experiment's significance. Actually, a multitude of problems still remain unsolved.

A basic question that needs consideration is about how well laboratory experiments really duplicate the hypothetical conditions on the early earth. Chemists in laboratories, using sophisticated equipment and purified chemicals, may not be providing good examples of the situation that would have existed on a raw primitive earth a very long time ago. Sometimes one can properly relate the observations in the laboratory to what theory assumes to have happened in the past, but sometimes one cannot. For example, the Miller experiment protected the desired products from the destructive effects of the spark energy source by collecting them in a special trap. Use of a protective trap would not really simulate what we would expect on a primitive earth.[12]

We need to keep in mind that we are talking about a world with no life, no laboratories, and no scientists. When scientists go into their laboratories and perform experiments based on their intelligence and employing information and equipment gleaned from centuries of experience, what they are doing is more like what we would expect from an intelligent God rather than an empty earth. In many ways the scientist is representing God's creative activities more than primitive chance conditions. Chemical evolution requires that all kinds of good things happen all by themselves, and not under the guidance of intelligent scientists in sophisticated laboratories.

PROBLEMS WITH CHEMICAL EVOLUTION

You may find this section a bit technical for your taste, but it is important and deserves special effort. If you do not follow every detail, you will still get the basic significance.

Where was the soup? Evolutionists need all the "warm organic soup" they can find. Organisms are so complex and the chance of them becoming organized by themselves so extremely remote that the more of the soup you have, the greater the possibility that somewhere life might have arisen spontaneously. The postulated soup would have been somewhat like consommé or broth, and to increase the potential for protein formation, let us have it equal to the volume of all the world's oceans. The problem is that if you had such organic soup on the primitive earth for many millions of years, so as to accumulate the needed molecules, you would expect to find lots of evidence for this in earth's oldest rocks. While they should contain all kinds of remains of organic matter, researchers have found virtually none.[13] The idea of a primitive soup has been very popular, and is often presented as fact.[14] So, as molecular biologist Michael Denton points out, "it comes as something of a shock to realize that there is absolutely no positive evidence for its existence."[15]

The need for the right kind of molecules. Experiments for producing the first molecules of life generate a host of additional kinds that are actually useless for life. For instance, the Miller experiment created many more kinds of amino acids that are worthless for making proteins than the 20 required for life forms.[16] The life-generating process would need somehow to sort out the trash ones before it could organize the first useful proteins of life. It is difficult to imagine how that could happen by itself. Besides that, the kinds of experiments used to duplicate the origin of life also create toxic molecules such as hydrogen cyanide and formaldehyde.[17]

Organic molecules would not survive. In order to get the first life to form, you need a heavy concentration of organic molecules, particularly the right ones. However, organic molecules are easily destroyed, especially by the ultraviolet light that supposedly provided the energy for their formation. At the California Research Corporation, chemist Donald Hull calculated the chance of survival of the simplest amino acid, glycine (NH_2CH_2COOH), on the primitive earth. He concluded that 97 percent would decompose in the primitive atmosphere before reaching the ocean where the remaining 3 percent would perish in the ocean water itself.[18] The more complicated amino acids that are even more delicate would have even less of a chance to survive. Thus we could expect only extremely dilute concentrations of the right kinds of organic molecules.[19]

Optical isomers. Your left hand and right hand are very similar, but the parts are arranged so that they are mirror images of each other. Organic molecules are also complicated three-dimensional structures that can exist in different forms even though they have the same kinds of atoms and basic chemical structure. Scientists call such different forms of similar molecules isomers, and like your hands they can be mirror images of each other (Figure 3.3).[20] One way of identifying the two mirror images of molecules is by noting the way they rotate light waves coming from polarized light that has its waves lined up. If rotation is to the left, they are the L (levo) type, and if to the right, they are the D (dextro) type. When one synthesizes such organic molecules in the laboratory, they turn out to be half L and half D. One exception is the amino acid glycine, which is so simple it does not have a mirror image of itself. In the Miller experiment half of the amino acids were L and half D, and that is what we would find in the primitive soup.[21] But when you look at living organisms, except for a few extremely peculiar molecules, all their amino acid molecules are of the L type. Living organisms do not

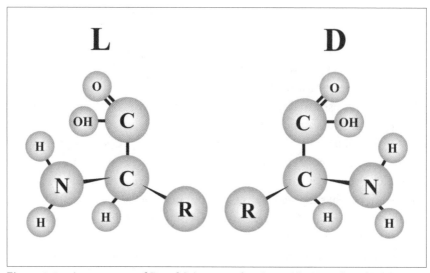

Figure 3.3   *Arrangement of D and L isomers of amino acids. Note that the pattern of the atoms in one form is in a three-dimensional mirror image of the other. R is a radical that varies considerably in chemical composition with the different kinds of amino acids, while the portion illustrated is the same for all amino acids.*

allow much in the way of substitutions. Just one D amino acid in a protein molecule will prevent it from forming into the right shape so that it can function properly.[22] The baffling question for evolution is: How could the first living forms of life assembling in the biologic soup just happen to pick only L amino acids for the first proteins from an equal mixture of L and D? The same problem applies to sugar molecules in DNA and RNA, except that they are of only the D type.

Through the years evolutionists have suggested a host of mechanisms, such as polarized light, magnetism, the effect of wind, etc., to explain why only L amino acids occur in living things.[23] But none solve the problem, so new ideas keep appearing. Researchers grasp even the minutest glimmers of hope from well-controlled artificial laboratory experiments (which could only vaguely resemble anything that might actually have happened in nature) as possible solutions. So far science has found no realistic resolution to the mystery.

Formation of large molecules. The amino acids, nucleotide bases, sugars, etc., are relatively simple when compared to the huge molecules they form when combining to create proteins, DNA, and RNA. We can make many of the simple molecules, but how did the large molecules ever become organized by themselves? A typical protein consists of 100 or more amino acids, and the DNA of *Escherichia coli* is a huge molecule containing more than 4 million bases. Recall that even the simplest kinds of independent organisms we know of have 500,000 bases in their DNA, coding for nearly 500 different proteins.[24]

How did the first life ever get organized? Organisms need proteins to produce DNA and they must have DNA to assemble proteins. Could this system all just result from happenstance, as interactions between atoms follow the laws of physics? Scientists have calculated the odds of forming just one specific kind of protein molecule, and they are incredibly small. One study[25] puts it at less than one chance out of the number 10^{190} (4.9×10^{-191}). Each of the 190 zeros increases the improbability 10 times that of the previous zero. But does not the possibility still exist that it could have happened without intelligent guidance? Although mathematicians sometimes define probabilities of less than one chance out of 10^{50} as impossible, one can still somewhat rationally argue that just once we just happened to get the right molecule on the first chance. However once you have one protein molecule, that is still not much help—you must have at least hundreds of different kinds for even the simplest form of life.[26] Then you need DNA or RNA molecules (often more complex than proteins) as well as carbohydrates and fats (lipids).

If you are going to invoke chance and unguided natural laws, you will need to think of more matter than we have in the known universe to accommodate the improbability! Bernd-Olaf Küppers, who favors the idea that somehow molecules organized themselves into life, has studied such probabilities. He comments that "even if all the matter in space consisted of DNA molecules of the structural complexity of the bacterial genome [i.e., microbe DNA], with random sequences, then the chances of finding among them a bacterial genome or something resembling one would still be completely negligible."[27] While a number of evolutionists recognize the problem, they have not come up with any plausible solutions. But life on earth is more than microbes. Eventually you will need to evolve the DNA of human beings which is 1,000 times larger than that of microbes.[28] We must also consider that the biological information in DNA must be very accurate.

Changing just one amino acid in a protein can spell disaster, as is the case for those afflicted with sickle-cell anemia. As far as the spontaneous origin of life is concerned, rationality would suggest that we look for other alternatives than chance. *You might as well believe in miracles instead of such improbabilities.*

The genetic code. One of the joys of childhood is to create secret codes whereby substituting letters or numbers you come up with a new language understood only by a select few. Warfare uses sophisticated codes and frequently changes them to protect information from the enemy, who has to spend considerable effort to break them. A few decades ago it also took considerable effort to figure out the genetic code.[29] It represents one of the great triumphs of science.

Earlier we mentioned how the bases A, T, G, and C along a DNA molecule direct the production of proteins by passing the information on to RNA and amino acids (Figure 3.2). How does the DNA communicate its information to the amino acids? Through special molecules that use the language of the genetic code. It is virtually impossible to think of any life as we know it without the genetic code, so it needs to exist before that kind of life can exist. Recall that in the genetic code it takes the combination of three bases (a codon) to code for one amino acid (Table 3.2). How such a language came to be is a vexing question for evolution. The primordial soup was no kind of alphabet soup! You would not expect that a multitude of DNA bases would arrange themselves in a meaningful coded order just by random changes. Furthermore, the system would have no usefulness to it, and no evolutionary survival value, until a system that matches the amino acids to the code itself had evolved.

On the other hand, many evolutionists feel that the very existence of a nearly universal genetic code indicates that all organisms are related to each other and have evolved from a common ancestor. As stated in a leading biology textbook: "The universality of the genetic code is among the strongest evidence that all living things share a common evolutionary heritage."[30] Evolutionists widely use the similarities of cells, genes, limb bones, etc., to support evolution, but upon reflection it is not at all convincing. One can easily counter it by suggesting that all such similarities are evidence that one Creator (God) employed the same workable design in producing various organisms. It would seem unusual for Him to conjure up a host of different genetic codes for various organisms when a good working one already existed. The argument from similarities does not carry much significance either for or against the evolution of organisms or the existence of God.

As is invariably the case in living things, the various systems are not simple, and that is also the case for the genetic code. Earlier we mentioned that in making proteins special molecules (aminoacyl-tRNA synthetases) combine the right kind of amino acid with the specific kind of transfer RNA that has the appropriate genetic code for that amino acid. Then the combined amino acid and coded transfer RNA gets matched to the coded information on messenger RNA. That information originally came from the DNA and results in the proper order of amino acids as they link to form a protein molecule in a ribosome (Figure 3.2). Unless the codes on the DNA and the codes used by transfer RNA match, you will not get the needed proteins. A simple analogy is that in order for a language such as the genetic code to be usable, both the speaker and the listener must employ and understand it. Furthermore, any attempt to change the code gradually would spell instant death for any organism.

Languages such as the genetic code just do not seem to appear spontaneously in either living or nonliving things unless purposefully crafted. In an evolutionary scenario of gradual evolutionary development the question arises as to which evolved first: the complicated code on the DNA or the ability to read it and match the amino acids to the code. Neither would seem to have any evolutionary survival value until both of them had begun to function. You need at least a separate DNA three-letter code for each of 20 amino acids. That code has to be matched to the amino acids by the 20 specific special molecules (aminoacyl-tRNA synthetases) that attach the right amino acids to 20 kinds of transfer RNA that then read the information on messenger RNA that came from the DNA. The whole system is not simple, and all of it has to work correctly in order to produce the right kinds of proteins. Actually the system is much more complicated than the minimum suggested above. So many parts associated with the genetic code depend on other parts before they can work that it all very much looks as if some intelligent mind must have created both the code and the complex process of making proteins.

Biochemical pathways and their control. Living organisms usually per-form a whole series of chemical steps to produce just one needed kind of molecule. The changes occur one step at a time in a specific order until the process has obtained the final product. Scientists call the sequence a bio-chemical pathway, and a different protein molecule labeled an enzyme pro-motes each step (Figure 3.4). Such assembly line-like biochemical pathways abound in living organisms. They raise the same problem for evolution as we mentioned for the development of the genetic code. It is implausible to think that a whole complex pathway just suddenly happened all at once by chance, thus giving it some evolutionary survival value. If it didn't come into being at once, how could such complex systems evolve gradually when they have no survival value until the final step is in place to manufacture the needed molecule?

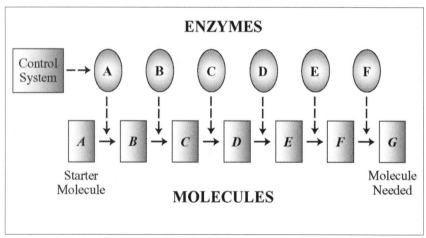

Figure 3.4 *Diagrammatic representation of a biochemical pathway. The enzymes are symbolized as ovals, while the molecules they modify are shown as rectangles. Enzyme A changes molecule A to molecule B, and enzyme B changes molecule B to C, etc., until the molecule needed (in this case, molecule G) is finally produced.*

Evolutionists have wrestled with the problem, and the standard solution presented in textbooks is to assume that all the various required molecules and their intermediates were already available in the environment. The evolu-tionary process thus proceeded backwards through the biochemical pathway. As the supply of a needed molecule (e.g., molecule G, Figure 3.4) became exhausted, an enzyme (enzyme F) evolved to change an earlier intermediate (molecule F) to the more advanced one (molecule G). This process continued backwards until all the different enzymes had evolved.[31] It is a clever suggestion, but because the needed intermediate molecules do not normally exist in earth's environment, it is a nonstarter.[32] Furthermore, it is highly improbable that the right kind of enzyme would be coded both at the right time and place on the DNA so as to provide a system that worked.

What if biochemical pathways just kept on going and going all the time? The result would be chaotic. Fortunately they usually have an elaborate control mechanism (associated with the first step) that regulates the production of the needed molecules. Such regulatory systems can respond in various ways as delicate sensors determine whether or not the organism needs the final molecule of the pathway. Without the regulatory mechanisms, life would not be possible. The enzymes would go on and on producing more and more molecules; and like a house on fire, everything would get out of control. This raises another problem for chemical evolution. Which evolved first— the biochemical pathway or the control system? If it was the biochemical pathway, what would provide the necessary control system? But if it was the control system, why would it ever come into existence since it did not have anything to regulate? *Living things require that very many things all appear at the same time.*

How did cells form? An incredibly huge chasm looms between the simple disorganized molecules of the much-acclaimed Miller type of experiment and the intricate structure of a living cell, including its multitude of controlled operating systems. Unfortunately, biology textbooks rarely note this fact. As the philosopher Michael Ruse points out: "If there is a nasty gap in your knowledge, then your best policy is to say nothing and say it firmly!"[33]

The tiny microbes we have been talking about represent organisms that are simpler than the cells of most living things we are familiar with. The cells in organisms from amoebas to human beings and from mosses to giant redwood trees tend to be larger, and it would take only around 100 of these cells side by side to equal a millimeter (2,500 for an inch). These larger cells have a central nucleus that harbors most of the DNA, and they are configured into all kinds of varieties from gland cells to nerve cells. We must also account for these kinds of cells in the great question of the origin of life.

We have mentioned proteins, DNA, RNA, enzymes, etc., but you don't have even a tiny microbe until you have something that encloses these special molecules, thus facilitating their interaction and control. The cell membrane performs this vital function. We are discovering that cell membranes are extremely complex. They include special parts that control and "pump" what goes in and out of the cell. How did the first living cell evolve its membrane?

Chemical evolutionists have suggested that aggregations of large organic molecules or even amino acids might have formed spherical masses that resulted in the first cells.[34] Such spheres would have no functioning cell membrane, no internal organization, or any other special characteristics necessary for life. Referring to this, William Day, who still argues for some kind of biological evolution, comments: "No matter how you look at it, this is scientific nonsense."[35] Besides that, life is not just a bunch of chemicals in a bag. They would soon reach what we call chemical equilibrium, and at equilibrium you are dead. Such a cell would not carry on the many metabolic changes characteristic of living things. As biochemist George Javor points out, for life you need to get a multitude of interdependent biochemical pathways started and operating.[36] You can have all the chemicals necessary, such as those that might be found in chicken soup, but life does not spontaneously appear there.

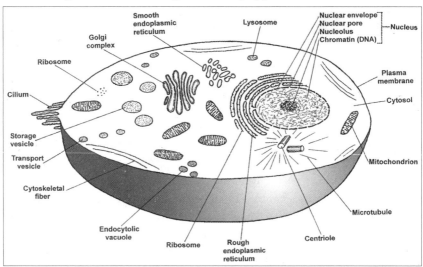

Figure 3.5   *Representation of a typical animal cell cut open to show some of the internal parts.*

We encounter all kinds of specialized structures in cells (Figure 3.5). They include: centrioles, which help in cell division; mitochondria, which provide energy; the endoplasmic reticulum, where the ribosomes make protein molecules; Golgi bodies, which collect synthesized products; lysosomes, which digest cell products; filaments, which protect the cell structure; and microtubules, which, along with special molecules, move cell parts to where they are needed. And this is just the beginning of what we are discovering to be an unbelievably small and intricate realm.

What is the probability that a cell could have just come about by chance? Some investigators have addressed the question, and the possibility is extremely remote. Sir Fred Hoyle[37] has calculated that the probability of getting at one time 2,000 enzymes (protein molecules) necessary to start life is one chance out of $10^{40,000}$. It is hard to conceive how small this possibility is. Just to write out the 40,000 zeros of this improbability using ordinary numbers would require more than 13 pages of zeros! It would be very boring reading. Remember that each zero added multiplies the improbability 10 times. It turns out that Hoyle was very optimistic. Using thermodynamics (the energy relationships of atoms and molecules), physical chemist Harold J. Morowitz,[38] who favors an evolutionary origin of life, calculates that the probability of a very tiny microbe (mycoplasma) appearing spontaneously is one chance out of $10^{5,000,000,000}$ ($10^{-5 \times 10^9}$). Cosmologist Chandra Wickramasinghe, who argues for an extraterrestrial source of life, is more graphic in describing the dilemma: "The chances that life just occurred on earth are about as unlikely as a typhoon blowing through a junkyard and constructing a [Boeing airplane] 747."[39]

Reproduction. To have just one living cell sitting there will not establish life on earth. Before it dies, that cell needs to duplicate itself again and again. Reproduction is one of life's leading identifying characteristics. In order to reproduce, all the necessary intricate parts of the cell have to be replicated, or life will cease. While how tiny cells do this challenges our imagination, science is now providing a host of fascinating details.

The most important part that needs duplicating is the DNA. A special mechanism, consisting of some 30 protein molecules called DNA polymerase, runs along the DNA and replicates it. When the cell starts dividing, the DNA, which in humans totals about three feet (about a meter) in length in each cell, compresses itself into 46 microscopic chromosomes. The cell accomplishes this by first coiling the DNA, next coiling the coil, then folding the coil and finally folding the folded double coil. This results in paired chromosomes that will get sorted to each new cell so each has a full complement of DNA. The chromosomes line up in the middle between the two newly forming cells, and microtubules hook on and pull them toward the centrioles that lie at opposite ends (Figure 3.6). There the chromosomes uncoil themselves in the new daughter cells, where they direct cell activity. What seems even more amazing is how the 1.6-millimeter-long circular loop of DNA in *Escherichia coli*, scrunched up in a cell only one eight-hundredth its length, gets duplicated. It does so without forming compressed chromosomes, as is the case for advanced organisms, and without getting tangled. The process takes about 42 minutes, and this means that the two DNA protein polymerase mechanisms, which move along the DNA, copy the genetic code bases at the rate of about 1,000 pairs per second. The marvels of microbes never cease to amaze us.

We have given only a general overview of a highly complicated process about which we know some details but still have much to learn. And then there are the rest of the parts of all kinds of cells, such as the cell membrane and lots of fibers that have to be duplicated. Could such complicated and necessarily integrated processes just arise by themselves? Many parts depend on still other parts and would have no evolutionary survival value unless all the needed aspects are present. For instance, what use would DNA be without the protein polymerase mechanism to duplicate it? And what value would the polymerase be with no DNA to replicate? Either would be meaningless without the other, and without both we would have no new organisms. And that is the case for most aspects of living organisms. You need an extensive array of interdependent parts before you could even start thinking about life. Biochemist Michael Behe has studied a number of systems of organisms that have many subunits that must work with others in order to function at all. To him these systems represent "irreducible complexity,"[40] and that very well describes what we are discovering.

Origin of the DNA proofreading and editing systems. When a cell divides, hundreds of thousands to thousands of millions of the bases that form the genetic code on the DNA have to undergo duplication. Some errors in copying are harmless and in rare cases may even be beneficial, but almost all

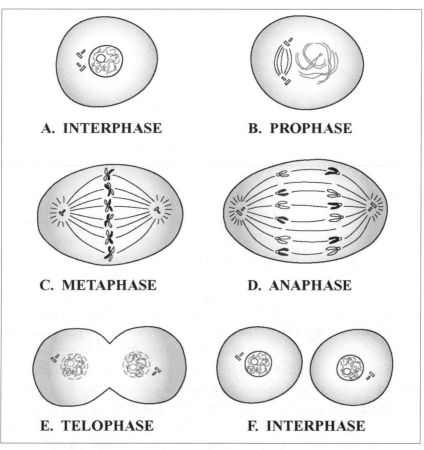

Figure 3.6 *Simple representation of the process of cell division. First the nuclear membrane breaks down and the DNA condenses into double rod-shaped chromosomes (prophase). The chromosomes are then lined up on a plane lying between the prospective cells, while the tiny paired centrioles become located at opposite poles (metaphase). The chromosome pairs separate and are drawn to opposite poles (anaphase). Constriction and separation begin, the nuclear membranes are restored (telophase) and the original cell becomes two normal functioning cells (interphase).*

others are detrimental and even fatal. Fortunately, living things have a number of special systems to proofread the copied code, remove the errors, and replace them with the correct bases.[41] Because such systems inhibit mutations, they would interfere with evolution. Without the editing and correcting process done by proteins, the rate of copying errors can be as high as

1 percent, and that is totally incompatible with life. Deactivating this corrective system in cells causes some forms of cancer. The elaborate correcting systems can improve the accuracy of copying by millions of times, and that permits life to continue as cells divide again and again while maintaining the accuracy of their DNA. This raises another question for the model of spontaneous generation of life. How did complex proofreading systems ever evolve in a system that would have been so inconsistent in copying before their existence? One scientist identifies such a difficulty as "an unsolved problem in theoretical biology."[42]

SOME OTHER IDEAS

Many scientists realize how improbable it is for life to arise spontaneously, so it is not surprising that they have proposed a number of alternative explanations. But like the examples given earlier, they border on the impossible. They include: 1. *Life originated from special information found in atoms.* We find no evidence for this. 2. *A much simpler kind of life gave rise to present life.* Unfortunately, we don't have much more evidence for that, either. 3. *A self-generating cyclic system of proteins and RNA might have started life.* However, the molecules involved are difficult to produce and tend to break down rapidly. Especially problematic is the fact that such synthesized RNA does not have the massive library of genetic information needed for even the simplest organism. 4. *Possibly life originated in hot springs in the deep oceans.* The heat of such a limited environment could easily destroy delicate molecules, and also it does not provide for the vast genetic information required for a living system. 5. *Life could have originated using patterns of minerals such as pyrite (fool's gold) or clay minerals as a template for the complex molecules of living organisms.* While such minerals have an orderly arrangement of atoms, the pattern repeats itself again and again, and thus could not provide the varied complex information needed for life. Unfortunately, scientists often confuse an abundance of orderliness (a characteristic of clay minerals) with the complexity found in DNA. It is a bit like having a book consisting of only the letters A, B, and C repeated constantly from beginning to end, while what you need for life is an Oxford dictionary loaded with meaningful information. 6. *Life originated as RNA because RNA has some enzyme properties and a minute suggestion of replication.* This idea has been a popular one. But while a well-educated chemist can make RNA in the laboratory, it does not appear that it was possible on the primitive earth before any life was present. Biochemist Gerald F. Joyce, who specializes in this area and is still sympathetic to the RNA model, warns that "you have to build straw man upon straw man to get to the point where RNA is a viable first biomolecule."[43] Furthermore, as for the other suggestions given above, where is the specific information necessary for life going to come from? 7. *If it is so difficult for life to start on earth, why not have it come from somewhere in outer space, perhaps traveling on a comet or a dust particle?* But this does not help much, because it simply shifts the same problems to somewhere else. The same improbabilities and problems we encounter on earth we also have to face elsewhere. All seven alternative suggestions have serious problems, and all totally fail to explain the origin of the vast integrated information we find on DNA that is so essential for the functioning and reproduction of even the most simple independent organism that we know of.

Some of the data presented above have generated one of the greatest shocks the scholarly community has faced in a long time. The legendary British philosopher Antony Flew has written nearly two dozen books on philosophy, has been a champion icon for atheists for decades, and has been called the world's most influential philosophical atheist. However, he has recently found some of the evidence from science quite compelling and has changed his view from atheism to believing that some kind of God must be involved to explain what science is discovering. In his words, he "had to go where the evidence leads." He points out that "the most impressive arguments for God's existence are those that are supported by recent scientific discoveries." Flew refers to the fine-tuning of the universe and in particular to the reproductive power of living organisms, indicating that evolutionists "must give some account" of such things. Furthermore, "it now seems to me that the findings of more than fifty years of DNA research have provided material for a new and enormously powerful argument to design."[44] While Flew is not adopting a traditional religion, he has given up atheism because of the nature of the scientific data itself.

CONCLUDING COMMENTS

One of the most profound questions we face is that of how life originated. Pasteur demonstrated that life comes only from previous life. Since then a veritable armada of scientists have been looking into how life could have arisen by itself, but that has not turned out to be a very fruitful search.

We are finding that a "simple" cell is immensely more complicated than anyone had imagined, and we still have much more to learn.

Scientists have had some success in creating simple organic molecules, such as amino acids, under assumed primitive earth conditions. However, the relationship of their laboratory experiments to what might have actually happened on a raw and empty earth is suspect. Beyond that questionable success, chemical evolution has encountered a plethora of insurmountable problems. Science has found no evidence of a primordial organic soup in the geological record itself. The molecules needed for life would be too delicate to survive the rigors of a primitive earth. Experiments producing the simple molecules of life do not provide the required optical configuration, and come mixed with all kinds of unnecessary and harmful molecules. How did just the right ones get selected? Nothing seems to provide the specific information needed for large molecules, such as proteins and DNA.

Many interdependent factors, such as those found in the genetic code, DNA synthesis, and controlled biochemical pathways challenge the idea that they could have developed gradually, with evolutionary survival value at each stage, until all necessary factors were present. Alternative models are unrealistic or unsatisfactory and totally ignore the fact that life requires an abundance of coordinated information. Then there is the question of forming all the parts of a cell and having those parts reproduce. Mathematical calculations all indicate essentially impossible probabilities. Researcher Dean Overman outlines the evolutionary dilemma: "One may choose on a religious basis to believe in self-organization theories, but such a belief must be based on one's metaphysical assumptions, not on science and mathematical probabilities."[45]

The failure of chemical evolution to provide a workable model, and the persistence of scientists in trying to make one, raises a serious question about the current practice of science. Many scientists have faith in models of the origin of life that follow a multitude of essentially impossible propositions, yet they will not consider faith in some cosmic designer. Why? Does such behavior reveal a prejudice against God in the current scientific mindset? Is this attitude preventing science from finding all truth? Something seems askew.

---

[1] Harold FM. 2001. The way of the cell: molecules, organisms and the order of life. Oxford: Oxford University Press, p. 251.

[2] This account of Semmelweis is based mainly on: Clendening L. 1933. The romance of medicine: behind the doctor. Garden City, N.Y.: Garden City Pub. Co., Inc., pp. 324-333; Harding AS. 2000. Milestones in health and medicine. Phoenix, Ariz.: Oryx Press, pp. 24, 25; Manger LN. 1992. A history of medicine. New York: Marcel Dekker, Inc., pp. 257-267; Porter R. 1996. Hospitals and surgery. In: Porter R., ed., the Cambridge illustrated history of medicine. Cambridge: Cambridge University Press, pp. 202-245.

[3] Behe MJ. 1996. Darwin's black box: the biochemical challenge to evolution. New York: Touchstone, pp. 69-72.

[4] See chapter 4 for further discussion of the complexity concept.

[5] Blattner FR et al. 1997. The complete genome sequence of *Escherichia coli* K-12. Science 277:1453-1474.

[6] Fraser CM et al. 1995. The minimal gene complement of *Mycoplasma genitalium*. Science 270:397-403.

[7] Farley J. 1977. The spontaneous generation controversy from Descartes to Oparin. Baltimore: Johns Hopkins University Press, p. 6.

[8] Vallery-Radot R. 1924. The life of Pasteur. Devonshire RL, trans. Garden City, N.Y.: Doubleday, Page and Co., p. 109.

[9] Darwin C. 1859. 1958. The origin of species by means of natural selection, or the preservation of favoured races in the struggle for life. New York: Mentor, p. 450.

[10] Darwin F, ed. 1888. The life and letters of Charles Darwin, vol. 3. London: John Murray, p. 18.

[11] Shapiro R. 1999. Prebiotic cytosine synthesis: a critical analysis and implications for the origin of life. Proceedings of the National Academy of Sciences 96:4396-4401.

[12] Thaxton CB, Bradley WL, Olsen, RL. 1984. The mystery of life's origin: reassessing current theories. New York: Philosophical Library, pp. 102-104.

[13] Among many references, see: Yockey HP. 1992. Information theory and molecular biology. Cambridge: Cambridge University Press, pp. 235-241.

[14] *Ibid.,* p. 240.

[15] Denton M. 1985. Evolution: a theory in crisis. London: Burnett Books Limited, p. 261.

[16] Thaxton, Bradley, Olsen, pp. 52, 53. [For publishing information, see note 12, above.]

[17] Giem PAL. 1997. Scientific theology. Riverside, Calif.: La Sierra University Press, pp. 58, 59.

[18] Hull DE. 1960. Thermodynamics and kinetics of spontaneous generation. Nature 186:693, 694.

[19] Overman DL. 1997. A case against accident and self-organization. Lanham, Md.: Rowman and Littlefield Pub., Inc., pp. 44-48; Thaxton, Bradley, Olsen, pp. 45-47 [see note 12]; Yockey, pp. 234-236 [see note 13].

[20] The identification of these forms for some complicated molecules is more difficult.

[21] For recent examples giving the same results, see: Bernstein MP et al. 2002. Racemic amino acids from the ultraviolet photolysis of interstellar ice analogues. Nature 416:401-403; Muñoz Caro GM et al. 2002. Amino acids from ultraviolet irradiation of interstellar ice ana-

logues. Nature 416:403-409.

[22] Yockey (p. 237) indicates that a mixture of the two kinds of amino acids would interfere with the folding process. [See note 13.]

[23] For a recent attempt, see: Saghatelian A et al. 2001. A chiroselective peptide replicator. Nature 409:797-801.

[24] Fraser. [See note 6.]

[25] Bradley WL, Thaxton CB. 1994. Information and the origin of life. In: Moreland JP, ed. The creation hypothesis: scientific evidence for an intelligent designer. Downers Grove, Ill.: InterVarsity Press, pp. 173-210.

[26] Discussed further in chapter 5.

[27] Küppers B-O. 1990. Information and the origin of life. Manu Scripta A, trans. Cambridge: MIT Press, p. 60.

[28] Some scientists debate the usefulness of the introns on genomes, but others suggest more and more functions for them. See: Brownlee C. 2004. Trash to treasure: junk DNA influences eggs, early embryos. Science News 166:243; Dennis C. 2002. A forage in the junkyard. Nature 420:458, 459; Standish TG. 2002. Rushing to judgment: functionality in noncoding or "junk" DNA. Origins 53:7-30.

[29] Nirenberg M, Leder P. 1964. RNA codewords and protein synthesis: the effect of trinucleotides upon the binding of sRNA to ribosomes. Science 145:1399-1407.

[30] Raven PH, Johnson GB. 1992. Biology, 3rd ed. St. Louis: Mosby-Year Book, Inc., p. 307.

[31] The classic paper is: Horowitz NH. 1945. On the evolution of biochemical syntheses. Proceedings of the National Academy of Sciences 31(6): 153-157.

[32] Behe, pp. 154-156. [See note 3.]

[33] Ruse M. 2000. The evolution wars: a guide to the debates. New Brunswick, N.J.: Rutgers University Press, p. 154.

[34] Oparin AI. 1938, 1965. Origin of life, 2nd ed. Morgulis S, trans. New York: Dover Publications, Inc., pp. 156-162; Fox SW, Harada K, Mueller, G. 1970. Chemical origins of cells. Chemical and Engineering News 48(26):80-94.

[35] Day W. 1984. Genesis on planet earth: the search for life's beginning, 2nd ed. New Haven, Conn.: Yale University Press, pp. 204, 205.

[36] Javor GT. 1998. What makes a cell tick? Origins 25:24-33.

[37] Hoyle F. 1980. Steady-state cosmology revisited. Cardiff, U.K.: University College Cardiff Press, p. 52; Hoyle F, Wickramasinghe, NC. 1981. Evolution from space: a theory of cosmic creationism. New York: Simon and Schuster, pp. 24, 26.

[38] Morowitz HJ. 1968. Energy flow in biology: biological organization as a problem in thermal physics. New York: Academic Press, p. 67.

[39] Anonymous. 1982. Threats on life of controversial astronomer. New Scientist 93(1289):140.

[40] Behe, p. 39. [See note 3.]

[41] Radman M, Wagner R. 1988. The high fidelity of DNA duplication. Scientific

American 259(2):40-46.

[42] Lambert GR. 1984. Enzymic editing mechanism and the origin of biological information transfer. Journal of Theoretical Biology 107:387-403.

[43] The quotation is from: Irion R. 1998. RNA can't take the heat. Science 279:1303. See also: Joyce GF. 1989. RNA evolution and the origin of life. Nature 338:217-224.

[44] Flew A, Habermas GR. 2004. My pilgrimage from atheism to theism: a discussion between Antony Flew and Gary Habermas. Philosophia Christi 6(2):197-211; see also: Flew A, Varghese RA. 2007. There is a God: how the world's most notorious atheist changed his mind. New York: Harper One.

[45] Overman, pp. 101, 102. [See note 19.]

Chapter Four

The Perplexity of Complexity

The challenge of fully elucidating how atoms assemble themselves—here on earth, and perhaps on other worlds—into living beings intricate enough to ponder their origins is more daunting than anything in cosmology.[1]

—Sir Martin Rees, Astronomer Royal

TRAGEDY

The news was bad, and a few days later it would be even worse. My friend Lloyd had worked late into the night and then started back to college. But it would be a very long time before he would get there. He was exhausted, and as he drove along a lonely country road, weariness overcame him, and his unguided car plunged into a stream. He survived the ordeal, but we soon learned that his injuries were extremely severe. The accident had severed the nerves in the lower part of his spinal cord, and he no longer had control of his legs. For the rest of his life he was confined to a wheelchair.

Healing, if you can call it that, was extremely slow. Fortunately he was no ordinary person, and he determined not to let his problems transform him into a burden on society. His strong mental capabilities and perseverance sustained him through college and for decades after. He served admirably as a teacher, chaplain, and editor. But the accident was not the end of his physical troubles. With their nerves severed, his legs became a constant source of problems until, five years later, he had them cut off.

INTERDEPENDENT PARTS

The trouble Lloyd had with his legs after the injury to his spinal cord illustrates how the parts of living organisms depend on each other. The muscles in his legs could not function without nerves sending the impulses that cause them to contract. Nerves all by themselves would also have no function without muscles to respond to the impulses sent, and both would be useless without a complicated control system in the brain to determine when motion is desirable and thus provide an appropriate stimulus to contract the muscles. These three parts—skeletal muscle, nerve, and control mechanism—provide a simple example of interdependent parts. None of them can work unless all necessary parts are present. In my friend's case the nerve was the missing part, and because of that, his legs were not only useless but a hindrance that he chose to get rid of.

As usual, we are grossly oversimplifying things. In our example we actually need even more vital parts, such as the special structures that transfer the nerve impulse from the nerves to the muscles. They secrete a specific chemical received by a special receptor on the muscle, and that receptor, when stimulated, changes the electrical charge on the muscle fibers and causes them to contract. And we could cite many more parts of this complex system.

As these systems assemble, nerves can originate from a central nerve area, but you need a plan that will associate each muscle with the right control mechanism, a fact that complicates the picture. The very fine elongated fibers that are part of the nerve cells and that carry the nerve impulses can be longer than three feet (one meter), yet they are only 1/25,000 inch (1/1,000 of a millimeter) in diameter. In order to keep these elongated cell fibers functioning properly, special transport systems carry chemicals back and forth along their great lengths.[2] The muscles are no simple structure either. Our muscular strength results from many thousands of units containing tiny protein molecules that crawl along fibers so as to pull and contract the muscles that activate most of the 206 bones of our body.

Control of muscular activity is also a very complex thing, with major parts of the brain or spinal cord regulating more than 600 muscles in our body. Many body movements involve the coordinated action of a number of muscles at the same time. Without adequate guidance, we can have muscle spasms and other serious conditions, such as cerebral palsy or epilepsy. To facilitate smooth action, the body has special spindle-shaped structures in the muscles that constantly monitor the operation of the muscles. Such spindles are especially abundant in those muscles that control precise motion, such as those that flex our fingers. The spindles have two kinds of modified muscle fibers that maintain tension so that special sensory nerves on the fibers can

97

monitor muscle length, tension, and motion. Somewhat like miniature muscle systems inside the muscles themselves, they have their own sets of interdependent parts. Not all parts of the spindles are dependent on all the other components, but most, if not all, will not function without something else being present.

A burglar alarm system also illustrates interdependent parts. Whether in a car or a house, it requires a certain number of basic parts. You must have: (1) a sensor that detects an intruder; (2) wires (or a transmitter) to communicate to a control system; (3) a control system; (4) a source of power; (5) wires to send a signal to an alarm; and (6) an alarm that is usually a siren. Like the muscle, nerve, and control mechanism example and several examples given in the previous chapter, these are systems of interdependent parts—the whole will not work until all the necessary components are present. They represent irreducible complexity,[3] sometimes also called irreducible structure.[4]

By complexity we refer specifically to systems such as a burglar alarm, which have interdependent parts. This is not at all the same as complicated. Many things can be complicated, but they are not complex because their parts are not related to each other and do not depend on each other. For instance, a mechanical watch with gears rotating and meshing with each other is complex—it consists of interdependent parts, necessary for the proper function of the timepiece. On the other hand, a pile of dirt can be very complicated, having many more parts than a watch, but it is not complex because the parts are not interdependent. Pages of various documents in a trash container can be complicated, but pages of a novel are complex, being related and dependent on each other as the plot of the novel develops.

Complex things are complicated, but complicated things need not be complex if the parts have no real connection or relationship with each other. In the great question about whether science is discovering God it is important to distinguish between complex and complicated. Unfortunately, many, including scientists, confuse the two terms. Most biological systems are complex. Like our example of muscles, nerves, and a control mechanism, they have many interdependent parts that will be useless unless other necessary related parts are also present.

Two centuries ago the English philosopher and ethicist William Paley (1743-1805) published a famous book entitled *Natural Theology*,[5] which became a popular philosophical icon, going through many editions. The book was a response to suggestions that life might have originated by itself and that there is no God. Paley argued that living things must have had some kind of maker, and he drew that conclusion long before we had any idea of how extremely complex they were. His most famous example relates to a watch. He pointed out that if on a walk we ran into a stone, we would probably not be able to explain how it originated. On the other hand, if we found a watch on the ground, we would immediately conclude that the watch had a maker. Someone who understood its construction and use had to put it together. Since nature is more intricate than a watch, it must also have a maker. In addition, he argued that since an instrument such as a telescope had a designer, the same thing also had to be the case for complex eyes. Paley challenged the idea that evolutionary advancement was the result of a multitude of small changes and illustrated his point by referring to that indispensable structure in our throats we call the epiglottis. When we swallow, it keeps food and drink out of our lungs by closing off our windpipe. If the epiglottis had developed gradually over a long time, it would have been useless most of that time, since it would not close the windpipe until it had evolved to full size.

People have criticized his arguments for a long time, often asserting that Darwin and his concept of natural selection took care of Paley's examples. In his book *The Blind Watchmaker*, famed Oxford University professor Richard Dawkins especially addresses the watch example, pointing out that "it is wrong, gloriously and utterly wrong." Also, the "only watchmaker in nature is the blind forces of physics," and furthermore "Darwin made it possible to be an intellectually fulfilled atheist."[6] But recent advances in modern biology, revealing a vast array of interdependent systems, have caused many to wonder if Paley and his ridiculed watch might have been right on target.

CAN EVOLUTION EXPLAIN COMPLEXITY?

Evolution has been unable to provide a satisfactory explanation for the gradual development of complex systems with their interdependent parts. Quite the contrary, the very process that supposedly drives evolution can actually interfere with the development of complexity. In 1859 Charles Darwin published his seminal volume *The Origin of Species*. He proposed that life evolved from simple to advanced forms, one minute step at a time, through a process he called natural selection. He reasoned that organisms constantly vary and that overreproduction results in competition for food, space, and other resources. Under such conditions those organisms that have some advantage will survive over inferior ones. Thus we have evolutionary advancement by survival of the fittest.

The system may at first seem quite reasonable and it is widely accepted, although some evolutionists opt for just changes without any natural selection to help out. Survival of the fittest should eliminate weak, aberrant organisms, but it does not provide for the evolution of complex systems with interdependent parts. Those systems do not work, and have no survival value, until *all* the necessary subunits are present. In other words, natural selection works to eliminate inferior organisms, but it cannot design complex systems. Besides that, natural selection is not a process that necessarily supports the concept of evolution. The fittest organisms would be expected to survive whether they evolved or were divinely created.

Scientists now attribute the variation we see in organisms to mutations that represent more or less permanent changes in DNA. We are discovering that a variety of factors cause such mutations. Scientific interest is shifting from tiny changes in one or a few DNA bases to the activity of transposable elements sometimes consisting of thousands of bases. Such segments move around, sometimes at great rates, from one part of the DNA to another and even between organisms. The shifts they produce can be useful in providing variety, but they can also be harmful. Other scientists also look at different kinds of mechanisms for providing variation, such as changes in control genes that direct development (homeobox genes).[7] Here is an area of biology in which we still have much to learn. Both creationists and evolutionists recognize that mutations occur and cause minor changes termed microevolution. Evolutionists also believe in much larger changes called macroevolution, while creationists tend to shy away from that concept. The evidence for microevolution is good, but that is not the case for macroevolution.

While without question some microevolution does take place, a number of the common examples used to depict it may not be what they are purported to be. The prime case, one illustrated in most basic biology textbooks, is the change in ratio of light and dark-peppered moths in England. It is sometimes called a "mutation,"[8] and some writers may refer to it as a "striking evolutionary change."[9] But it turns out that it is probably neither. The polluted environment darkened the trees during the industrial revolution by killing the light-colored lichens on their bark. When this happened, it seems that the proportion of dark-peppered moths increased. The darker moths received more protection because they were less visible to predators. As the trees became lighter again in the past half century, the proportion of lighter peppered moths appears to have increased. However, the example has more recently faced serious scientific challenges.[10] Studies in other regions give conflicting results, and researchers now consider the original experiment to be totally unrepresentative of normal conditions. Furthermore, it appears that the moth populations are just changing ratios of genes that already exist.

When new insecticides are tried out, they kill off most of the insects, but a few odd individuals will survive, reproduce, and reclaim the territory. They are resistant to the chemicals, and because they face less competition, rapid reproduction ensues until they dominate.

The same kind of situation seems often to apply for the frequently reported "development" of resistance to antibiotics by germs. Our "new" super germs, untouched by many antibiotics, have apparently been around resisting antibiotics for a very long time, and they are in reality quite common organisms.[11] Antibiotics are also abundant, coming from organisms that live in soil. The super germs now tend to invade us more frequently mainly because we have increased their relative abundance by using too many antibiotics to kill off their more susceptible counterparts.

Leading scientists have questioned the concept that the three examples given above really represent recent evolutionary mutation or advancement.[12] It appears that the genes providing the "changes" are nothing new, and the cases do not represent rapid evolution in action, as sometimes claimed. The genes were already present in small numbers in the various populations and *only the proportions changed* because of natural selection responding to the changes in the environment.

For evolutionary advancement you need new genetic information, not just shifts in the proportions of already existing genes, as commonly appears to be the case for moths, insecticides, and antibiotics. Mutations that involve real new information changes in DNA do occur,[13] and natural selection can favor some of them, and in some cases they too can provide resistance to antibiotics. The viruses that cause flu and AIDS are notorious for rapid changes, but these are only minor variations,[14] not new complex designs. It also appears that organisms, including the simplest ones, possess many varied protective systems, as our three examples illustrate. Such systems make life on earth a persistent thing, but may not represent any novel evolutionary advancement. Many of the proposed examples of rapid evolutionary adaptation are not that.

Mutations are notoriously detrimental. A commonly mentioned proportion is just one beneficial mutation per 1,000 bad ones, but we really do not have solid data on the subject. However, there is little question that as far as random mutations are concerned, natural selection has to contend with many more harmful changes than good ones. Evolution needs to go in the direction of improvements, not degeneration. In view of this, some calculations raise the question as to how the human race has ever survived for so long despite such dangerous odds.[15] We would expect that almost any kind of accidental random change, such as a mutation, would be harmful, since we are dealing with complex living systems. Changes in such systems usually cause them not to work as well or to cease functioning altogether. Changing just one aspect of a complex system can be detrimental to several other parts that are dependent on the action of the altered part. As an illustration, how much improvement would you expect on the complex page that you are now reading by inserting accidental typographic changes? The more you introduce, the worse it gets. The more complex a system is, the more difficult it is to change and still have it work.[16]

One of the most severe challenges the evolutionary model faces is its inadequacy to explain how complex organs and organisms with interdependent parts ever evolved. The basic problem is that random mutations cannot plan ahead to gradually design intricate systems, and the appearance of a multitude of the right kind of mutations, all emerging at the same time, to produce a new organ is implausible. If you are going to produce such complex things gradually, the very process of natural selection by survival of the fittest proposed by Darwin would tend to prevent their evolution. Until all the necessary parts of a complex system have assembled so that the system can actually work, it has no survival value. Before that, the functionless extra parts of an incomplete developing system are useless—a cumbersome impediment.

One would expect natural selection to get rid of them. As an example, what survival value would a newly evolving skeletal muscle have without a nerve to stimulate it to contract, and what purpose would a nerve have without an intricate control mechanism to provide the necessary stimulus?

In systems with interdependent parts, in which nothing works until all necessary components are present, natural selection would eliminate misfit organisms with extra useless parts. Such seems to be the case with the degeneration or loss of eyes by species of fish and spiders that live in the total darkness of caves where their eyes are useless. Like the legs of my friend, mentioned earlier, which ceased to function when an accident severed their nerves, these are parts that we are better off without. As a crude analogy, you are more likely to win a bicycle race with a bicycle that has no supplemental engine than with one that has most of a heavy engine but not enough of it to function. In order for natural selection to preserve a structure, the biological change must have some superiority that provides survival value, but partial, nonfunctional systems that can't work have none—they are useless excess baggage. It turns out that the proposed evolutionary process of survival of the fittest can eliminate weak organisms, but it cannot plan ahead to form new complex systems, and it would tend to eliminate gradually developing complex systems, because they would not have any survival value until all necessary parts were present.

It is not always possible to determine if a certain part or process in a complicated system is essential, and researchers have suggested a lot of evolutionary advantages for puzzling situations. For instance, some evolutionists suggest that the reason that some animals gradually evolved wings is that the forelimbs of some animals were first used to glide down from trees before they evolved powered flight. Other evolutionists totally disagree, proposing that flight evolved from animals on the ground trying to go faster and faster as they chased their prey.[17] Strangely, in the evolutionary discussion the pronounced disadvantage of the loss of use of good forelimbs, as they gradually change through stages that are neither true limbs nor wings, hardly ever receives serious consideration. Speculation is an easy exercise, and one can postulate usefulness for almost anything. If you find a bulldozer sitting in the middle of a tennis court, you could claim that it is there to add variety to the game! The problem lies with authentication. Much more than we do, we need to identify what is fact and what is interpretation.

Scientists have been concerned about the problem that complexity poses to evolution. An article in the journal *Nature* tries to show how evolution can explain the origin of "complex features."[18] But the suggestion has serious problems,[19] not the least of which is that a huge gap exists between the simple "digital organisms" programmed on the computer used for the study, and real live organisms in a normal environment. The authors were able to obtain some simple evolutionary advantages by using sequences arbitrarily defined as beneficial. This kind of exercise represents intelligent designing rather than the random changes occurring out in raw nature all by themselves, as expected for evolution. Researchers have used other computer-based programs to try to explain the evolution of complexity, but leading biologists have criticized such attempts as too simplistic and not at all related to the really complicated world of biology.[20]

Prominent evolutionists, including Douglas Futuyma[21] (of the University of Michigan and the State University of New York at Stony Brook) and others, have also addressed the problem of the evolution of complexity. Their suggestions are not very encouraging. Some propose natural selection as the solution, but as we have already seen, that would tend to eliminate the not yet functional developing stages of evolving systems with interdependent parts. Others have argued that simple systems can gradually evolve into complex ones. A commonly used example is that we have simple, more complex, and very complex kinds of eyes in a variety of animals. Supposedly such a series illustrates how eyes can gradually transform into more complex ones. But the suggestion overlooks the facts that simple eyes work on different principles than the more advanced ones, and the latter have complex characteristics such as automatic focusing and aperture regulating systems that have many interdependent parts that would not work until all are present. The proposed solution is too simplistic compared to the facts. Another proposed evolutionary explanation for complexity is that evolution has modified certain complex structures to produce other structures with a different function.[22] This begs the question of the origin of complexity, because in this model you need a complex system to start out with. Evolution thus has no valid mechanism for dealing with the problem of complexity.

Furthermore, one can ask the question: If the evolution of complexity is a real thing, why is it that as we look at far more than a million living species on our earth, we don't see all kinds of complex systems in the process of development? Why do we not find some gradually evolving legs, eyes, livers, etc., on those organisms that do not yet have them? This is a serious indictment against the concept of an evolutionary process that is alleged to be real.[23] Complex systems pose several severe challenges to the evolutionary scenario.

COMPLEX SYSTEMS ABOUND

Earlier we described the complex process of cells replicating themselves.[24] Most simple organisms such as microbes commonly reproduce by ordinary cell division, resulting in two organisms with the same DNA formula. More advanced organisms usually create the next generation by the more complex process of sexual reproduction, which involves a more extensive array of interdependent or irreducible processes. For instance, to form sperm and eggs requires two special successive divisions. The first involves an exchange of DNA, and the second reduces the number of chromosomes, so that when the sperm and egg eventually come together to start a new organism the normal amount of DNA is again present. Evolving sperm and egg and bringing them together in the fertilization process is not simple. It requires many highly specialized and complex steps before the system of sexual reproduction can work. Again we have another example of a series of interdependent processes that we would not expect to appear suddenly, and that would not have any survival value until all the necessary steps had begun functioning. As a consequence it would not seem possible that complex sexual reproduction could ever evolve.

We could go on and on describing hundreds of complex systems with intricately linked parts. If they lack just one essential component, the whole system is useless. Our ability to taste, smell, detect warmth, etc., all involve systems with interdependent units. For instance, a taste bud on our tongue is useless unless it has some special cells sensitive to a certain taste, such as the sweetness of sugar. But those cells have no value unless the sensation gets passed on to the brain. In the case of humans the response to sweetness travels from a cell in a taste bud on our tongue through an elongated nerve cell to the gustatory nucleus at the base of the brain. From there it goes by another nerve cell to the thalamus in the brain, and by a third nerve cell to the cortex of the brain which analyzes the stimulus and generates a response, it-self a complex process.

The tasting system is simple compared to the ability to hear and analyze sounds. Our ears have an intricate spiral-shaped cochlea consisting of a host of necessary specialized parts that includes feedback systems. It is a marvel of microscopic engineering. The cochlea passes the sounds detected to a variety of special nerve cells that respond to different ranges of auditory changes. Then other nerve cells integrate that information for further analysis. The analyzing systems themselves consist of many interdependent units.

It is not just we who are complex; all living things are that way. The lowly caterpillar performs a real tour de force when it alters into a flying butterfly—literally a complete transformation. In an evolutionary context, could such a process have any survival value until all the mutations necessary to produce a successful butterfly had appeared? It takes a lot of specific changes to develop a flying system. How many random mutations involving mostly unsuccessful attempts would be expected to have occurred? The number would be huge. Some evolutionists try to resolve the mystery by proposing reproductive crossing of a worm type with a butterfly type, but this seems rather impossible.[25] And why don't we see any other kinds of organisms in the process of trying to evolve such a miraculous feat? We can also wonder about how many interdependent processes are involved when a tiny spider designs a well-engineered web.

When we face the fact of an overwhelming number of complex systems with many essential interdependent parts, it becomes difficult to think that all of them arose gradually by chance. Recall that they lack survival value until complete. We are dealing with what seems like an overwhelming abundance of unquestionable irreducible complexity. The data strongly suggests a demand for some kind of perceptive reasoning to produce what we keep finding.

THE PERSISTENT CONTROVERSY ABOUT THE EYE

The ongoing controversy about the origin of the eye has been seething for two centuries. Those believing in a Creator God claim that it is implausible to imagine that a complicated instrument such as the eye could arise by itself; while those of a more naturalistic bent claim that given enough time it could happen. Charles Darwin was very much aware of the problem and devoted several pages in *The Origin of Species* to that question under the title "Organs of Extreme Perfection and Complication." He introduces the problem by admitting that "to suppose that the eye with all its inimitable contrivances for adjusting the focus to different distances, for admitting different amounts of light, and for the correction of spherical and chromatic aberration, could have been formed by natural selection, seems, I freely confess, absurd in the highest degree." Then he points out that throughout the animal kingdom we observe all kinds of varieties of eyes, from a simple light-sensitive spot on up to the eye of an eagle. Small changes could, he believed, bring about gradual improvements. Furthermore, he argues, it is not unreasonable to think that "natural selection or the survival of the fittest" operating for millions of years in millions of individuals might produce a living optical instrument "superior to one of glass."[26] To him, the natural selection process that he was proposing was what would cause eyes to get more and more advanced one little step at a time.

A century later George Gaylord Simpson of Harvard University fame would use about the same kind of argument, suggesting that since eyes from simple to complex are all functional they must have survival value.[27] More recently, the fervent advocates of evolution, Futuyma and Dawkins, also employ the same approach.[28] But the entire argument bypasses the crucial issue of the lack of survival value of incomplete systems that do not function until all the necessary interdependent parts are present. As an example, most evolutionary advancements in the eye, such as the ability to distinguish between colors, would be useless until the brain itself could interpret different colors.[29] Each process depends on the other in order to have a useful function. Furthermore, just because we can place eyes in a sequence that appears to go from simple to complex is not evidence that they evolved from each other. One can arrange many things in the universe, such as women's hats (Figure 5.5), from simple to complex. We hardly need to mention that humans design and create hats, and that they did not evolve by themselves from each other or from a common hat ancestor!

Many animals have some kind of "eye" that detects light. Such fascinating structures vary greatly. A simple marine worm has what we would consider a highly advanced eye, and the famed chambered nautilus has an

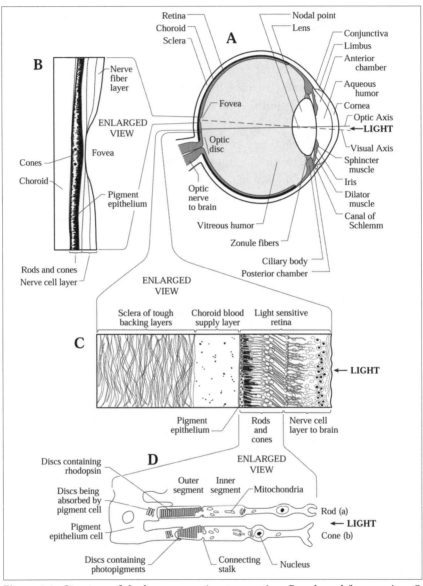

Figure 4.1 *Structure of the human eye. A, cross-section; B, enlarged fovea region; C, enlarged wall of the eye; D, enlarged rods (a) and cones (b) of the retina. Note that in all diagrams light comes from the right. Discs are being absorbed into the pigment cell at the left end of D.* Based in part on Figure 1, p. 16: Dawkins R. 1986. The blind watchmaker. New York, London: W. W. Norton and Company.

extremely simple one. The degree of complexity of eyes does not follow an evolutionary pattern. Some one-celled animals (protists) have a simple light-sensitive spot. Earthworms have light-sensitive cells, especially at the ends of their bodies. Certain marine worms can have more than 10,000 "eyes" on their tentacles, and the lowly limpet has an intriguing eye in the shape of a cup. Organisms such as crabs, some worms, squids, octopuses, insects, and vertebrates (fish, amphibians, reptiles, birds, and mammals) have eyes that not only detect light, but form images. Although squids are a quite different kind of animal from human beings, their eyes are remarkably similar to ours. Giant squids, which can reach a length of 70 feet (21 meters), and which dive into deep water where little light penetrates, need large eyes so as to gather as much light as possible. These behemoths possess the largest eyes that we know of. The eye of a squid that washed up on the shore of New Zealand had a diameter of 16 inches (40 centimeters). This is significantly larger than our ordinary 12-inch (30-centimeter) world globes! Such an eye will harbor an estimated billion light-sensitive cells. By way of comparison, our eyes (Figure 4.1A) are only about one inch (2.5 centimeters) in diameter.

Eyes employ many different systems to form images. Vertebrates (and that includes humans) have a lens in the front part of the eye that focuses the incoming light on the light-sensitive retina in the back, resulting in a sharp image. Other animals such as the chambered nautilus have no lens. Instead, a small pinhole helps to localize the incoming light on various parts of the retina. Insects form images in an entirely different way, using small "tubes" called ommatidia (Figure 4.2) that point in slightly different directions. The light from each tube is then combined to put a picture together. Dragonflies can have as many as 28,000 ommatidia in their bulging eyes. A variety of other intricate eye systems have their own specific arrangements of interdependent parts, including the amazing system of a small crablike copepod that puts a picture together somewhat like a television system does, by rapid scanning.[30] All such different and complex arrangements with their interdependent parts challenge the idea that small gradual changes evolved the eye.

To change from one system to the other requires an entirely different approach in order to put a picture together, as we can see by comparing the eyes in Figures 4.1A and 4.2. Most evolutionists recognize the fundamental differences and propose that the eye evolved independently for each system.

But this would negate the suggestion of other evolutionists, mentioned earlier, that complex eyes evolved from simple ones.[31] The systems are so varied, or similar systems appear in such widely different kinds of animal groups, that *some propose that the eye may have evolved independently many times*—not from each other, and perhaps even as many as 66 times.[32]

On the other hand, researchers have discovered a master gene in the DNA of a variety of organisms that stimulates eye development. Evolutionists consider the widespread presence of such a gene to reflect common evolutionary ancestry. Conversely, those who believe in a Creator see the gene as the imprint of an intelligent mind efficiently using a system that works in different organisms. For instance, scientists can take the master control gene for eye development from a mouse, insert it in a lowly fruit fly, and cause the development of extra eyes on the wings, antennae, and legs.[33] Now the fruit fly has a quite different kind of eye than a mouse, as we see illustrated in Figures 4.2 and 4.1A, respectively, but the same kind of master gene can stimulate the development of either. Biologists estimate that several thousand genes are associated with the embryonic development of the eye of the fruit fly. As a result, it appears that we are dealing with a master control gene that turns on many other genes that cause the formation of different kinds of eyes in varied organisms. The differences between the various eye types come from the many other genes, and the master control gene does little to explain how the various kinds of visual systems might have evolved. The concept of a few master genes ("Evo Devo") simplifying the evolutionary process is actually complicated by the discovery that multiple tiers of both activators and

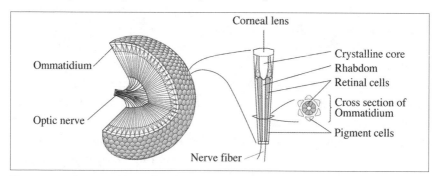

Figure 4.2 *Compound eye of an insect. After: Raven PH, Johnson GB. 1992. Biology, 3rd ed. St. Louis: Mosby-Year Book, p. 831.*

repressors are necessary to get the master genes to function properly. Timing of activity is very important, and control of proper timing itself would also have to evolve.[34]

The study of trilobites has revealed some amazing facts about their eyes. The lower part of Figure 5.1 illustrates a small one. They are remotely similar to horseshoe crabs. Evolutionists consider trilobites to be among the most ancient of animals, yet some have remarkable eyes of the same basic type illustrated in Figure 4.2. Their lenses consist of crystals of the mineral calcite (calcium carbonate). Calcite is a complicated mineral that bends light rays entering or leaving it at different angles depending on the orientation of the crystal. Trilobite eyes orientate the calcite of the lenses in just the proper direction so as to give the right focus. Furthermore, the lens is shaped in a special complicated curved way that corrects the blurring of the focus (spherical aberration) that occurs with ordinary simple lenses. Such design reflects highly sophisticated optical knowledge.[35] This is very remarkable since as you go up through the fossil record, trilobite eyes are among the first eyes you encounter, and they don't seem to have any evolutionary ancestry. One researcher refers to the lenses of these eyes as "an all-time feat of function optimization."[36]

INTRICATE EYES

Advanced eyes such as ours, about which we have learned quite a bit, are marvels of complexity. The following description is a bit technical, but by just following through it you will get a general idea of the fascinating organ that permits you to read this. In envisioning the arrangement of layers of a spherical eye, try to keep in mind what is toward the inside, i.e., toward the center of the sphere of the eye, and what is toward the outside surface of the eye. This will become important in later discussion about the reversed or "inverted" retina.

The eye is largely a somewhat empty sphere with extremely complex things forming the outside wall (Figure 4.1A). Lining the inside of most of the eye is the all-important retina, the organ that senses the light entering the eye through the black opening called the pupil. The retina is quite complicated and consists of many layers of cells, as illustrated in Figure 4.1C, D. The layer closest to the outer surface of the eye is the important pigment epithelium. It contains pigment that collects stray light and also nurtures the cells of the next layer on the inside, which consists of rods and cones. The rods and cones are the all-important photoreceptor cells that detect the light entering the eye. The rods respond especially to dim light, while three kinds of cones serve for brighter and colored light.

As illustrated in Figure 4.1D, the end portion of the elongated rods and cones that lies closest to the pigment epithelium—in other words, the end toward the outside of the eye—contains many discs. The discs have a special kind of protein molecule called rhodopsin, and one rod may contain 40 million such molecules. When light strikes a rhodopsin molecule, it causes the molecule to change its shape. That response gets passed on to many more of several different kinds of molecules, resulting in an "avalanche" type of reaction that quickly modifies the electrical charge on the surface of the rod or cone, thus indicating that the cell has detected light. Then the whole process reverses itself to prepare for receiving more light. The entire operation involves at least a dozen different kinds of protein molecules.[37] Many of them are specific and necessary for the visual process. Again we have another example of the irreducible complexity that we referred to in the previous chapter, and one that severely challenges evolution.

The change in electrical charge on the surface of the rod or cone is passed on as an impulse to a complex network of nerve cells. Those cells form a layer that lies on the inside (i.e., toward the center of the eye) of the layer of rods and cones ("nerve cell layer" of Figure 4.1C). From the nerve cell layer the information travels to the brain through the optic nerve (Figure 4.1A).

The human retina contains more than 100 million light-sensitive cells (rods or cones), and the information from these cells is partially processed in the nerve cell layer. Scientific studies have identified more than 50 different kinds of nerve cells in this layer.[38] Through careful research we are beginning to find out what some of the cells do. For instance, if a particular area is stimulated, the information from cells around it is suppressed so as to sharpen the contrast. This type of processing occurs at several levels of analysis of the incoming light. It is very complex and includes feedback systems. We know that some other circuits in the nerve cell layer deal with the detection of motion, but we still have much more to learn about what the different kinds of cells in this layer do.

We do not actually see in our eyes, although we might intuitively think so. The eye only collects and processes information that is sent on to the back part of our brain, which puts the image together. Without our brains, we would perceive nothing. Millions of bits of information rapidly travel from the eye to the brain by way of the optic nerve. The brain apparently analyzes the data for various components such as brightness, color, motion, form, and depth. Then the brain puts it all together in an integrated picture. The process is incredibly complex, incredibly fast, and goes on without conscious effort. Vision researchers comment that "the simplest visual tasks, such as perceiving colors and recognizing familiar faces, require elaborate computations and more neural circuitry than we have yet imagined."[39]

Advanced eyes include a number of other systems with interdependent parts that also would not function unless they had all the necessary basic components. One example is the mechanism that analyzes the brightness of light and controls the size of the pupil. The system that determines if the focal point of the incoming light is in front or behind the retina so as to change the shape of the lens to keep the picture in sharp focus on the retina itself is another. And a number of additional complex systems help us see better, such as the mechanism that keeps both eyes looking at the same thing.

All these factors raise questions about a multitude of interdependent parts. For instance, what would be the use of a system that can detect that a picture in the eye is out of focus without a corresponding mechanism that can adjust the shape of the lens and bring the image back into focus? In a gradual evolutionary scenario, these developing mechanisms would not have survival value, since most if not all of their parts would be useless without the others. Here as in many other places we have a typical chicken-and-egg conundrum: which came first, the chicken or the egg? Each is necessary for survival.

At times Darwin did not hesitate to challenge the critics of his theory. Right after discussing the evolution of the eye in *The Origin of Species,* he commented: "If it could be demonstrated that any complex organ existed, which could not possibly have been formed by numerous, successive, slight modifications, my theory would absolutely break down. But I can find no such case."[40] While Darwin tried to protect his theory by demanding that one show that it "could not possibly" happen, he walks right into the problem of the lack of survival value of developing interdependent parts as he talks of "numerous . . . slight modifications." Slight modifications are *especially* a problem for his mechanism. Slowly developing interdependent parts that do not work until other necessary parts are present will not have survival value for an extremely long time. Unfortunately, as Darwin suggests, his theory has "absolutely broken down."

EVOLUTION'S INCOMPLETE EYE

Two researchers, Dan-E Nilsson and Susanne Pelger at Lund University in Sweden, have published an interesting article on the evolution of the eye. Entitled "A Pessimistic Estimate of the Time Required for an Eye to Evolve,"[41] it appeared in the prestigious *Proceedings of the Royal Society of London*, and comes to the surprising conclusion that the eye could have evolved in just 1,829 steps of arbitrary 1 percent improvements. Taking some natural selection factors into account, they conclude that it would have taken less than 364,000 years for a camera eye (eye with a small hole) to evolve from a light-sensitive patch. Furthermore, since the ancient Cambrian time period, estimated at 550 million years ago, we would have enough time "for eyes to evolve more than 1500 times!" Their model of the evolution of the eye starts with a layer of light-sensitive cells sandwiched between a transparent layer on top and a pigment layer below. The layers are gradually bent first to form a cup and then an eye with a lens (Figure 4.3). Each step provides an optical advantage over the previous stage, thus giving evolutionary survival value throughout the process. Voilà: the eye has evolved in a very short time!

While one can appreciate the analytical approach employed, it is difficult either to take their model seriously or to accept the claim that there has been enough time for an eye with a lens to have evolved more than 1,500 times. In reality, they are talking about an eye that is so simple that it will not work. The concept has many major problems:

1. The model omits the evolution of the most important and most complex part of the eye, the light-sensitive retina. As mentioned previously, the retina has a host of different kinds of cells for the detection and processing of light information. All kinds of new special protein molecules have to emerge. Sooner or later in the evolutionary scenario all the parts of advanced eyes have to evolve, and to exclude the most complicated and important part

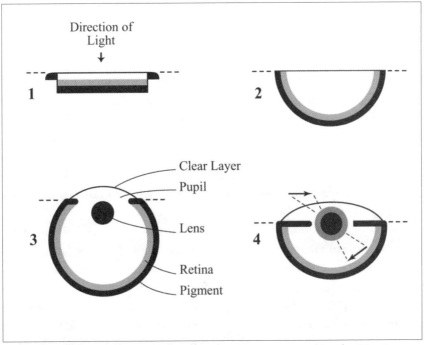

Figure 4.3 *Proposed model for the evolution of the eye. Four stages of development appear in cross section. For each stage light comes from above, while the rest of the body of the animal lies below the eye. The gray layer represents the retina. Above it is a clear layer, and the black layer below is a pigment layer.*
Diagrams based on: Nilsson D-E, Pelger S. 1994. A pessimistic estimate of the time required for an eye to evolve. Proceedings of the Royal Society of London B 256:53-58.

of the eye from the time calculations is a serious omission that completely invalidates the main conclusion.

2. A complex eye, as proposed, is useless without a brain to interpret the visual data, yet the model does not consider the problem of the evolution of the necessary areas of the brain. At least in human beings, the parts of the brain that deal with seeing are much more complex than the retina itself, and the visual area of the brain needs to be closely correlated with the retina if there is to be significance to what the eye sees.

3. In order for an eye to be useful, it has to have a connection between the brain and the eye, which in the case of humans involves an optic nerve that has more than 1 million nerve fibers per eye, and the fibers must be

properly connected. The optic nerve of one eye crosses with the optic nerve of the other eye, and a complex sorting of visual information takes place. A little further along in the system, a much more complex sorting occurs as the nerve cells carry impulses toward the brain. One would expect a lot of random trials before evolution established the right patterns of connection.

4. The suggested model ignores the evolution of the mechanism that focuses the lens. Even some worms have this capability.[42] As we have already noted, it is a complex system that detects when the image on the retina is out of focus and then adjusts the lens to the degree necessary to create a sharp focus. The system involves a number of special elements. In some animals the focusing results from moving the lens, while in others it occurs by changing the shape of the lens itself.

5. Nor does the model consider the time needed for the development of the mechanism that regulates the size of the pupil. Here we have still another complex system of advanced eyes that involves muscles, nerves, and a control system. It would take a very long time to produce such a system even just once, if it ever could. We must include such important elements in any realistic estimate of how long it would take for the eye to evolve.

6. About halfway through the proposed evolutionary process a lens begins to appear. It requires a most fortuitous set of circumstances for this new part to work properly and have survival value.[43] You need a lens with the right protein, shape, and position, all coming together at the right time. It would take an immense amount of time for essentially random mutations to bring all this about at once so as to provide true survival value.

7. In embryos of vertebrates—as, for instance, the fish, frog, or the chicken—the eye does not form by the folding in of superficial layers on the surface of the head, as proposed by the Nilsson and Pelger model. It arises as an outgrowth from the developing brain that then induces the formation of the lens from a superficial layer. Hence we must also consider the time required to evolve one system of development into a different one.

8. Furthermore, the eyes of vertebrates and some invertebrates employ a complex muscular system to coordinate the movement of the two eyes. Some birds are capable of adjusting the direction of their eyes to give either a closely focused binocular vision or a broad panoramic view as the eyes look in different directions.[44] These are not simple systems. The octopus has

six muscles to control the motion of each eye, as is the case for your eyes. In the octopus we find some 3,000 nerve fibers that conduct impulses from the brain to those six muscles so as to control carefully the movement of the eyes. Again all of these systems would also need lots of time to evolve, and we should take that fact into account in estimating how many times the eye could evolve.

Nilsson and Pelger recognize a very few of these omissions in their report, but regrettably ignore them both in their title and conclusions. Their "pessimistic estimate" does not deal with most of the complex parts of the eye, all the hosts of nerve cells, and almost all of the special kinds of proteins that have to be formulated. Recently researchers have discovered a special protein molecule in the cornea of the eye that prevents the development of blood vessels. The substance keeps the cornea free of the blood vessels found in most tissues so light can get right into the eye.

You cannot just bend a few layers around, arbitrarily add a lens, and then claim you have determined that the eye could have evolved "more than 1500 times" in evolutionary history. This kind of exercise borders on what one could describe as *fact-free science.*

Surprisingly, the model has received some strong endorsement. In the renowned journal *Nature,* Richard Dawkins published a favorable review titled "The Eye in a Twinkling,"[45] pointing out that Nilsson and Pelger's results were "swift and decisive" and that the time required for the evolution of the eye "is a geological blink." Furthermore, Daniel Osorio of Sussex University in England, who studies all kinds of eyes, suggests that the article appeases the problem of the evolution of the eye that Darwin was so much concerned about—a problem sometimes referred to as "Darwin's shudder."[46] Nilsson and Pelger's article has given some encouragement to evolutionists expounding on the Internet. One correspondent commented that "the eye has turned into the BEST PROOF of evolution."[47] Considering the real facts of the case, all of this is a sobering revelation of how subjective human concepts can be.

The exuberance of some evolutionists about the Nilsson and Pelger model probably reflects how serious the problem of the eye has been for evolution through the years. A model that essentially ignores all its complex systems may encourage the committed evolutionist, but it can do little for the serious seeker after truth who wants to consider as much of the available data as possible. Unfortunately, studies such as those of Nilsson and Pelger reduce confidence not only in evolution but also in science as a whole. Sir Isaac Newton, who served as president of the Royal Society for 24 years, and who was so thorough in his work, would probably be disappointed to see an article such as this published in the journal of his beloved Royal Society.

IS THE EYE WIRED BACKWARDS?

"There would be no blind spot if the vertebrate eye were really intelligently designed. In fact it is stupidly designed."[48] "However, the vessels and nerves aren't located behind the photoreceptors, where any sensible engineer would have placed them, but out in front of them, where they screen some of the incoming light. A camera designer who committed such a blunder would be fired immediately. By contrast, the eyes of the lowly squid, with the nerves artfully hidden behind the photoreceptors, are an example of design perfection. If the Creator had indeed lavished his best design on the creature he shaped in his own image, creationists would surely have to conclude that God is really a squid."[49] "The human eye has a 'blind spot.'. . . It is caused by the functionally nonsensical arrangement of the axons of the retinal cells which run forward into the eye."[50] "Vertebrates are cursed with an inside-out retina in the eye. . . . Did God at the time of the 'Fall' turn the vertebrate retina inside-out. . .?"[51] "Any engineer" "would laugh at any suggestion that the photocells might point away from the light, with their wires departing on the side *nearest* the light. . . . Each photocell is, in effect, wired in backwards."[52] The preceding plethora of diatribes from respected scientists, including some leading evolutionists, refers to another controversy about the eye. To some the retina is so badly arranged that it could not represent any thoughtful planning. It is inside out, and no competent God would do that, and by implication, an intelligent God does not really exist.

We see the problem well illustrated in Figure 4.1, in which the orientation of all the diagrams is such that the light comes into the eye from the right and travels toward the left. Evolutionists suggest three problems. First, as mentioned earlier, the rods and cones are buried deep in the retina, with their light-sensitive ends turned away from the light and into the dark pigment epithelium. Note especially Figure 4.1D, in which the main body (nucleus, etc.) of the rod or cone cell is toward the right, while the light-sensitive discs are toward the left, some buried into the pigment epithelium. It is comparable to turning a surveillance camera toward a wall instead of toward an open area. Second, the complicated nerve cell layer of the retina lies between the incoming light and the light-sensitive rods and cones. Why not place the light-sensitive parts of the rods and cones toward the light (on the right part of the retina, in Figure 4.1C), so that the incoming light from the lens will hit them first without having to go through all those nerve cells? The presence of the nerve cells on the inside of the layer of rods and cones is also the cause of the third problem. The information the nerve cells process has to get out of the eye, and this occurs by way of the optic nerve. The spot where that nerve goes through the retina has no rods or cones, and causes a blind spot where we can't see (labeled "optic disc" in Figure 4.1A). Some evolutionists reason that if the eye had been designed properly, the arrangement of the layers of the retina would have been reversed from the present situation. Thus the nerve cell layer and nerve would be behind the rods and cones, and the eye would not have a blind spot.

Some creatures, such as the squid, octopus, and many simpler animals, do not have a reversed retina. Their eyes employ different kinds of light-sensing cells that point with their sensitive portion toward the light. In all vertebrates (fish, amphibians, reptiles, birds, and mammals), including you, the retinas are what many evolutionists consider to be inverted or reversed.

However, when you know a little more about the physiology and the details of how the advanced eye of vertebrates works, it becomes apparent that the inverted retina is actually a good design, and a number of evolutionists support such a conclusion.[53] When we examine the most important region of the eye, where we do our most acute viewing, the objection that the nerve cells lie in front of the rods and cones loses much of its force. That region, called the *fovea* (Figure 4.1 A, B), harbors some 30,000 cones that provide the sharp type of vision you are using as you read these words. There the nerve cells and their fibers are especially small, and the fibers radiate away from that region, leaving the cones of the fovea more open to direct light coming from the lens (Figure 4.1B). Other nerve fibers and rare blood vessels in the region of the fovea go around it, thus further avoiding any blockage of the incoming light. The eye is constructed so as to give a sharp image just where needed. Furthermore, the nerve cells and fibers are not that much of an obstruction to the incoming light. If you remove the dark pigment epithelium from the backside of the retina, what remains, which includes the rods and cones and the nerve cell layer, is "almost perfectly transparent."[54] Furthermore, scientists have discovered some long cells that seem to transfer light from the inside surface of the eye, directly to the rods and cones. The blind spot of the eye does not seem to be the major impediment claimed. It is hard to find, and most of us are not even aware of its existence since it is located to the side, and one eye compensates for the blind spot of the other.

In addition, there appears to be a very good reason the retina is inverted, and that is because of the special nutritional requirements of the rods and cones. Among the most active cells in our body, they are constantly replacing their discs, probably so as to maintain a fresh supply of the protein molecules that detect light. A single rod cell can have close to 1,000 discs—many more than illustrated in Figure 4.1D. Studies on the rhesus monkey indicate that each rod produces 80 to 90 new discs per day, and it is probably about the same for humans. (Parenthetically, this rate is very slow compared to the 2 million red blood cells formed in our bodies every second!) The discs develop in the region of the rod or cone cell close to the nucleus and are disposed of at the end most intimately associated with the pigment epithelium. That epithelium absorbs the old discs and recycles some of their parts to the rods. For several reasons, separation of the retina from its pigment epithelium results in blindness, hence that connection is essential. Just on the outside of the pigment epithelium is the choroid blood supply layer (Figure 4.1C), which provides the pigment epithelium with some of the nutrients needed by the active rods and cones as they manufacture more discs.

Should we reverse the retina, as some evolutionists suggest that God should have done, it appears that we would have a visual disaster. The discs of the rods and cones would face into the light, but what would perform the essential function of the pigment epithelium in absorbing the old discs? Rods and cones take no vacation, generating some 10 billion discs per day in each of our eyes. They would accumulate in the transparent vitreous humor of the eye (Figure 4.1A), and their great numbers would soon impair our ability to see. Also, the rods and cones would lack the necessary pigment epithelium and blood supply of the choroid needed to make the discs, so the disc replacing system would not work at all. If we should then try to provide the disc ends of the rods and cones pointed toward the light with their necessary pigment epithelium and choroid blood supply layer, the layers would have to lie on the *inside* of the layer of rods and cones. In other words, they would lie closer to the center of the eye than the rest of the retina. As a result the light coming into the eye would first have to get through the blood-supplying choroid layer before reaching the light-sensitive discs. A blood hemorrhage in the retina is extremely debilitating and illustrates how disruptive blood can be to the visual process. The pigment in the pigment epithelium that absorbs light would also be in the way and would contribute further to complete blindness. Like playing tennis with ripe tomatoes, this is not a great idea!

The present structure of the retina seems to be an excellent design that provides the active rods and cones of advanced organisms with the blood supply and nutrients they must have. Besides that, it is hard to argue with success—the eye works very well! If, as some evolutionists suggest, the eye is so badly designed and if, as others argue, the eye can evolve in a twinkling, why didn't natural selection produce a better eye a long time ago?

THE HUMAN BRAIN

Each of the cells in our body, of which we have many trillions, has more than 3 billion DNA bases. The DNA in each cell, if stretched out, would be about three feet (one meter) long. In fact, the DNA in the average human would extend from the earth to Jupiter and back more than 60 times. However, such complexity as seen in our cells pales into insignificance when compared to our brains. Many consider the brain to be the most intricate structure that we know of in the universe.

When it comes to living organisms, human beings stand on the top of life's ladder. Not because of our bodies, which are neither the strongest nor the largest, but because we have brains that exceed those of all other living things. We can, within limits, manipulate all other creatures, to say nothing of our capability to destroy their environment and ours also!

Each of our brains consists of about 100 billion nerve cells (neurons) connected with each other by an almost unbelievable 248,000 miles (400,000 kilometers) of nerve fibers. Such fibers often branch repeatedly as they attach to other nerve cells. One large nerve cell can link to as many as 600 other nerve cells, with some 60,000 connections. Researchers conservatively estimate the total number of connections in the brain at 100 million times a million, which is the same as 100,000 billion (10^{14}). Such large numbers are difficult to envision. It may help if we realize that a single cubic millimeter of the main part of the brain (cortex of cerebrum), where the cells are especially large, has an estimated 40,000 nerve cells and 1 billion connections. We are finding that the brain is much more than a lot of linkages, such as we have in a computer. The brain is capable of moving various functions from one area to another and of growing where it needs more brainpower.

A flurry of mental and coordinating activity goes on in our brains as changes in electrical charge travel along the nerve fibers that conduct impulses between cells. At least 30 different kinds of chemicals, and probably many times more, work to transfer the impulses at the contact from one nerve cell to another. The whole process is amazing, because the different kinds of chemicals have to be assigned to the right connections. We are just beginning to learn about the intricacies of the brain, and we are finding it challenging to think about the organ with which we do our thinking! The great question that the brain poses to evolution is Could all those 100,000 billion connections ever get the pattern to connect the right way with just trial-and-error random changes going through the slow and laborious process of natural selection? Also, it is not at all clear that humanity's unique mental capabilities provide evolutionary survival value, since baboons seem to do quite well without them. Several leading thought leaders have wondered about that.[55] Stephen Hawking candidly states, "It is not clear that intelligence has much survival value. Bacteria do very well without intelligence."[56] Perhaps no evolutionary process created our brains.

Darwin, who lived in England, had a good friend and supporter in the United States, the noted Harvard botanist Asa Gray. Sometimes Darwin shared some of his deeper feelings with Gray, who himself was sympathetic to evolution but very much believed in a God active in nature.[57] In a letter to Gray, Darwin confided that "I remember well the time when the thought of the eye made me cold all over, but I have got over this stage of the complaint, and now small trifling particulars of structure often make me very uncomfortable. The sight of a feather in a peacock's tail, whenever I gaze at it, makes me sick!"[58]

Why would the feather of a peacock bother Darwin? I cannot answer that question with certainty, but I suspect that few can reflect on the intricate structure and especially the beauty of a peacock's iridescent tail feather without wondering if it is not the result of some kind of design. Furthermore, why do we even appreciate beauty, enjoy music, or realize that we exist? This raises the question of origins to a different level—that of our mysterious minds. It is an awesome fact that in our three-pound (1.4-kilogram) brain is the seat of "who I am." How did the multitude of connections in the brain get programmed so that we can think logically (we hope that most of us are thinking straight!), have curiosity to ask questions about our origins, learn new languages, create mathematical theorems, and compose operas? Even more challenging to a naturalistic worldview are the issues of our power of choice, and characteristics such as moral responsibility, loyalty, love, and spirituality. The particle physicist, Cambridge University administrator, and Anglican priest John Polkinghorne expresses the concern of many. In referring to the physical world, he states that "I cannot believe that our ability to understand its strange character is a curious spin-off from our ancestors having had to dodge saber-toothed tigers."[59]

The debate about the mind frequently focuses on the nature of the enigmatic phenomenon of consciousness, which is the self-awareness that we all have—in other words, the feeling that we exist. Such awareness seems intimately related to our ability to think, to our curiosity, emotions, and judgment, and to other phenomena of the conscious mind. Is our consciousness evidence of a reality beyond a simple mechanistic (naturalistic) explanation? Or is consciousness simply highly complicated and purely mechanistic? The battle between these two views has waged for centuries, and often relates to whether or not mechanistic explanations, which exclude God, are sufficient to explain all of reality.

Those defending the view that consciousness is a purely mechanistic phenomenon suggest that there is nothing special about consciousness. In fact, it does not even exist. It is just a great amount of simple activity. In recent years some have emphasized the analogy that we can draw between a computer and the brain. Some flippant comparisons deride any difference between the two. The brain is a computer made of meat,[60] and such rudimentary devices as thermostats have beliefs![61] But thought leaders such as the

Table 4.1		
THE LONG SEARCH FOR AN EVOLUTIONARY MECHANISM		
DESIGNATION AND DATE	MAIN PROPONENTS	CHARACTERISTICS
Lamarckism 1809–1859	Lamarck	Use causes development of new characteristics that become inheritable.
Darwinism 1859–1894	Darwin, Wallace	Small changes, acted upon by natural selection, lead to survival of the fittest. Inheritance by gemmules.
Mutations 1894–1922	Morgan, de Vries	Emphasis on larger mutational changes. Natural selection not as important.
Modern Synthesis (neo-Darwinism) 1922–1968	Chetverikov, Dobzhansky, Fisher, Haldane, Huxley, Mayr, Simpson, Wright	Unified attitude. Changes in populations important. Small mutations acted upon by natural selection. Relation to traditional classification.
Diversification 1968–present	Eldredge, Gould, Grassé, Henning, Kauffman, Kimura, Lewontin, Patterson, Platnick	Multiplicity of conflicting ideas. Dissatisfaction with modern synthesis. Emphasis on cladistics. Search for a cause for complexity.

Nobel laureate Sir John Eccles have countered such simplistic reductionism when he observes that "one can ... recall the poignant question by computer lovers: At what stage of complexity and performance can we agree to endow them with consciousness? Mercifully this emotionally charged question need not be answered. You can do what you like to computers without qualms of being cruel!"[62] The famed mathematician-cosmologist Roger Penrose at Oxford University comments that "consciousness seems to me to be such an important phenomenon that I simply cannot believe that it is something just 'accidentally' conjured up by a complicated computation. It is the phenomenon whereby the universe's very existence is made known."[63]

Nothing about the laws of science requires that we should have consciousness.[64] Consciousness is something that eludes present analysis. We have no evidence that it is a characteristic of matter. The existence of consciousness points to a reality beyond our ordinary mechanistic understanding.

However, we need not rely on the phenomenon of consciousness to conclude that purposeful planning is necessary for the existence of our minds. Comparison of the brain with computers only strengthens the evidence for a designer God, because we all know that computers do not just happen to organize themselves. They result from intentional design involving foreknowledge leading to correlated complexity. The same applies to our extremely complex brains. They contain 1,000 times as many connections as our galaxy has stars. It stretches credulity even to suggest that such an organized assembly originated just as a result of accident or chance. How could any random process provide anything close to this magnitude of complexity? As we have already noted, natural selection is detrimental to the gradual evolution of systems with interdependent parts. Moreover, for most, the brain houses minds that process and integrate information rapidly and extremely well.

THE LONG SEARCH FOR AN EVOLUTIONARY MECHANISM

How do evolutionists explain the origin of complexity? For two centuries they have been searching for an evolutionary mechanism. Although they have proposed one idea after another (Table 4.1), they have not been able to agree on any particular model, especially one that will realistically explain the origin of complexity. Most scientists agree that evolution has taken place, but a satisfactory explanation of how the various systems of advanced organisms evolved still awaits discovery. Some traditionalists cling to Darwin's idea that natural selection by survival of the fittest is adequate. Others prefer models of more pure chance or randomness. Many feel that evolution proceeds by small changes, while others believe in larger jumps, but the latter concept would require a host of fortuitous mutations all at once. Still others argue about the criteria used to determine evolutionary relationships. The more rigorous methodology of cladistics, an approach which especially considers unique characteristics, has been gaining considerable approval. However, as we will discuss in the next chapter, cladistics is not at all an evolutionary mechanism—it is only a way of testing hypotheses about relationships. As mentioned earlier, computer-simulated attempts to explain complexity do not provide any realistic representation of what actually occurs in nature.

Evolution is the best model that science can come up with if one is going to exclude God, but it falls far short of plausibility. The perseverance that evolutionists have shown is highly commendable, but after two centuries of an essentially fruitless search, it would seem that it is time for scientists to give serious consideration to nonnaturalistic alternatives. The involvement of some reasoning intelligence such as God seems necessary to explain a lot of what science is discovering.

CONCLUDING COMMENTS

Advanced organs give us many examples of complex systems with interdependent parts. Natural selection poses a problem for the evolution of such systems. While natural selection can eliminate weak aberrant types, it cannot plan ahead so as to gradually develop the various parts required for complex interrelationships. Natural selection limits itself to immediate success in survival. As a result, we would also expect it to eliminate the various new parts of gradually evolving complex systems with their interdependent subunits. Such new elements would be useless and cumbersome impediments until all the necessary aspects were present to provide a working system with some inherent survival value. Organisms with useless extra parts would have less survival potential. Hence it appears that Darwin's system of survival of the fittest actually interferes with the evolutionary advancement of complex systems.

Most biological systems are complex, but the eye and the brain are examples of organs that are exceedingly intricate. It does not appear that either organ could have developed without intelligent planning. Here we find scientific data that definitely favors the idea that there is a God.

[1] Rees M. 2000. Just six numbers: the deep forces that shape the universe. New York: Basic Books, p. 19.

[2] Schnapp BJ et al. 1985. Single microtubules from squid axoplasm support bidirectional movement of organelles. Cell 40:455-462.

[3] Behe, MJ. 1996. Darwin's black box: the biochemical challenge to evolution. New York: Touchstone.

[4] Polanyi M. 1968. Life's irreducible structure. Science 160:1308-1312.

[5] Paley W. 1807. Natural theology; or, evidences of the existence and attributes of the deity, 11th ed. London: R. Faulder and Son.

[6] Dawkins R. 1986, 1987. The blind watchmaker: why the evidence of evolution reveals a universe without design. New York: W.W. Norton and Co., Inc., pp. 5, 6.

[7] Schwartz JH. 1999. Sudden origins: fossils, genes, and the emergence of species. New York: John Wiley and Sons, Inc., pp. 12, 13.

[8] For example: Sagan C. 1977. The dragons of Eden: speculation on the evolution of human intelligence. New York: Ballantine Books, p. 28.

[9] Keeton WT. 1967. Biological science. New York: W.W. Norton and Co., Inc., p. 672.

[10] For many problems with this scenario, see: Wells J. 2000. Icons of evolution: science or myth? Why much of what we teach about evolution is wrong. Washington, D.C. Regnery Publishing, Inc., pp. 137-157.

[11] D'Costa VM et al. 2006. Sampling antibiotic resistance. Science 311:374-377.

[12] Amábile-Cuevas CF. 2003. New antibiotics and new resistance. American Scientist 91:138-149; Ayala FJ. 1978. The mechanism of evolution. Scientific American 239(3):56-69; Jukes TH. 1990. Responses of critics. In: Johnson PE. Evolution as dogma: the establishment of naturalism. Dallas: Haughton Pub. Co., pp. 26-28. For further discussion, see: Anderson KL. 2005. Is bacterial resistance to antibiotics an appropriate example of evolutionary change? Creation Research Society Quarterly 41:318-326.

[13] Hall BG. 1982. Evolution on a Petri dish. In: Hecht MK, Wallace B, Prance GT, eds. 1982. Evolutionary Biology. New York: Plenum Press, vol. 15, pp. 85-150. For a perceptive evaluation of the significance of this report, see: Pitman SD. 2005. Why I believe in creation. College and University Dialogue 17(3):9-11.

[14] For instance, see: Chen H et al. 2005. H5N1 virus outbreak in migratory waterfowl. Nature 436:191, 192.

[15] Beardsley T. 1999. Mutations galore: humans have high mutation rates. But why worry? Scientific American 280(4):32, 36; Nachman MW, Crowell SL. 2000. Estimate of the mutation rate per nucleotide in humans. Genetics 156:297-304.

[16] Futuyma DJ. 1998. Evolutionary biology, 3rd ed. Sunderland, Mass.: Sinauer Associates, Inc., p. 684.

[17] See chapter 6 for further discussion.

[18] Lenski RE et al. 2003. The evolutionary origin of complex features. Nature 423:139-144.

[19] For example: Pitman SD. 2003. Computers and the theory of evolution. http://www.naturalselection.0catch.com/Files/computerevolution.htlm. (Viewed March 20, 2005.)

[20] Horgan J. 1995. From complexity to perplexity. Scientific American 272(6):104-109; Lewin R. 1992. Complexity: life at the edge of chaos. New York: Collier Books, Macmillan Pub. Co.; Oreskes N, Shrader-Frechette K, Belitz K. 1994. Verification, validation, and con-

firmation of numerical models in the earth sciences. Science 263:641-646.

[21] Futuyma, pp. 681-684, 761. [For publishing information, see note 16, above.]

[22] Gould SJ. 1980. The panda's thumb: more reflections in natural history. New York: W. W. Norton and Co., pp. 19-26.

[23] Some evolutionists generalize and suggest that everything in the living world is in the process of evolving. But this concept does little to answer the problem of lack of new evolving organs.

[24] See chapter 3.

[25] For some speculative ideas, see: Margulis L, Sagan D. 2002. Acquiring genomes: a theory of the origins of species. New York: Basic Books, pp. 165-172; Williamson DI. 2003. The origins of larvae, rev. ed. Dordrecht, Netherlands: Kluwer Academic Publishers; Williamson DI. 2001. Larval transfer and the origins of larvae. Zoological Journal of the Linnean Society 131:111-122. These sources suggest that the complex life cycle of butterflies evolved by some worm types and butterfly types first evolving independently, then combining their genes by hybridization resulting in a caterpillar-butterfly life cycle. Such speculation has no experimental authentication and borders on fact-free science. Furthermore, it does not address the serious problem of the origin of all the new coordinated gene activity, especially the formation and timing of the many hormones that we find necessary for the successful *conversion process* of changing from a caterpillar to a butterfly. For more traditional interpretations and questions, see: Hall BK, Wake MH, eds. 1999. The origin and evolution of larval forms. San Diego: Academic Press.

[26] Darwin C. 1859, 1958. The origin of species by means of natural selection, or the preservation of favoured races in the struggle for life. New York: Mentor, pp. 168-171.

[27] Simpson GG. 1967. The meaning of evolution: a study of the history of life and of its significance for man, rev. ed. New Haven, Conn.: Yale University Press, pp. 168-175.

[28] Dawkins. The blind watchmaker, pp. 15-18, 77-87 [see note 6]; Futuyma, pp. 682-684 [see note 16].

[29] Evolutionists sometimes propose that detectors for various colors would have evolved to enhance the total ability to see various types of objects although they had different colors, thus enhancing a "color constancy." This is not what we are considering here. Our concern is the ability to distinguish between different colors and putting that information together in a meaningful picture in the brain. For further discussion, see: Goldsmith TH. 1991. The evolution of visual pigments and colour vision. In: Gouras P, ed. The perception of colour. Boca Raton, Fla.: CRC Press, Inc., pp. 62-89; Neumeyer C. 1991. Evolution of colour vision. In: Cronley-Dillon JR, Gregory RL, eds. Evolution of the eye and visual system. Boca Raton, Fla.: CRC Press, Inc., pp. 284-305.

[30] Gregory RL, Ross HE, Moray N. 1964. The curious eye of *Copilia*. Nature 201:1166-1168.

[31] Some evolutionists such as D. J. Futuyma (p. 683 [see note 16]) and L.V. Salvini-Plawen and E. Mayr (1977. On the evolution of photoreceptors and eyes. Evolutionary Biology 10:207-263) recognize that the eye evolved many times, and at the same time suggest that the eye evolved within limited groups. Their example from the eye of mollusks presents relatively minor changes in eye development, and thus does little to explain the evolution from the eyespot of a protist to the eye of an eagle.

[32] Salvini-Plawen, Mayr. [See note 31.]

[33] Halder G, Callaerts P, Gehring WJ. 1995. Induction of ectopic eyes by targeted expression of the *eyeless* gene in *Drosophila*. Science 267:1788-1792.

[34] For a simple rendition of "Evo Devo" from an evolutionary perspective, see: Carroll SB. 2005. Endless forms most beautiful: the new science of evo devo and the making of the animal kingdom. New York: W. W. Norton and Co.

[35] Clarkson ENK, Levi-Setti R. 1975. Trilobite eyes and the optics of Des Cartes and Huygenes. Nature 254:663-667; Towe KM. 1973. Trilobite eyes: calcified lenses in vivo. Science 179:1007-1009.

[36] Levi-Setti R. 1993. Trilobites, 2nd ed. Chicago: University of Chicago Press, p. 29.

[37] Behe, pp. 18-22. [See note 3.]

[38] Kolb H. 2003. How the retina works. American Scientist 91:28-35.

[39] Shapley R et al. 1990. Computational theories of visual perception. In: Spillmann L, Werner JS, eds. Visual perception: the neurophysiological foundations. San Diego: Academic Press, Inc., pp. 417-448.

[40] Darwin C. 1859, 1985. The origin of species. London: Penguin Books, p. 219.

[41] Nilsson D-E, Pelger S. 1994. A pessimistic estimate of the time required for an eye to evolve. Proceedings of the Royal Society of London, B, 256:53-58.

[42] Duke-Elder S. 1958. The eye in evolution. Volume 1 of: Duke-Elder S, ed. System of Ophthalmology. St. Louis: C.V. Mosby Co., pp. 143, 192, 591.

[43] Baldwin JT. 1995. The argument from sufficient initial system organization as a continuing challenge to the Darwinian rate and method of transitional evolution. Christian Scholar's Review 24:423-443.

[44] Pettigrew JD. 1991. Evolution of binocular vision. In: Cronly-Dillon JR, Gregory RL, eds.: Evolution of the eye and visual system. Boca Raton, Fla.: CRC Press, Inc., pp. 271-283.

[45] Dawkins R. 1994. The eye in a twinkling. Nature 368:690, 691.

[46] Osorio D. 1994. Eye evolution: Darwin's shudder stilled. Trends in Ecology and Evolution 9(7):241, 242.

[47] http://www.geocities.com/evolvedthinking/evolution_of_the_eye.htm. Statement downloaded in 2003, where it appeared in the second paragraph. Probably, for good reason, it was later found to be no longer on the Web page.

[48] Williams, GC. 1992. Natural selection: domains, levels, and challenges. Oxford: Oxford University Press, p. 73.

[49] Diamond, J. 1985. Voyage of the overloaded ark. Discover 6(6):82-92.

[50] Futuyma, p. 123. [See note 16.]

[51] Thwaites WM. 1983. An answer to Dr. Geisler—from the perspective of biology. Creation/Evolution 13: 13-20.

[52] Dawkins. The blind watchmaker, p. 93. [See note 6.]

[53] For instance, see: Duke-Elder, p. 147 [see note 42]; Kolb [see note 38].

[54] Maximow AA, Bloom W. 1957. A textbook of histology, 7th ed. Philadelphia: W. B. Saunders Co., p. 566.

[55] For example: Maynard Smith J. 1988. Did Darwin get it right? New York: Chapman and Hall, p. 94.

[56] Hawking SW. 2001. The universe in a nutshell. New York: Bantam Books, , p. 171.

[57] For further elucidation, see: Ruse M. 2001 The evolution wars: a guide to the debates. New Brunswick, N. J.: Rutgers University Press, pp. 93-96.

[58] Darwin C. 1860. C. Darwin to Asa Gray. In: Darwin F, ed. 1888. The life and letters of Charles Darwin, Volume II. Reprinted 2001, Honolulu: University Press of the Pacific, p. 90.

[59] Polkinghorne J. 1996. Beyond science: the wider human context. Cambridge: Cambridge University Press, p. 79.

[60] Ruse, p. 197. [See note 57.]

[61] Brown A. 1999. The Darwin wars: the scientific battle for the soul of man. London: Touchstone, p. 153.

[62] Eccles J. As quoted in: Horvitz LA. 2000. The quotable scientist: words of wisdom from Charles Darwin, Albert Einstein, Richard Feynman, Galileo, Marie Curie, and others. New York: McGraw-Hill, p. 68.

[63] Penrose R. 1989. The emperor's new mind: concerning computers, minds, and the laws of physics. New York: Oxford University Press, pp. 447, 448.

[64] For a recent and unimpressive attempt, see: Ramachandran VS. 2004. A brief tour of human consciousness: from impostor poodles to purple numbers. New York: Pi Press.

Chapter Five

So Little Time for Everything

Leaders in science, speaking ex cathedra, should stop polarizing the minds of students and younger creative scientists with statements for which faith is the only evidence.[1]

—*Hubert P. Yockey, molecular biologist*

HOW FAST WAS THE PAST?

The strange smell of sulfur fumes startled the crew of the fishing vessel *Isleifur II* as it glided quietly in the North Atlantic south of Iceland. In the dim light of the breaking dawn of November 14, 1963, smoke appeared on the southern horizon. Was another boat on fire? A check for radio messages indicated no SOS call. The boat started rolling in an unusual pattern, and as the captain scanned the horizon with his binoculars he saw black eruption columns rising out of the sea just a half mile (one kilometer) away. The ship's crew members who were from Iceland, where volcanic activity is almost a way of life, immediately suspected that an underwater volcano was rising from the floor of the ocean. They happened to be navigating over the volcanically active Mid-Atlantic Ridge, which at that location lay only a scant 300 feet (100 meters) below the ocean's surface.

All day the disturbance continued as ashes, steam, and smoke rose up in the air while stones and flashes of light could be seen below. Five days later an island 2,000 feet (600 meters) long had formed right above where earlier fish had been freely swimming in the open ocean. The new island, which eventually grew to a diameter of 1.2 miles (two kilometers), received the name Surtsey after the mythological giant Surtur. Later when investigators checked out the island it amazed them how old it looked. In just five months wave action had formed a huge mature-looking beach and cliff. One researcher commented: "What elsewhere may take thousands of years" "may take a few weeks or even a few days here.

"On Surtsey only a few months sufficed for a landscape to be created which was so varied and mature that it was almost beyond belief."[2]

On our usually placid earth, events such as the creation of Surtsey remind us that sometimes things happen rapidly. The question "How fast was the past?" has fueled a controversy that has raged for two centuries. Some have considered major catastrophes as extremely important while others essentially ignore them.

TWO OPPOSING VIEWS: CATASTROPHISM AND UNIFORMITARIANISM

The controversy between uniformitarianism and catastrophism[3] has historically been closely associated with the God question in science. Catastrophism refers to large-scale rapid events and implies that such events have been the main factor shaping the earth's crust. Uniformitarianism holds that the present crust of the earth is the result of many small, prolonged events more typical of day-to-day geologic processes. Catastrophism fits better with the biblical concept of a major catastrophic flood and with a God not constrained by time. Uniformitarianism corresponds better with the proposed eons of geologic ages and the time needed for a slow, gradual evolutionary process.

Well accepted through most of human history, catastrophism dominated ancient mythology. During medieval times interest waned a little, although the Arabs closely followed Aristotle, who very much believed in catastrophes. Interest renewed in the Western world during the revolutionary Renaissance and Reformation periods. Scholars regarded the biblical flood as the catastrophic event that explained such interesting geological features as fossils of animals that normally live in the ocean occurring high in the Alps. However, before long, some new interpretations appeared on the horizon.

Two centuries ago the Scottish geologist James Hutton, renowned for being controversial, published a famous book entitled *Theory of the Earth*. The book defended uniformitarianism as he emphasized the importance of slow geological changes during long periods of time. His strong naturalistic approach (no God involved) surfaces as he asserts that "no powers [are] to be employed that are not natural to the globe, no action to be admitted of except those of which we know the principle, and no extraordinary events to be alleged in order to explain a common appearance."[4] He concludes the book with his famous phrase "we find no vestige of a beginning—no prospect of an end."[5] His assertion boldly confronted the then-prevailing biblical idea that God was the Creator, and that He had created the earth in six days a few thousand years ago. Furthermore, it set aside the great catastrophic flood described in the Bible that was endorsed by several leading geologists in England. Not long afterward another book quickly became the most influential geology treatise ever written. It would not only revolutionize geology—it would also profoundly alter scientific thinking as a whole.

Charles Lyell's *Principles of Geology* first came off the press in 1830 and eventually went through 11 editions. Strongly endorsing uniformitarianism, it advocated the permanent effects of slow, gradual changes. By the middle of the century uniformitarianism had become the dominant view in intellectual circles as catastrophism dwindled. Lyell's book was one of Charles Darwin's "most treasured possessions"[6] during his epic worldwide discovery voyage aboard the H.M.S. *Beagle.* The long geologic ages advocated by the book provided some of the time needed for Darwin's slow evolutionary changes.

Lyell trained as a lawyer, and part of the success of his book can be attributed to his skill in presenting his views, a fact illustrated in a letter he wrote to his friend and supporter George Poulett Scrope. "If we don't irritate, which I fear that we may . . . we shall carry all with us. If you don't triumph over them, but compliment the liberality and candor of the present age, the bishops and enlightened saints will join us in despising both the ancient and modern physico-theologians [catastrophists]. It is just the time to strike, so rejoice that, sinner as you are, the Q. R. *[Quarterly Review]* is open to you." "If Murray [the publisher of Lyell's book] has to push my vols., and you wield the geology of the Q. R., we shall be able in a short time to work an entire change in public opinion."[7] As Lyell had hoped, he accomplished his goal, at least in the geological community. For more than a century geology did not tolerate catastrophic interpretations.

While both Hutton and Lyell opposed the biblical model of origins, and they faced a lot of opposition from religious factions, neither appears to have denied the existence of God. Historians have characterized Hutton as actually being a "pious man of conservative views,"[8] and he defined God as "that Mind which formed the matter of this globe."[9] Lyell may have leaned toward deism,[10] but he appears to have believed in a God that was a little more involved than that viewpoint usually holds. He accepted some aspects of evolution, but believed that human beings had a special status in Creation, and "always denied that humankind could have evolved from apelike creatures."[11] Moreover, Lyell is reported as being "frightened of losing all touch with Jehovah [God] if he followed Darwin to what seemed to him the bitter end."[12]

By the turn of the century the long ages postulated for uniformitarianism and evolution were firmly established, and catastrophism became kind of a dirty word in the scientific community. But all was not well. Some things observed in the rocks did not agree with the prevailing mindset of slow changes that did not allow for major catastrophes. In the southeastern quarter of the state of Washington we find an amazing washed out region consisting of some 15,000 square miles (40,000 square kilometers) of huge buttes and wide canyons cut into hard volcanic rock. Mounds of stream gravel at various levels and the remnants of hundreds of ancient waterfalls, some as high as 300 feet (100 meters) with large eroded plunge pools at their base, testify to a most unusual past. How did such a landscape, referred to as Channeled Scabland, ever develop? The independent-minded geologist J. Harlen Bretz started studying the area and had an idea that was so outrageous for that time that it sparked a controversy that lasted for 40 years. Bretz was indulging in the outdated heresy of catastrophism!

In 1923 he published his first scientific report about the area[13] but did not divulge his suspicion of a major catastrophic flood, suggesting only that its formation involved prodigious amounts of water. Later that year in a second publication[14] he proposed that a short-lived widespread flood had eroded the channels and deposited the immense gravel bars. This was blatant catastrophism; it was in the same category in which creation now finds itself in most scientific circles—totally unacceptable. The geologic community had to deal with this young upstart who was proposing ideas dangerously close to the biblical flood.[15] Adopting Bretz's ideas implied retreating to the catastrophism of "the dark ages. . . . It could not, it must not be tolerated."[16]

Bretz, who was a geology professor at the University of Chicago, became the object of focused persuasion efforts from the geologic community. Their wayward colleague, who kept on publishing in a catastrophic mode, needed conversion. His fellow geologists invited him to present his views to the Geological Society of Washington, D.C. To oppose him, "a veritable phalanx of doubters had been assembled to debate the flood hypothesis."[17] After Bretz's presentation, five scientists from the prestigious United States Geological Survey presented alternative explanations such as the action of ice and other slow processes. Amazingly, two of the objectors had not even visited the Channeled Scabland! Apparently no one at the meeting changed their minds. As for Bretz himself, he continued his research with a catastrophic flavor while facing continued opposition. In his words, this "heresy must be gently but firmly stamped out."[18] Then geologists found evidence of a large ancient lake that had likely served as the source of the floodwaters that washed the Channeled Scabland,[19] and tensions started to abate as more and more geologists acknowledged that Bretz's explanation was the correct one.

Eventually the data from the rocks won out. In 1965 the International Association for Quaternary Research organized a geologic field trip to the area to view the evidence. At the end of the trip Bretz, who was unable to attend, received a telegram from the participants giving him their greetings and concluding with the sentence: "We are now all catastrophists."[20] A few years later Bretz received the Penrose Medal, the United States' most prestigious geologic award. Catastrophism had won, and so had Bretz. This modern-day "Noah" and his likewise unwanted flood had been vindicated.

By the middle of the twentieth century a few daring souls started suggesting other catastrophic events to explain the rocks and the fossils they contained. We can thank dinosaurs for the coup de grâce for strict uniformitarianism. How did those behemoths all disappear? Scientists have proposed many ideas. One scientific article listed 40 possible reasons ranging from stupidity to a change in the gravitational constant.[21] Then in 1980 Nobel laureate Louis Alvarez, from the Berkeley campus of the University of California, and others,[22] suggested that the unusually widespread abundance of the element iridium in deposits at the top of the Cretaceous Period (i.e., top of Mesozoic in Figure 5.1) came from an asteroid that had killed off the dinosaurs. The startling idea became especially popular with the public media and geophysicists, but other groups of scientists, especially paleontologists (who study fossils), had strong reservations. Some questioned the asteroid interpretation because certain dinosaurs seem to disappear earlier in the fossil layers and the rocks also contain evidence for widespread volcanic activity, global fires, or a rise in temperature that might explain the

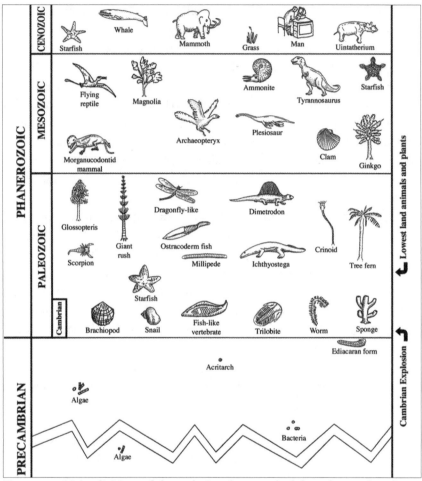

Figure 5.1 *Major divisions of the geologic column at the left, and examples of some representative organisms to the right. Note the sharp contrast between the Precambrian, which has few small organisms, and the Phanerozoic, which has a great variety of large organisms.*

dinosaurs' demise.[23]

Details continue to be debated, but the door to catastrophic interpretations has swung wide open. Some have characterized the change as "a great philosophical breakthrough,"[24] and it allows the possibility of catastrophes all through the rock record. One geologist acknowledges that "the profound role of major storms throughout geologic history is becoming increasingly recognized."[25] Another geologist speaks of "extreme events . . . with magnitudes so large and devastating that they have not, and probably could not, be observed scientifically."[26] Catastrophism has made a strong comeback, but it is not the classical approach of two centuries ago, in which the biblical flood was a dominant geologic factor. At present geologists readily consider many kinds of catastrophic events, but they assume that lots of time took place between them. The term neocatastrophism (new catastrophism) is gaining acceptance as a way of identifying the emerging perspective.

More important is the lesson that we can learn from the changes in interpretations. For millennia, thinkers accepted catastrophes as a normal part of earth history. Then for more than a century catastrophes virtually vanished from geologic explanations. Geologists had to view changes as gradual and within the range of currently active processes. Now major catastrophes are again welcome. Sometimes older rejected ideas can turn out to be correct after all!

THE GEOLOGIC COLUMN—WHAT IS IT?

Nowhere can you go looking into the rock layers of the earth and find a tall geologic column. The geologic column is more like a representation or a map, often in some kind of a vertical column format. It illustrates one small portion of a geologic layer stacked on top of another, showing the order and main divisions of the widespread rock layers found across the surface of the earth. The lowest layers of the column consist of rocks that would have been deposited first, and the most recent at the top. The geologic column has played a major role in the disputations about God and time.

As is usual in the study of nature, the picture is more complicated than what first appears and what our minds tend to envision. Any particular area often lacks many parts of the geologic column. We can tell that they are missing, because we find them in other regions. Geologists put the total geologic column together by painstakingly comparing the rocks, and especially the fossils found in them, from one locality to the other. Figure 5.1 gives a broad outline of the geologic column and some of the characteristic fossils occurring at different levels. The figures to the left represent the generally accepted geologic ages for specific fossil and rock sequences, but such datings face serious challenges. We will consider one example toward the end of this chapter. While probably no single spot on earth has a complete geologic column, the main divisions are well represented in many places.

One of the stark realities of the geologic column is the rather sharp contrast in fossils between the lower Precambrian layers and the higher Phanerozoic ones (see Figure 5.1). Only rare, very small, usually microscopic, organisms appear in the lower portion, advanced ones being essentially limited to the higher Phanerozic. It is not what we would expect from gradual evolution, and we will discuss the implications later. One also sees a moderate trend toward increasing complexity of organisms as one goes up through the Phanerozoic part, and evolutionists regard this as strong evidence of evolutionary advancement through millions of years.

Some creationists interpret the geologic column as representing repetitive creation events during long ages; others see the biblical flood as a major rapid, catastrophic event responsible for a major part of the geologic column. They interpret the slight trend in increasing complexity of fossils as one goes up through the geologic column as reflecting the order of burial of the original distribution of organisms before that flood.[27] Other creationists deny any validity to the order in the geologic column,[28] but some of their attempts to invalidate it have turned out to be erroneous.[29]

SO LITTLE TIME IN THE GEOLOGIC COLUMN FOR THE ORIGIN OF LIFE

Evolutionists depend on lots of time for the highly improbable events they postulate, a reliance well illustrated by a famous quotation by Nobel laureate George Wald. Referring to 2 billion years for the origin of life, he stated, "Given so much time, the 'impossible' becomes possible, the possible probable, and the probable virtually certain. One has only to wait: time itself performs the miracles."[30] Unfortunately for the evolution model, even eons of time such as the 15-billion-year assumed age of the universe is virtually no help at all when evaluated against our knowledge of the chemistry of life and mathematical probability. In chapter 3 we talked about the very low probability of forming a protein or a small cell given a one-chance event. But if we had lots of time, which would allow for many tries, it would seem to dramatically improve the possibility of an evolutionary success. However, when it comes to the origin of life, the probabilities are so minute and the time required so immense that the effects of the billions of years of geologic time can scarcely be noticed. Time itself does not perform the miracles that evolutionists expect. When carefully evaluated we find that evolution has very little time compared to what it really needs. Two examples of how long it would take to make just a single specific protein molecule illustrate the challenge evolution must face.

When I was an undergraduate student, one of my treasured possessions was the book *Human Destiny*, by the French biophysicist Lecomte du Noüy. The book presents a number of outstanding and challenging questions about the traditional views of the origin of human beings. In the early part of the book du Noüy discusses the origin of life and offers some calculations about the average amount of time required to produce a specific protein molecule. Despite his conservative approach to the question, he uses figures that are generous for the evolution case. Starting with a quantity of atoms equivalent to the number making up our earth, he estimates that it would take 10^{242} billion years to produce one specific protein molecule.[31] Now keep in mind that astronomers assume the earth to be less than 5 billion (5×10^9) years old and that each digit of the "242" exponent in "10^{242}" multiplies the amount of time 10 times. Even if you had an infinite amount of time, you would have, on an average, only one specific kind of protein molecule for each 10^{242} billion years. However, since fragile protein molecules would not last long under primitive conditions, *it is going to be essentially impossible to accumulate the many molecules required.* You need a lot of protein molecules for life. Perhaps you may recall from Table 3.1 that the tiny microbe *Escherichia coli* has 4,288 different kinds of protein molecules. The various types are replicated many times for a total of 2,400,000 protein molecules in one microbe, and the microbe also must have many other kinds of organic molecules. As mentioned previously, while *E. coli* is not the smallest organism we know of, we have a greater knowledge of it. Even for the smallest form of independent life that we have discovered, we still need at least several hundred different kinds of specific protein molecules, so an infinite amount of time trying to accumulate fragile protein molecules does not appear to be a plausible solution. You cannot postulate that such molecules would have evolved from each other, because life has not yet started. We are dealing with conditions before any life has occurred. Furthermore, you have to get all those molecules together in the same place. As an illustration, if you have all the parts of a car spread over the earth, after zillions of years, they still will not have assembled themselves in the same place to make a car.

Some evolutionists point out that since organisms have so many different kinds of protein molecules, any one of them could serve as the first protein molecule, hence the initial kind of protein molecule need not be that specific. But the suggestion has two problems. First, it can work only for a short time at the beginning of life, because very soon in the process of organizing life you will need a specific protein molecule to work with the first one so as to provide a meaningful arrangement that actually functions. Second, proteins are extremely complicated. The total number[32] of possible kinds of protein molecules is 10^{130}. It is a number so great that the chance of producing any one of the hundreds of different kinds of specific proteins found in the simplest microorganisms is a virtual impossibility. Recall that the whole known universe has only 10^{78} atoms.

Another more recent study by the molecular biologist Hubert Yockey[33] of the Berkeley campus of the University of California does not give much more encouraging results than the one reported on above by du Noüy. Yockey asks somewhat the same kind of question about how long it would take to form a specific protein molecule. He includes more advanced mathematical information and assumptions, but instead of starting from atoms, as du Noüy did, he addresses only the question about the time required to assemble a protein from amino acids assumed to be already available. While he does come up with a shorter time, it is still extremely long. The figure given by du Noüy reflects more what one would expect on a primitive earth. Yockey proposes that evolution's postulated primordial soup[34] was the size of our present oceans and contained 10^{44} amino acid molecules.[35] His calculations indicate that in that soup it would take, on average, 10^{23} years to form a specific protein molecule. Now, since the assumed age of the earth is less than 5 billion years (5 x 10^9 years), that age turns out to be at least 10,000 billion times too short a time to produce one specific protein molecule. One can assume that just by chance the needed protein molecule assembled at the beginning of that extended period of time, but then you would have only one molecule, and on average, a specific kind would emerge only once every 10^{23} years. Geologic time is way, way too short.

Figure 5.2 *Grand Canyon of the Colorado River. The left arrow points at the location of the Cambrian explosion. The layers below the arrow are Precambrian and those above, Phanerozoic. The right arrow points to an assumed gap of 100 million years in the geologic column. Here both the Ordovician and Silurian are missing, but the underlayer shows little or no erosion.*

Of course, you do not even have the 5 billion years mentioned above for the first protein to form, let alone for life to originate on earth. The current scientific scenario proposes that the earth is 4.6 billion years old, and that originally it was so hot that it had to cool down for more than 600 million years before life could start.[36] Some scientists assume that life started as early as 3.85 billion years ago,[37] although their evidence is debatable. However, many agree that, based on the carbon isotope evidence for life and arguable fossil finds, life originated on earth at least 3.5 billion years ago. The carbon isotope evidence employs the fact that living things tend to absorb slightly more of the lighter form of carbon (carbon-12) over the heavier forms (carbon-13 or -14), and that selection appears in the rocks. However, these results could be caused by contamination of carbon coming from life in other places. Being generous to the theory of evolution, we can state that according to its various proposals the first life should have started in less than 500 million years, which would be between 4 and 3.5 billion years ago. That time is only one tenth of the 5 billion years mentioned in our calculations above. However, keeping in mind the extreme improbabilities under consideration, such minor adjustments make hardly any difference anyway. There just isn't enough time.

In such probability studies one can always propose other assumptions and conditions to improve the chances of success, but when you face such essentially impossible odds, it is hard to not conclude that there is a real problem and that one should consider other alternatives. A number of scientists have done so and proposed other models that we discussed earlier.[38] But they are all unsatisfactory explanations because they do not provide any solution to the very same problem that protein molecules pose, namely, the complex and integrated specific requirements that life demands. Furthermore, it is not just proteins that we must account for—there are fats (lipids) and also carbohydrates. But even all those are relatively simple compared to the DNA that stores the essential information for life.

Related to the question of the origin of life are recent discussions about how to identify early forms of life. Stalwart icons of the earliest life on earth have become shrouded in controversies playing out in a number of scientific journals[39] and elsewhere. What science once considered to be plain simple facts have turned out to be quite different after further study. One leading researcher in this area appropriately comments that "for every interpretation there is an equal and opposite interpretation."[40] It seems that some of the most important rocks where the earliest life had been assumed to occur are not the kinds they were claimed to be, and their fossils are just some things that may resemble fossils but are really something else. This latter problem has plagued much of the study of Precambrian fossils. Only a few findings are clearly indisputable. One researcher reports on nearly 300 different named species that are likely either dubious or false fossils.[41] This is not an area of study in which you want to automatically accept what you read in the scientific literature.

THE CAMBRIAN EXPLOSION: EVOLUTION'S BIG BANG?

Does the fossil record in the rocks suggest that life gradually evolved during 3.5 billion years? Not at all! As mentioned above, most paleontologists—i.e., those scientists who study fossils—believe that life originated around 3.5 billion years ago. The amazing thing is that for most of the suggested time since then there is virtually no evolutionary advancement. An assumed 3 billion years later, which is five-sixths of evolutionary time, most organisms continue to consist of only one cell (Figure 5.1). The whole long Precambrian time does not show any significant increase in complexity.

Going further up the geologic column, you reach the Phanerozoic part, and all of a sudden you run into what evolutionists call the Cambrian explosion (Figure 5.1 and 5.2, Grand Canyon, left arrow), in which a large number of the basic animal types appear suddenly. Biologists refer to these types as phyla, and they represent the fundamental groups of the animal kingdom. Major differences in body plan define each group. Familiar examples of different phyla are those of snails (mollusks), sponges, starfish (echinoderms), and animals with backbones, such as fish and you and me (chordates).

Evolutionists speak of only 5 to 20 million years for the Cambrian explosion,[42] but the time limits are ill-defined. Being generous to evolution, we can state that the Cambrian explosion took less than 2 percent of all of evolutionary time! Proportionately, if evolutionary time were one hour, most animal phyla would appear in less than one minute. Figure 5.3 (black arrow) and Figure 5.1 (lower black arrow) put the time relationship for the Cambrian explosion in graphic perspective. Samuel Bowring of the Massachusetts Institute of Technology, a specialist in dating rocks, wryly comments: "And what I like to ask some of my biologist friends is How fast can evolution get before they start feeling uncomfortable?"[43] A comprehensive study[44] of fossil distribution reports that only three definite animal phyla body plans (Cnidaria, Porifera, and some kind of worm tracks) appear in the Precambrian, and they do not appear deep down, but close to the Cambrian layers.[45] Nineteen fossil phyla body plans appear in the Cambrian (about 50 million years) and

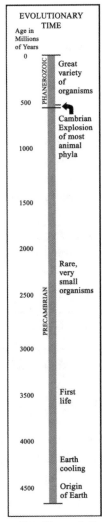

Figure 5.3 *The evolutionary time scale. The black arrow points to the Cambrian explosion, in which most animal phyla first appear. It took less than 2 percent of the total postulated time. Time scale not endorsed by author.*

only six in all the later geologic periods that represent half a billion years!

There are other explosions. Some suggest a small Avalon explosion of odd Ediacaran animals (Figure 5:1) just below the Cambrian explosion. Higher up in the fossil layers we encounter minor bursts of change, such as the Paleocene placental explosion"[46] of most modern mammal groups. We find the same situation for most living bird groups. According to the standard geologic time scale those explosions took less than 12 million years each, hardly any time at all for all the changes envisioned. A species typically lives in the fossil record 1 to 3 million years, so according to that evidence there is time for only a dozen successive species to produce all the varied types of most living mammals or birds! Reflecting on such a short time for the evolution of so many varied kinds of mammals, one evolutionist comments that "this is clearly preposterous,"[47] and he suggests some kind of rapid evolution as a solution. Other evolutionists try to solve the problem by suggesting that new species budded off from the fossil species generation at an early period, thus reducing the time for a new species to appear. However, to reduce the time paradox significantly, one has to postulate a tremendous amount of very fortuitous budding. We would expect an abundant fossil record of all this activity, but virtually none at all seems to be there.[48] Trying to explain such biological explosions this way is definitely in the category of special pleading.

The severe problem evolution faces is how to get several random mutations to occur all at once so as to provide survival value for evolving interdependent parts of new systems. While rapidly reproducing microorganisms can undergo minor changes in a short time, such is not the case for advanced organisms that can sometimes require years between generations. Calculations by Michael Behe[49] indicate that the extremely long geologic ages are way too short to accommodate the improbabilities involved. This is an especially acute problem for advanced organisms such as reptiles, birds, and mammals, which reproduce slowly, and such organisms appear abundantly in the fossil record.

The abrupt appearance of major kinds of animals and plants looks more like creation by God rather than gradual evolutionary development. Evolution needs a lot of time to accommodate the virtually impossible events necessary for producing such varied and complex life forms. However, the many fossil types that appear suddenly suggest hardly any time at all. On the other hand, those who favor the God hypothesis see the Cambrian explosion as evidence of His creative ability. Some specifically interpret it as evidence of the first group of organisms buried during the catastrophic biblical flood.

A NEW EVOLUTIONARY TREND: CLADISTICS

A quiet revolution has been going on in biology, one which the public is scarcely aware of. Our ordinary way of viewing organisms by their traditional groupings is being replaced by a "wholly evolutionary way of looking at nature."[50] It is a very different way of interpreting the variety of organisms we find. The assumed evolutionary ancestry of an organism, instead of its appearance, is becoming the determining factor in grouping organisms. Such reasoning permits evolutionists to claim that birds are dinosaurs, because they consider the two groups to share more unique characteristics (derived factors or synapomorphies) with each other than with other groups.[51] These newer studies have introduced sophisticated improvements in analysis with special emphasis on certain unique characteristics, such as long neck bones, etc., that do not appear in other groups. This is in contrast to looking at overall general characteristics, as we have usually done when classifying such organisms as snakes and birds.

These comparisons consider a great variety of different factors, and in living organisms the similarities in DNA often emerge as leading criteria. Researchers assume that the more identical the structure of the DNA in two kinds of organisms, the closer the evolutionary relationship and the less time that has occurred since the organisms evolved from each other. That seems to make good sense if you assume evolution. But the similarities in DNA are also just what you would expect from creation by God. DNA determines what the organism will be like, and it goes almost without saying that similar organisms will have similar DNA, and the closer the similarities the closer the DNA pattern, whether the organisms evolved or were created.

Sometimes scientists illustrate evolutionary relationships through connecting lines in diagrams called cladograms, that can come in somewhat different forms and interpretations. In these diagrams, organisms related by evolution form a group called a clade, which can be any size, depending on what unique characteristics are under consideration. It is possible, by using the right kind of "unique" characteristics, to make a huge clade of all living organisms, and that

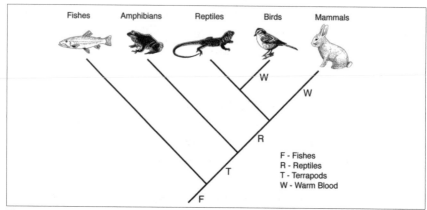

Figure 5.4 *Illustration of a simple kind of cladogram for living vertebrates. It considers evolution to proceed upward through the lines in the diagram to the living forms illustrated at the top. The letters along the lines designate the appearance of new unique characteristics. In this model, note that the warm-blooded feature, W, evolved independently for birds and mammals by parallel evolution. As one focuses on more details of the characteristics of the different groups, it leads to different and more complicated relationships. Reptiles are no longer regarded by some as a valid group.*

fits with the evolutionary belief that all living forms are related. Figure 5.4 is a simplified cladogram of our living vertebrates. Vertebrates provide a familiar example, and a basic paleontology textbook used this cladogram to introduce the concept. As you go *up* through the lines of the cladogram, they suggest the unique characteristics focused on. In that diagram the designation "tetrapods" refers to the four appendages of all the groups as you follow the lines up from that point. But the actual picture becomes more complicated. When dealing with more detailed unique factors *within* vertebrates one gets a different and more complex relationship for the vertebrates than portrayed in Figure 5.4.[52] For instance, the traditional reptile class (lizards, crocodiles, turtles, snakes) is not now considered by many as a valid group (clade) because it shares too many characteristics with other groups, especially birds.[53] We need to keep in perspective that the indiscriminate use of unique characteristics can sometimes suggest very peculiar evolutionary relationships, such as lungfish (fish with an odd kind of lung) being more closely related to cows than to other fish.[54]

Cladograms usually indicate on the diagram what specific factors they regard as important in determining the suggested pattern of evolution. The selection of these factors can be difficult, and too often, similar characteristics, such as the eye of a squid and of a fish that have the same basic structure, are just assumed to have evolved independently more than once (parallel evolution, convergence), and thus are not related. That kind of thinking introduces a lot of conjecture in trying to determine evolutionary relationships. On the other hand, cladograms can be highly sophisticated and represent a complicated process that carefully analyzes the unique similarities found among groups of organisms by using the shortest pathway possible to represent relationships. The real problem with cladograms is that the patterns do not mean that the organisms necessarily evolved the way suggested or any other way, and some evolutionists point this out. Their use usually implies evolution but they actually show unique similarities, not evolution. You can play the cladogram "game" with any variety of things, such as toys or houses. Figure 5.5 illustrates a proposed "cladogram" for the evolution of women's hats, but we all know they did not evolve by themselves from each other or from a common hat ancestor. Instead, someone designed them. The reality about the relationship of organisms can be very different than cladograms illustrate.

IGNORING THE FOSSILS

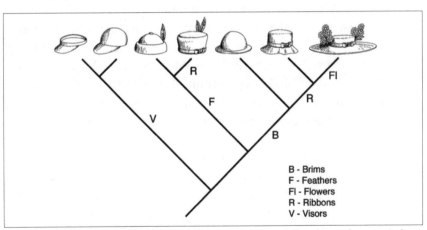

Figure 5.5 *Illustration of a simple cladogram for the relationships of women's hats. Evolution would proceed upward through the lines in the diagram. Note that ribbons, R, evolved independently twice for separate types of hats by parallel evolution. The diagram illustrates that you can make cladograms for many things, including such created items as women's hats. Some evolutionists point out that cladograms need not necessarily represent evolutionary relationships, although this is often inferred.*

Another recent scientific trend is especially related to time. While fossils give us the best clues we have about past life on earth, researchers will ignore some important evidence from the fossil record when it seems expedient. Such an approach has triggered much controversy. While one expert favoring it comments that "we don't see time as particularly important," another who is more cautious claims that "so much of this is just hot air."[55] This may turn out to be one of those great bad ideas! We do not know which way science will go, but just the trend itself is alarming.

This new approach permits evolutionists to explain problems such as the Cambrian explosion, since in their paradigm[56] the DNA indicates to them that animal phyla evolved from each other much earlier.[57] Their reasoning is that since changes in DNA are very slow, and since the differences between the DNA of the various animal phyla are great, the phyla must have evolved long before their fossils first show up in the rocks. Again this borders on fact-free science.

To determine how fast DNA changes, scientists use the molecular clock that frequently employs assumed geologic time to estimate rates of change. Sadly, the molecular clock has turned out to be rather unreliable.[58] Researchers refer to the "extreme rate variation in the molecular clock"[59] and that the "problems of establishing accurate calibration points, correctly rooted phylogenies, and accurate estimates of branch length remain formidable."[60] The well-respected paleontologist James Valentine of the Berkeley campus of the University of California points out that "unfortunately, the rates of molecular evolution are not clocklike; different parts of molecules evolve at different rates, molecules within the same lineage vary in their rates of change over time, different molecules evolve at different rates, and homologous molecules in different taxa evolve at different rates."[61]

In spite of such shortcomings, suggestions are that the evolution of some of the basic animal types may have taken place as early as 500 million to 1 billion years earlier than the Cambrian explosion[62] despite the fact that we have essentially found no relevant fossils for that immense period of time. That is as long as or even twice as long as all the time proposed for the evolution of almost all organisms from the Cambrian explosion to the present. Paleontologists, who study the fossils and pay more attention to their significance, have been more cautious in their estimates of how long before the Cambrian the various animals evolved from each other. Recall that it is at the base of the Phanerozic that you have the Cambrian layers and the Cambrian explosion, and there you find an abundance of different kinds of well-preserved animal species, but a virtual absence below them. To explain this sudden appearance, evolutionists report on rare minute fossils and dubious animal tracks found in the Precambrian. If evolution of the animal phyla had taken place before the Cambrian explosion, we should at least encounter thousands of good Precambrian animal fossils, representing animals evolving into other kinds, but virtually none are found.

It is particularly depressing to see a number of researchers ignoring the good data we have about fossil distribution because of the new trends in evolutionary classification. That so many scientists are willing to do so reveals how easily theory instead of the facts of nature can drive science. More than 50 years ago Richard Lull, a famed paleontologist and director of the world-renowned Peabody Museum at Yale University, hailed fossils as "the final court of appeal when the doctrine of evolution is brought to the bar."[63] That may have been the case then, but now when the fossil record is affirming serious problems for evolution, a number of scientists are paying no attention to it. The final court of appeal for evolution may become only a dubious application of the supposed molecular clock and the undisputed assumption that evolution took place.

THE MISSING LINKS

When you look down through the rock layers, you find many hundreds of fossil turtles. Some are huge, more than 10 feet (three meters) long. Then below the lowest turtles you don't find the evolutionary links between them and an assumed lizardlike evolutionary ancestor of the turtle. Turtles as a specific kind of animal appear suddenly and fully formed in the fossil record. The same is the case for fossils of those forbidding flying reptiles called pterosaurs, as well as fossil bats and many other groups, including the many animal phyla in the Cambrian explosion (Figure 5.1). The evolutionary problem of the Cambrian explosion is not just that a multitude of animal phyla show up in relatively no time at all; it is also that below the Cambrian explosion you don't find the fossils of the intermediate forms from which the various phyla should have evolved. Other major groups of organisms also tend to appear abruptly in the fossil record. Again, if they had really evolved, we should find the fossils of all kinds of intermediate forms below them as evolution slowly developed a great variety of phyla.

Charles Darwin was quite aware of the problem and candidly acknowledged it in *The Origin of Species.* "But just in proportion as this process of extermination has acted on an enormous scale, so must the number of intermediate varieties, which have formerly existed on the earth, be truly enormous. Why then is not every geological formation and every stratum full of such intermediate links? Geology assuredly does not reveal any such finely graduated organic chain; and this, perhaps, is the most obvious and gravest objection which can be urged against my theory."[64] Darwin then devotes many pages explaining that the reason we don't have the intermediate links is that the geological record is so imperfect. He speaks of parts of the geologic column missing in many places across the earth and casually refers to the striking feature that the underlying layer at such gaps does not show the effects of time. In so doing he is inadvertently posing a significant problem for the long ages of time necessary for the slow evolutionary process he proposes. You can tell that you have a gap in the geologic column because the missing parts, especially the characteristic fossils, occur elsewhere on the earth in the appropriate sequence. Furthermore, Darwin speaks of "the many cases on record of a formation conformably covered, after an enormous interval of time, by another and later formation, without the underlying bed having suffered in the interval any wear and tear."[65] By "conformably" Darwin means that the layer just below the gap, the one assumed to be much older, and the much younger layer just above the gap lie in flat contact with each other. Since the underlayer is flat, this implies that the "enormous interval of time" he suggests never occurred, because the ravages of time, such as the irregular erosion expected, are not there. Geologists call these major gaps, where there is no or little evidence for them in the rocks, paraconformities. But if they do find evidence of slight erosion they tend to refer to them as disconformities. The lack of "wear and tear" at these flat gaps makes them hard to identify, and you need to study the fossils carefully to spot them. Like the proverbial hole in a doughnut, there is nothing there to represent the gap. But their abundance in the fossil record, and the smoothness of their contacts, raises a serious question about the validity of the long geologic ages, including the complicated process of radiometric dating often used to establish them. [66]

Adam Sedgwick, Darwin's old professor of geology at Cambridge University, had no problems with long geologic ages, but had serious doubts about evolution. He did not let Darwin get away with the suggestion that the missing layers indicated enormous intervals of time without any wear and tear of the underlayer. Darwin tried to explain these as regions at the bottom of the sea, but that does not fit either the fossils or the kind of rocks we find above and below the gaps. In a critique published in *The Spectator,* Sedgwick not too subtly comments that "you cannot make a good rope out of a string of air bubbles," and, speaking specifically about the gaps, asks, "Where have we a proof of any enormous lapse of geologic time to account for the change? . . . Physical evidence is against it. To support a baseless theory, Darwin would require a countless lapse of ages of which we have no commensurate physical monuments."[67] You can easily see the problem in the Grand Canyon (Figure 5.2, right arrow), where the Ordovician and Silurian periods, representing more than 100 million years, are absent, and yet we find only slight evidence of erosion of the underlayer at this gap. The Grand Canyon has a number of similar gaps, but as you can see, the layers in this part of the geologic record are all extremely flat. The contrast of the flat underlayer at such gaps with the dramatic irregular carving of the Grand Canyon itself illustrates the conundrum. Time produces a lot of irregular erosion like the Grand Canyon, and we don't see much of it at these gaps.[68] Through time the ravages of erosion become dramatic. Based on average rates of erosion for the continents of the earth, you would expect their surface to lower by two miles (three kilometers) in 100 million years, and that is twice the depth of the whole Grand Canyon![69] The problems that Sedgwick had with the lack of physical evidence for the very long time proposed at such gaps remains unresolved.[70] Any shortening of the standard geologic time scale leaves even less time for the improbabilities of evolution. Such flat gap data lends strong support to the biblical model of origins.

Almost a century and a half later Darwin's concerns about the lack of intermediate fossil forms still remains very much alive. We have collected multitudes of fossils since then, and when we go up through the layers, major kinds appear suddenly and don't seem to have evolved from different ancestors. Some researchers acknowledge the problem. Famed paleontologist Robert Carroll, who defends evolution, points out that "fossils would be expected to show a continuous progression of slightly different forms linking all species and all major groups with one another in a nearly unbroken spectrum. In fact, most well-preserved fossils are as readily classified in a relatively small number of major groups as are living species." Speaking of the features of various kinds of flowering plants, he comments that "in no cases can the gradual evolution of these characters of groups be documented."[71] And discussing the relationship between paleontology and biology theory, David Kitts at the University of Oklahoma observes that "despite the bright promise that paleontology provides a means of 'seeing' evolution, it has presented some nasty difficulties for evolutionists, the most notorious of which is the presence of 'gaps' in the fossil record. Evolution requires intermediate forms between species, and paleontology does not provide them."[72] Paleontologist T. S. Kemp of Oxford University reaffirms the problem we find as he states that "the observed fossil pattern is invariably not compatible with a gradualistic evolutionary process. Fossils only extremely rarely come as lineages of finely graded intermediate forms connecting ancestors with descendants."[73] He opts for a variety of explanations for evolution and for the fossil record.

Some evolutionists such as Stephen Gould at Harvard have suggested that evolution proceeds by quick little jumps and that not much of a fossil record gets preserved during them (i.e., the punctuated equilibrium model). But it does little to resolve the problem that evolution faces in the fossil record, because the real lack of intermediates is most pronounced between the major groups, such as the animal phyla, and the problem seems to be even more severe in the plant kingdom. At the big gaps between major groups of organisms you would expect the greatest number of evolutionary intermediates to bridge the gaps, and that is precisely where the intermediates are notably absent.[74] Where you should find lots of small jumps the record is instead virtually, if not totally, barren. In spite of this, some evolutionists, including spokespersons for the National Academy of Sciences, claim that research has filled many of the gaps.[75] But this is simply not the case. Paleontologists can suggest intermediates for only a few minor gaps. Furthermore, we need to keep in mind that even finding an intermediate does not demonstrate evolution—it could be just another created variety that has traits that evolutionists would interpret as intermediate.

A lot of evolutionists don't seem to understand the real problem of the fossil record. They point to isolated suggestions of intermediate parts or forms. Unfortunately, that is not what they must have in order to demonstrate that evolution actually occurred. By now we have identified many millions of fossils, comprising more than 250,000 different species. The more we find, the surer it appears that the lack of intermediates is a real fact. With that many species classified you would of course expect some to be considered as intermediates and paleontologists do suggest a few examples, and we can expect more. However, those few exceptions do little to solve evolution's problem. Indeed, many of them are not real intermediates but are what we call mosaics, in which the organism displays several characteristics from the two groups it supposedly bridges, but each character (such as a feather or type of ankle) is completely developed and not transitional in structure.

If evolution had actually taken place, as organisms tried to evolve through billions of years, with the occasional successes and the many failures expected, we should find a solid continuity of intermediates, not just a few questionable exceptions. Such continuity should be especially pronounced in the geologic column just below where major groups arise suddenly, such as with the Cambrian explosion or the appearance of modern mammals and birds. The rocks should be filled with many thousands of intermediates instead of the few that paleontologists too often find themselves debating over.[76] Charles Darwin was really asking the right question when, as discussed earlier, he asked, "Why then is not every geological formation and every stratum full of such intermediate links?"[77]

CONCLUDING COMMENTS

The question of how fast was the past has raised a large number of questions with deep implications for the God question as well as equally deep ramifications for how science operates. We find ourselves faced with a plethora of conflicting conclusions about time. In science we have seen the concept of catastrophism at first accepted, then buried, and more recently, resurrected.

It makes little difference whether or not one invokes billions of years for evolution. All of geologic time is totally inadequate. Those who believe in creation, however,[78] have an omnipotent God not bound by time and who does not need much time to create. Evolution, on the other hand, requires far, far more time than it has available. Essentially there is not enough time to produce even a single specific protein molecule in a huge early primordial soup, let alone evolve all the various forms of life from microbe to whale. It does not look as though science is trying to find God. Its present idealism is a strong defense of naturalistic evolution. The disregard for the implications of the fossil record is pronounced. Problems include: the brief time in the geologic column for the origin of life; the lack of time for complete changes in advanced organisms; the fact of the Cambrian and other explosions; and the lack of intermediates between major kinds of fossils. These all illustrate how easily science can ignore data. Is this same kind of thinking involved when science turns its back to the evidence that there is a God? In the chapters ahead we will give special attention to some of science's special attributes.

[1] Yockey HP. 1981. Self-organization origin of life scenarios and information theory. Journal of Theoretical Biology 91:13-31.

[2] Thorarinsson S. 1964. Surtsey: the new island in the North Atlantic. Eysteinsson S, trans. New York: Viking Press, p. 39.

[3] For further discussion, see: Gould SJ. 1970. Is uniformitarianism useful? In: Cloud P, ed. Adventures in earth history. San Francisco: W. H. Freeman and Co., pp. 51-53; Hallam A. 1989. Great geological controversies, 2nd ed. Oxford: Oxford University Press, pp. 30-64; Palmer T. 1999. Controversy: catastrophism and evolution, the ongoing debate. New York: Kluwer Academic/Plenum Publishers.

[4] Hutton J. 1795. Theory of the earth: with proofs and illustrations, volume II. Edinburgh: n.p. Reprinted 1959 by H. R. Engelmann (J. Cramer) and Wheldon and Wesley, Ltd., p. 547.

[5] This famous statement is quoted in many references, including: Cohn N. 1996. Noah's flood: the Genesis story in Western thought. New Haven, Conn.: Yale University Press, p. 102.

[6] Hallam, p. 55. [For publishing information, see note 3, above.]

[7] Lyell KM, ed. 1881. Life, letters and journals of Sir Charles Lyell, Bart., vol. 1. London: John Murray, p. 271 (14 June 1830), p. 273 (20 June 1830).

[8] Cohn, p. 102. [See note 5.]

[9] Hutton, p. 551. [See note 4.]

[10] Ruse M. 2000. The evolution wars: a guide to the debates. New Brunswick, N.J.: Rutgers University Press, p. 34.

[11] Palmer, p. ix. [See note 3.]

[12] Bailey E. 1963. Charles Lyell. Garden City, N.Y.: Doubleday and Co., Inc., p. 191.

[13] Bretz JH. 1923. Glacial drainage on the Columbia Plateau. Geological Society of America Bulletin 34:573-608.

[14] Bretz JH. 1923. The Channeled Scablands of the Columbia Plateau. Journal of Geology 31:617-649.

[15] Allen JE, Burns M, Sargent SC. 1986. Cataclysm on the Columbia: a layman's guide to the features produced by the catastrophic Bretz floods in the Pacific Northwest. Scenic trips to the Northwest's geologic past, No. 2. Portland: Timber Press, p. 44.

[16] Bretz JH. 1978. Introduction. In: Baker VR, ed. 1981. Catastrophic flooding: the origin of the Channeled Scabland. Benchmark Papers in Geology 55. Stroudsburg, Pa.: Dowden, Hutchinson, and Ross, pp. 18, 19.

[17] Baker VR. 1981. Editor's Comments on papers 4, 5, and 6. In: Baker, p. 60. [See note 16.]

[18] Bretz JH, Smith HTU, Neff GE. 1956. Channeled Scabland of Washington: new data and interpretations. Bulletin of the Geological Society of America 67:957-1049.

[19] For current disputations about the number of floods involved, see: Clague JJ et al. 2003. Paleomagnetic and tephra evidence for tens of Missoula floods in southern Washington. Geology 31:247-250; Shaw J et al. 1999. The Channeled Scabland: back to Bretz? Geology 27:605-608.

[20] Bretz JH. 1969. The Lake Missoula floods and the Channeled Scabland. Journal of Geology 77:505-543.

[21] Jepsen GL. 1964. Riddles of the terrible lizards. American Scientist 52:227-246.

[22] Alvarez L et al. 1980. Extraterrestrial causes for the Cretaceous-Tertiary extinction: experimental results and theoretical interpretations. Science 208:1095-1108.

[23] Dobb E. 2002. What wiped out the dinosaurs? Discover 23(6):36-43; Hallam, pp. 184-215. [See note 3.]

[24] Kauffman E. 1983. Quoted in: Lewin R. Extinctions and the history of life. Science 221:935-937.

[25] Nummendal D. 1982. Clastics. Geotimes 27(2):22, 23.

[26] Brett CE. 2000. A slice of the "layer cake": the paradox of "frosting continuity." Palaios 15:495-498.

[27] Clark HW. 1946. The new diluvialism. Angwin, Calif.: Science Publications; Roth AA. 2003. Genesis and the geologic column. Dialogue 15(1):9-12, 18.

[28] For further discussion and references, see: Numbers RL. 1992. The creationists. New York: Alfred A. Knopf, pp. 79-81, 123-219.

[29] See: Chadwick AV. 1987. Of dinosaurs and men. Origins 14:33-40; Kuban GJ. 1989. Retracking those incredible man tracks. National Center for Science Education Reports 9(4): 4 pages, unpaginated special supplement; Neufeld B. 1975. Dinosaur tracks and giant men. Origins 2:64-76; Numbers, pp. 265-267. [See note 28.]

[30] Wald G. 1954. The origin of life. Scientific American 191(2):45-53.

[31] du Noüy L. 1947. Human destiny. New York: Longmans, Green, and Co., pp. 33-35.

[32] Meyer SC. 1998. The explanatory power of design: DNA and the origin of information. In: Dembski WA, ed. Mere creation: science, faith, and intelligent design. Downer's Grove, Ill.: InterVarsity Press, pp. 113-147.

[33] Yockey HP. 1992. Information theory and molecular biology. Cambridge: Cambridge University Press, pp. 248-255.

[34] Discussed in chapter 3.

[35] This is a well-accepted figure, e.g., Eigen M. 1971. Self-organization of matter and the evolution of biological macromolecules. Die Naturwissenschaften 58:465-523.

[36] Morowitz HJ. 1992. Beginnings of cellular life: metabolism recapitulates biogenesis. New Haven, Conn.: Yale University Press, p. 31.

[37] Hayes JM. 1996. The earliest memories of life on earth. Nature 384:21, 22; Mojzsis SJ, Harrison TM. 2000. Vestiges of a beginning: clues to the emergent biosphere recorded in the oldest sedimentary rocks. GSA Today 10(4):1-6.

[38] See chapter 3.

[39] For some general reviews and references, see: Copley J. 2003. Proof of life. New Scientist 177:28-31; Kerr RA. 2002. Reversals reveal pitfalls in spotting ancient and E.T. life. Science 296:1384, 1385; Simpson S. 2003. Questioning the oldest signs of life. Scientific American 288(4):70-77.

[40] Copley. [See note 39.]

[41] Hofmann HJ. 1992. Proterozoic and selected Cambrian megascopic dubiofossils and pseudofossils. In: Schopf WJ, Klein C, eds. The Proterozoic biosphere: a multidisciplinary study. Cambridge: Cambridge University Press, pp. 1035-1053.

[42] For example: Bowring SA, Erwin DH. 1998. A new look at evolutionary rates in deep time: uniting paleontology and high-precision geochronology. GSA Today 8(9):1-8; Bowring SA et al. 1993. Calibrating rates of early Cambrian evolution. Science 261:1293-1298; Zimmer C. 1999. Fossils give glimpse of old mother lamprey. Science 286:1064, 1065.

[43] As quoted in: Nash M. 1995. When life exploded. Time 146(23):66-74.

[44] Meyer SC, Ross M, Nelson P, Chien P. 2003. The Cambrian explosion: biology's big bang. In: Campbell JA, Meyer SC, eds. Darwinism, design, and public education. East Lansing, Mich.: Michigan State University Press, pp. 323-402; see also: Appendix C, Stratigraphic first appearance of phyla body plans, pp. 593-598; Appendix D, Stratigraphic first appearance of phyla-subphyla body plans, pp. 599-604.

[45] Valentine JW. 2004. On the origin of phyla. Chicago: University of Chicago Press; Valentine JW. 2002. Prelude to the Cambrian explosion. Annual Review of Earth and Planetary Sciences 30:285-306.

[46] Benton MJ. 2000. Vertebrate paleontology, 2nd ed. Oxford: Blackwell Science, Ltd., p. 327.

[47] Stanley SM. 1981. The new evolutionary timetable: fossils, genes, and the origin of species. New York: Basic Books, Inc., Publishers, p. 93.

[48] For further study, the reader may want to consult the insightful mathematical implications of: Foote M. 1996. On the probability of ancestors in the fossil record. Paleobiology 22(2):141-151.

[49] Behe MJ. 2007. The edge of evolution: the search for the limits of Darwinism. New York: Free Press, pp. 44-63,

[50] Padian K. 2000. What the media don't tell you about evolution. Scientific American 282(2):102, 103.

[51] Chapter 6 will further consider the question of bird evolution.

[52] Cowen R. 2000. History of life, 3rd ed.. Malden, Mass.: Blackwell Science, Inc., Figure 3.9.

[53] Benton, p. 32 [see note 46]; Cowen, p. 50 [see note 52].

[54] Gee H. 1999. In search of deep time: beyond the fossil record to a new history of life. New York: Free Press, p. 145.

[55] As quoted in: DiSilvestro RL. 1997. In quest of the origin of birds. BioScience 47:481-485.

[56] Chapter 6 will extensively discuss the paradigm concept.

[57] Fortey RA, Briggs DEG, Wills MA. 1996. The Cambrian evolutionary "explosion": decoupling cladogenesis from morphological disparity. Biological Journal of the Linnean Society 57:13-33; Smith AB, Peterson KJ. 2002. Dating the time of origin of major clades: molecular clocks and the fossil record. Annual Review of Earth and Planetary Sciences 30:65-88;

Valentine. Prelude to the Cambrian explosion. [See note 45.]

[58] Ayala FJ. 1997. Vagaries of the molecular clock. Proceedings of the National Academy of Sciences (USA) 94:7776-7783; Ayala FJ. 1986. On the virtues and pitfalls of the molecular evolutionary clock. Journal of Heredity 77:226-235; Smith, Peterson [see note 57].

[59] Vawter L, Brown WM. 1986 Nuclear and mitochondrial DNA comparisons reveal extreme rate variation in the molecular clock. Science 234:194-196.

[60] Smith, Peterson. [See note 57.]

[61] Valentine. Prelude to the Cambrian explosion. [See note 45.]

[62] Ibid.; Wang DY-C, Kumar S, Hedges SB. 1999. Divergence time estimates for early history of animal phyla and the origin of plants, animals and fungi. Proceedings of the Royal Society of London, B, 226(1415):163-171; Wray GA, Levinton JS, Shapiro LH. 1996. Molecular evidence for deep Precambrian divergences among Metazoan phyla. Science 274:568-573.

[63] Lull RS. 1931, 1935. Fossils: what they tell us of plants and animals of the past. New York: The University Society, p. 3.

[64] Darwin C. 1859. On the origin of species. London: John Murray. In: Burrow JW, ed. 1968 reprint. London: Penguin Books, pp. 291, 292.

[65] Ibid., p. 298.

[66] For a knowledgeable evaluation, see: Giem PAL. 1997. Scientific theology. Riverside, Calif.: La Sierra University Press, pp. 111-190. Also: http://www.scientifictheology.com.

[67] Anonymous article unquestionably credited to Adam Sedgwick. Darwin referred to Sedgwick as the author in his correspondence. 1860. Objections to Mr. Darwin's theory of the origin of species. The Spectator, Apr. 7, 1860, pp. 334, 335.

[68] Roth AA. 2003. Implications of paraconformities. Geoscience Reports No. 36:1-5; Roth AA. 1998. Origins: linking science and Scripture. Hagerstown, Md.: Review and Herald Pub. Assn., pp. 222-229, 262-266; Roth AA. 1988. Those gaps in the sedimentary layers. Origins 15:75-92.

[69] North America is now being eroded away at an average rate of 2.4 inches (61 millimeters) per 1,000 years, and this figure appears close to the average for the rest of the continents. [See: Judson S, Ritter DF. 1964. Rates of regional denudation in the United States. Journal of Geophysical Research 69(16):3395-3401; for some other estimates, see: McLennan SM. 1993. Weathering and global denudation. Journal of Geology 101:295-303; more references in Roth. Origins, pp. 263-266, 271-273 [see note 68].] At that rate you would expect 3.8 miles (6.1 kilometers) of erosion in 100 million years. Modern agricultural practices have doubled the rate of erosion, so the expected erosion in the past 100 million years, without agriculture, would be about 1.9 miles (3 kilometers).

[70] For an attempted resolution, that fits only a special case, see: Newell ND. 1967. Paraconformities. In: Teichert C, Yochelson EL, eds. Essays in paleontology and stratigraphy. Department of Geology, University of Kansas Special Publication 2, pp. 349-367.

[71] Carroll RL. 1997. Patterns and processes of vertebrate evolution. Cambridge: Cambridge University Press, pp. 8, 9.

[72] Kitts DB. 1974. Paleontology and evolutionary theory. Evolution 28:458-472.

[73] Kemp TS. 1999. Fossils and evolution. Oxford: Oxford University Press, p. 16.

[74] Simpson GG. 1967. The meaning of evolution: a study of the history of life and its significance for man, rev. ed. New Haven, Conn.: Yale University Press, pp. 232, 233.

[75] Futuyma DJ. 1998. Evolutionary biology. 3rd ed. Sunderland, Mass.: Simaur Associates,

Inc., p. 761; National Academy of Sciences. 1998. Teaching about evolution and the nature of science. Washington, D.C.: National Academy Press, Internet version, chapter 5.

[76] For instance, a recent article: Prothero DR. 2005. The fossils say yes. Natural History 114 [9]:52-56), claiming that the fossil record is no longer an embarrassment to evolution, lists only a few examples of supposed intermediates, and some of those are of dubious validity. Furthermore, it does not even mention the Cambrian explosion problem.

[77] Darwin C. On the origin of species, p. 292. [See note 64.]

[78] I favor the old universe, old earth, and young life variety. For further elaboration, see Roth. Origins. [See note 68.]

Chapter Six

Fashions in Science

Almost anyone can do science; almost no one can do good science.[1]

—L. L. Larson Cudmore, biologist

PARADIGMS

One day my professor of physical geology discussed the amazing "jigsaw puzzle" type of match between the east and west coasts of the Atlantic Ocean. He commented that decades earlier a man by the name of Alfred Wegener had proposed that, long ago, Europe and Africa had been next to North and South America with no Atlantic Ocean between them. Since that time this major supercontinent had split apart into smaller continents, creating the Atlantic Ocean between. My professor also mentioned that while the idea was interesting, no one paid much attention to it anymore. What he did not realize is that six years later the geological community would have made a complete reversal from nearly complete rejection to almost total acceptance of Wegener's idea.

The concept that the continents had moved was revolutionary and affected many geological interpretations, especially ideas about how the world's land masses, mountains, and oceans had formed. The textbooks all had to be rewritten. Living through this major shift in thinking was both exciting and sobering. It was exciting because it stimulated so many new interpretations and because Wegener, who had endured such severe criticism, especially from American geologists,[2] turned out to be right after all. Unfortunately, he died long before his ideas received their vindication. The shift was also sobering because it left a number of us wondering how many currently ridiculed ideas would soon become accepted dogma. The change to belief that continents moved was dramatic and striking. Ridicule and satire often entered into the debate. Before acceptance, you were not a part of the geological community if you believed that continents shifted. Afterward, to believe that they did not slide across the surface of the earth made you a geological outcast. Sociological factors seem to have dominated. What was puzzling was how such large groups of scientists could be so sure the continents did not move, and then very soon thereafter be positive that they did. It suggests that scientists tend to act as unified groups whose members are loyal to each other or to an idea, instead of behaving as independent investigators. But scientists are not the only ones who do such things—we also see the tendency in many areas, such as nationalism, politics, and religion. Such a realization can have profound implications as we try to interpret science. Is science a steady progress toward truth, as some scientists tend to believe it is, or is it at the mercy of the gregarious behavior of scientists as they shift from one idea to another?

Some years ago I attended a conference of the International Association of Sedimentologists. It consisted of all kinds of technical presentations about how to identify and interpret physical structures and various changes going on over time in geological sediments. However, arguably the most important presentation of the conference was not about details of the way sediments behave, but about how sedimentologists (those who study sediments) themselves act. Under the title of "Fashions and Models in Sedimentology: A Personal Perspective,"[3] the president of the association addressed the scientists, pointing out how they tended to shift from one fashionable interpretation to another. By looking back at past concepts about sediments he showed how for a few years one idea dominates, then a few years later another captivates the limelight, only to get replaced later by still another, etc. He also identified what helps an idea to become fashionable. Especially important in gaining recognition were timing, simplicity, and publicity. It is gratifying to see that some leading scientists recognize the fact that other factors, besides the sometimes-purported unbiased search for truth, can drive the scientific process. Popular acceptance of an idea may reflect sociological factors instead of compelling evidence.

In 1962 Thomas Kuhn published a book that a number of scholars consider to be the most influential analysis of the behavior of scientists. Entitled *The Structure of Scientific Revolutions,*[4] it challenged the "immaculate perception" of science as a steady advancement toward truth. Instead Kuhn proposed that the social behavior of scientists has a greater influence than the facts of science themselves. As expected, it received criticism from many perspectives, and some scientists were especially unimpressed. Several philosophers, including the Hungarian philosopher of science Imre Lakatos, came to the rescue of science by proposing a less-radical scenario in which scientific ideas do get revised, but more on the basis of rational correction than social behavior.[5]

Kuhn proposed that normally scientists pursue their investigations and shape their conclusions under the influence of broad concepts that he calls paradigms. He defines paradigms as concepts "that for a time provide model problems and solutions."[6] While paradigms can be either true or false, scientists accept them, at least for a while, as true. Examples would be evolution, or the idea that continents move. Earlier the broadly accepted concept that continents do not shift would also be a paradigm. Because scientists (or any group, for that matter) accept paradigms as true, they regard any explanations that do not fit the accepted view as false and interpret the data supporting such unacceptable explanations as anomalous. In addition, they reject those who propose ideas outside the paradigm. Such a closed attitude tends to restrict innovation and helps perpetuate the life of the paradigm.

Fitting data under an accepted paradigm is what Kuhn considers normal science. Occasionally a change in paradigm occurs, and he calls that a scientific revolution. The change from belief that continents do not move to belief that they do was a scientific revolution. Kuhn characterized a scientific revolution as a "conversion experience,"[7] a term that did not endear him to a scientific community that sees objectivity and reason as its hallmarks. Transformation from one paradigm to another is usually difficult, and may represent a shift toward either truth or error. Kuhn's views are probably extreme and tend to minimize the accomplishments of science. On the other hand, on the basis of what we learn from the history of science, his paradigm concept is a perceptive analysis of the behavior of scientists.

Sometimes a paradigm change can revert back to one previously rejected. An example mentioned earlier is the idea that life can arise spontaneously all by itself. Scholars generally accepted that idea for a long time, then abandoned it as the result of the work of Louis Pasteur, and now it has

161

again gained support as part of the naturalistic evolutionary scenario.[8] The same applies to the role of major catastrophes in earth history (catastrophism) as it fell from favor only to come back once again and help shape geology.[9] Any evaluation of science needs to take into account the influence of dominating paradigms on the conclusions it reaches.

SCIENTISTS ARE HUMAN!

In the *Edinburgh Review* of April 1860 there appeared a long and scathing anonymous review of Charles Darwin's *The Origin of Species*. It raised questions about many of Darwin's ideas, especially about the progressive development of life forms through natural selection, in which the fittest were the ones that survived. The author pitched a barrage of arguments, some of dubious value, against Darwin's proposals. One of the more cogent ones was the simple comment that if evolutionary advancement occurred by survival of the fittest, how come the simpler organisms are now so much more abundant than more advanced ones? The fittest should replace the less fit, or at least outnumber them. Furthermore, the article was quite complimentary of the ideas of the most renowned English naturalist of that time, Sir Richard Owen. Owen, who had founded London's monumental Natural History Museum, believed in a modified form of creation, in which God had originated the major kinds of organisms and they later changed into a variety of other organisms while keeping the same basic characteristics. Vertebrates are an example of one of Owen's major created kinds. Owen originated the term *dinosaur,* recognizing these peculiar organisms as a distinct group. In fact, he supervised the creation of life-size models of dinosaurs at the Crystal Palace. Twenty-two people, including Owen, attended a New Year's dinner inside one of the dinosaur models, and a crowd of 40,000 joined Queen Victoria at the display's inauguration ceremony.[10]

It did not take long to solve the mystery of the critical anonymous review. Richard Owen himself, one of Charles Darwin's fiercest opponents, had written it. As expected, the review did not please Darwin. In a letter to the Harvard University botanist Asa Gray, he commented that "no one fact tells so strongly against Owen, considering his former position at the College of Surgeons, as that he has never reared one pupil or follower."[11] Historian Nicolaas Rupki comments about the assertion: "this was of course nonsense; Owen had a wide following, in the museum movement, as a Cuvierian [Cuvier was a French naturalist], and as a transcendentalist."[12]

Owen's anonymous subterfuge in support of his views and Darwin's distortion of the facts illustrate that scientists are undeniably human, and that they can get very personally involved in their science. This raises an important question about the practice of science: Is it an open search for truth about nature, or is it a hunt for evidence to support the hypotheses and theories of the scientist? It turns out to be a mixture of both.

A prolonged conflict over the famous *Archaeopteryx* fossil further demonstrates how scientists get personally wrapped up in their science. Earlier[13] we referred to Charles Darwin's comment that probably the gravest objection that could be raised against his theory was the fact that the geologic record did not display countless intermediate links between various kinds of organisms. Not only did the rocks lack an abundant supply of such intermediates, paleontology did not have even one accepted example despite the fact that at that time fossils fascinated the public, adorning the shelves of many museums and lurking in many homes and basements. Then, with almost immaculate timing, just two years after the publication of *The Origin of Species,* someone discovered a hopeful intermediate that acquired the name *Archaeopteryx.*[14] Not only did it appear to be a good transition between reptiles and birds, it was at the right place in the geologic layers. Soon it became one of the most famous fossils known.

Archaeopteryx had been uncovered in the Solnhofen limestone of Germany. This limestone readily splits into thin slabs and is sometimes of such fine quality that it has been used for precise lithographic printing, hence the scientific name of the fossil *Archaeopteryx lithographica.* Fossils are not abundant in the Solnhofen, but it has yielded some of the most exquisitely preserved examples found anywhere, and they can command an exhorbitant price on the collector's market. Of special interest have been fossils of the reptiles called pterosaurs. They had huge leathery wings and do not resemble any known living animal. *Archaeopteryx* also turned out to be very peculiar (Figure 6.1). Looking like a bird, it had birdlike feet and well-preserved feathers, including the typical asymmetrical flight feathers of modern birds. In flight feathers the vane on one side of the feather shaft is wider than on the other. In contrast, such flightless birds as the ostrich, rhea, and kiwi have symmetrical feathers. *Archaeopteryx* also has

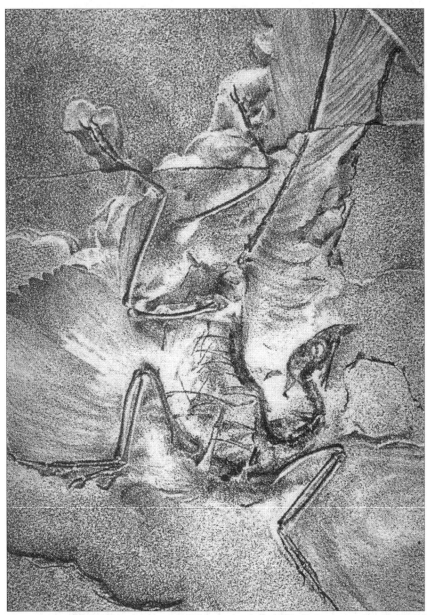

Figure 6.1 *Fossil of Archaeopteryx. This is the famed "Berlin" specimen, considered by many to be the best example. Note the well-developed feathers on the wings and elongated tail. Courtesy of the Linda Hall Library of Science, Engineering and Technology.*

some especially reptilian characteristics such as claws on the forelimbs, which in this case are the wings. In addition, it has a long bony tail and fine teeth, traits not found in modern birds. On the other hand, many fossil birds have teeth, and a couple of modern birds have claws on their wings. So far about 10 described specimens of *Archaeopteryx* have turned up in the Solnhofen limestone. One consists only of a feather, and one specimen is lost.

The first good specimen of *Archaeopteryx* fell into the hands of a physician who appears to have been more interested in monetary gain than most other things. Sufficiently familiar with fossils to know that he had something unusual, he allowed specialists to view the fossil, but they could not take any notes about it. People soon began to recognize the specimen's importance. It might be the missing link that Darwin's supporters sought. Johann Andreas Wagner, a professor of zoology in charge of the Munich Bavarian State Collection, was especially interested. Because his health was waning, he sent his talented assistant to look at *Archaeopteryx*. The assistant drew from memory what he saw, and after several visits produced a remarkably accurate rendition of the fossil. Wagner, who, like most scientists of his time, believed in the biblical account of creation, became concerned that Darwinists might interpret the fossil as a missing link. In spite of his ill health, he delivered an official report to the Munich Bavarian State Collection on the novel creature. He classified it as a reptile with features that resembled feathers. At the conclusion of his presentation he declared that the fossil was not a missing link, and challenged the Darwinians to provide the intermediate steps expected between animal classes. "If they cannot do this (as they certainly cannot), their views must be at once rejected as fantastic dreams, with which the exact investigation of nature has nothing to do."[15]

A short time later Wagner died, but the growing acrimony between creation and evolution continued. Triumphalism sometimes prevailed. The paleontologist Hugh Falconer wrote to Charles Darwin that Darwinism had "killed poor Wagner. [B]ut on his death-bed, he took consolation in denouncing it as a *phantasia*."[16] We need to keep in perspective that Charles Darwin was not the atheist people sometimes infer him to be. During his last year of life he severely remonstrated with two atheists for being so belligerent about their beliefs. Regarding the question of God's existence, Darwin advocated passive agnosticism and not aggressive atheism. However, secularists did not give up. After Darwin's burial in Westminster Abbey, one of them quipped that though the church had Darwin's corpse, it did not have his ideas! These ideas were undermining the very foundation of the church.

Much earlier, Darwin's opponent Richard Owen was intensely aware of the controversy swirling around *Archaeopteryx*, and there were few things in the world that he wanted more than the actual *Archaeopteryx* specimen. Using his powerful position at the British Museum, and after considerable negotiations with both the board and with the physician who owned the specimen, he reached an agreement to purchase it and a few less-important fossils for around £700. After extensive study of *Archaeopteryx*, Owen reported his findings to the Royal Society. He predictably concluded, as Wagner had, that *Archaeopteryx* was no intermediate between birds and reptiles. However, in contrast to Wagner's view that the creature was a reptile, he decided that it was a bird, not all that different from some modern birds, and that it flew quite well. His conclusion did not deter the then minority Darwinians from promoting it as the example of a missing link that they desperately needed. Later Darwin included it in future printings of *The Origin of Species*. However, evolutionists really needed a host of intermediates to authenticate the gradual transition from reptiles to *Archaeopteryx* and then from *Archaeopteryx* to more modern kinds of birds. To those who believed in creation by God, *Archaeopteryx* could just represent another created variety.

FEATHERS FLYING OVER THE ORIGIN OF BIRDS

A few years after the publication of *The Origin of Species* evolution gained wider approval, but the question of the evolutionary origin of birds did not resolve itself with *Archaeopteryx*. Evolutionists explored many other ideas. Some wondered if birds might not have evolved from the winged reptiles called pterosaurs, but the basic differences between pterosaurs and birds are so great that the concept had few supporters. Possibly birds developed from dinosaurs, and some such ideas included *Archaeopteryx* in the line of ancestors. An approach that received a great deal of acceptance, especially early in the past century, was that both birds and dinosaurs emerged from some as yet-undiscovered ancestor. The Danish naturalist Gerhard Heilmann played the crucial role in the adoption of that view. Early in life Heilmann rejected his parents' religious views, developing a strong anti-religious attitude. Becoming interested in science and more specifically the evolution of birds, he published a number of articles and books on the topic. He began looking for an ancestor to birds much earlier in the geological layers than the ones containing *Archaeopteryx*. Also Heilmann was an excellent illustrator, having designed some Danish bank notes. In his publications he included exquisite illustrations of what he thought a possible missing link of birds would look like. The lifelike representation that he called *Proavis* had lots of scales and developing feathers, especially on the forelimbs and tail. The high quality of his illustrations no doubt contributed to the general adoption of his views of bird evolution. The scientific community widely held them as valid for decades.

In 1964 Yale University paleontologist John Ostrom was assiduously searching through the rocks of the Cloverly Formation (lower Cretaceous; upper part of Mesozoic in Figure 5.1) in Montana when he noticed a fossil claw. When the rest of the accompanying skeleton was excavated, it turned out to be a small, lightweight animal about three feet (one meter) high, with a prominent claw. Ostrom called it *Deinonychus,* which means "terrible claw." The lethal claw meant that the two-legged theropod dinosaur was a fast hunter, something that was not at all the prevailing image for dinosaurs at that time. Furthermore, Ostrom noted that the wrists of his new discovery were remarkably close to those of *Archaeopteryx.* The similarity helped propel the well-feathered *Archaeopteryx,* which had by this time been almost relegated to oblivion, back into the sequence of the evolution of birds.[17] Many now considered *Archaeopteryx* to have evolved from a theropod dinosaur. Ostrom came to the conclusion that birds were just feathered dinosaurs. Supposedly a common ancestor to both *Deinonychus* and *Archaeopteryx* existed some time before the Solnhofen limestone was laid down. While the idea was not all that different in principle from Heilmann's postulated ancestor, the fact that Heilmann's crucial ancestor still remained undiscovered made any other suggestion welcome. Some even speculated that birds may have sprung from crocodiles or mammals.[18] Nevertheless, Ostrom's idea that birds evolved from dinosaurs gained significant acceptance, especially among paleontologists.[19] That idea triggered a lively intellectual tribal warfare within the scientific community between the paleontologists (the fossil specialists), who claim that birds emerged from dinosaurs, and the ornithologists (the bird specialists), who prefer some other kind of reptilian ancestor for birds.

The controversy has included shouting down opponents at conferences and seeing to it that opposing views did not get published.[20] The ornithologists have consolidated themselves under the "BAND" banner. BAND is an acronym for "birds are not dinosaurs," and at important conferences BAND supporters proudly sport buttons declaring their position. Both sides claim not to understand why the other is so naive, and both sides are prone to claim victory. The paleontologists, who are in a moderate majority, have the advantage of some kinds of representative intermediate fossils, and they have had the public media on their side. Dinosaur stories are wonderful attention catchers, and a close relationship often exists between dinosaur finders and the public media.

Alan Feduccia of the University of North Carolina has been one of the leaders in the anti-dinosaur origin of birds view promoted by BAND. He feels that the other viewpoint overlooks certain details. "If you mount a dinosaur skeleton and a chicken skeleton next to each other and then view them both through binoculars at fifty paces then they look very similar. However, if you look at them in detail, then you suddenly find that there are huge differences in their jaws, teeth, fingers, pelvis, and a host of other regions."[21] There have been, and continue to be, endless debates about the evolution of the wrists of the assumed intermediate fossils and their associated fingers, the ornithologists claiming that you cannot change the wrist of a dinosaur into that of a bird.[22] Creationists who think that God created the main kinds of birds tend to sympathize with some of the arguments of the ornithologists, who in turn are dismayed when the paleontologist camp accuses them of being like creationists.[23]

How did the ability to fly evolve? The issue has been another point of contention in the saga of bird evolution. Veteran paleontologist Michael Benton, who specializes in dinosaurs, candidly mentions that "the origins of bird flight must be entirely speculative."[24] Another noted paleontologist, Robert Carroll, in discussing evolutionary problems, perceptively comments: "How can we explain the gradual evolution of entirely new structures, like the wings of bats, birds, and butterflies, when the function of a partially evolved wing is almost impossible to conceive?"[25]

The lack of hard data has not deterred ornithologists and paleontologists from persisting in heated debates, each side arguing from a perspective that fits their evolutionary interpretation. The BAND ornithologists favor the idea that flight developed from animals climbing in trees and leaping and gliding down, using their forelimbs eventually to develop a powered flapping-wings type of flight. This "trees down" idea contrasts with the "ground up" idea of the paleontologists, who suggest that animals jumping around on the ground chasing insects would eventually evolve their forelimbs into wings that could generate powered flight. While some animals, such as rare flying squirrels and lizards, do some gliding using expanded folds of skin between their appendages, and others, such as frogs and lizards, relish insects, we don't see animals now in the process of acquiring powered flight from their forelimbs. Powered flight requires the kind of extremely specialized structures seen in birds, insects, and bats.

The persistent disagreement between the BAND ornithologists and the paleontologists received a welcomed but nevertheless shocking interlude when, in 1985, two highly respected astronomers claimed that *Archaeopteryx* was a fraud. Sir Fred Hoyle and Chandra Wickramasinghe of the University of Wales studied the London specimen that Richard Owen had purchased at a then staggering price. They reported that the impression of feathers had been added to an existing fossil skeleton and that it had probably been done as an attempt to produce a needed missing link to substantiate Darwin's theory of evolution. The story quickly spread over the world. Evolutionists were not at all amused. Some creationists responded with delight because they assumed that finally this enigmatic missing link had been dethroned. The curators of the London Natural History Museum mounted a comprehensive defense. After thorough study they were able to credibly refute the forgery arguments.[26] Some creationists also sided with this latter study,[27] lending their support to the authenticity of the famous fossil.

In the past decade some marvelous fossil finds have given hope to the paleontologists who think birds evolved from dinosaurs. They have come largely from a rich fossil source in Liaoning province in northeast China. The fine grains of the sediments entombing the fossils originate from volcanoes and provide excellent preservation. Paleontologists usually classify these deposits as early Cretaceous. Although precise assignment has not been possible, it means that according to the standard geologic time scale they are possibly of the same age or most likely younger than the Jurassic *Archaeopteryx*.

A striking discovery from Liaoning is a small theropod dinosaur named *Sinosauropteryx.*[28] While only 2.2 feet (68 centimeters) long, it caused quite a sensation because of a dense black fringe found especially along its back and tail. Paleontologists interpreted the fringe, that appeared to be made of filaments, as feathers or some form of evolving feathers called protofeathers, but the preservation was not good enough to permit definite identification. The protofeather interpretation favors the "ground up" evolutionary concept. On the other hand, researchers from the BAND side suggested that the fringe is not feathers and might only be degenerating muscles or some kind of fibrous connective tissue.

Still more enigmatic is *Protarchaeopteryx,*[29] which many paleontologists regard as a dinosaur while the BAND ornithologists think it is a bird. The conflict illustrates the technique of trying to win arguments by changing definitions. A BAND supporter cautions that a chicken would be a dinosaur to the paleontologists,[30] and paleontologists who think that dinosaurs had feathers point out "that feathers are irrelevant in the diagnosis of birds."[31] The name *Protarchaeopteryx* actually means "before" *Archaeopteryx,* but that hardly applies since *Protarchaeopteryx* would be considered to be younger than, or at most only as old as, *Archaeopteryx.* Besides, *Archaeopteryx* has unquestionable fully developed feathers, while *Protarchaeopteryx* has elongated structures that slightly resemble feathers but lack evidence of a real feather shaft. Also on the fossil specimen the best feathers may not have been attached to the body and could have come from another organism. Although *Archaeopteryx* is more advanced, those who study *Protarchaeopteryx* describe it as a missing link in the evolution of birds.

What probably we can best understand as a cultural conflict emerged during the early study of *Protarchaeopteryx.* Four Western scientists, one of the BAND variety and three of the paleontology variety, were touring in China and received the privilege of viewing the fossil before its official publication. A significant discussion ensued, and their hosts told the Western scientists that the tour would not continue unless they would identify the puzzling flat structures on the fossil as feathers. A calamity was in the making, since none of the Western scientists could endorse the feather interpretation. They resolved the issue by deciding to call the structures *protofeathers.* Since protofeathers had no established definition, the tour continued as a great success.[32]

The Chinese have made many more fossil finds in Liaoning, and more dinosaurs have been described as having featherlike structures such as long branching filaments.[33] Storrs Olson, a BAND ornithologist at the National Museum of Natural History in Washington, D.C., is not impressed: "They want to see feathers . . . so they see feathers." "This is simply an exercise in wishful thinking."[34] He suggests that the filaments might just be hair. After all, *Archaeopteryx,* generally recognized as the earliest known bird, most likely lies lower down in the fossil layers and has fully developed flight feathers.

Both the BAND and paleontologist camps are sure that birds somehow evolved and do not even consider the possibility that they might not have. The different interpretations that they apply to the evolution of birds illustrate how their assumptions combine with those of evolution as the science driven by hypotheses gets more speculative. We need to dig deeper and learn to distinguish between good explanations supported by data and those based on speculation.

Fairly modern-looking bird fossils (*Confuciusornis*) have also turned up at Liaoning. They have good feathers and no teeth, as is the case for modern birds.[35] However, the most startling discovery to date is *Microraptor,* which some describe as a four-winged dinosaur. Several specimens seem to have large feathers on four appendages, and they do not have legs designed for walking. Some paleontologists regard the animal as a gliding kind of organism, living in trees, on its way to evolving powered flight.[36] But thus far the creature leaves almost everyone totally baffled.

Finding fully developed feathers in this part of the geologic column as seen in *Archaeopteryx* and *Confuciusornis* plainly points out that it is the wrong place to look for the evolution of feathers. Evolution would require that the feathers would have emerged earlier, and a few evolutionists point this out.[37] However, the desire to evolve birds from dinosaurs is so strong that interpretations describing the early evolution of feathers on dinosaurs in these layers that already have fully developed feathers continue to appear in the scientific literature.[38] It offers still another illustration of how theory, instead of the facts, can drive a science.[39]

You cannot just stick feathers on a dinosaur or some other kind of animal and expect it to fly. Birds have numerous special features that permit

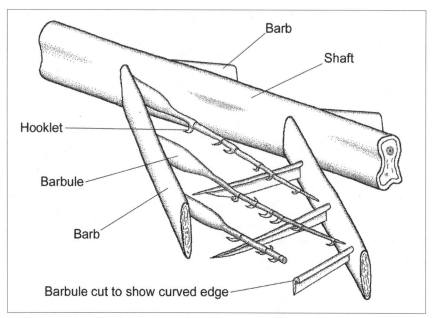

FIGURE 6.2 *Details of the structural features of a small part of a contour feather. The shaft is the middle spine we see in normal feathers. Barbs branch out from the shaft and smaller branches called barbules branch out to form the barbs. Some barbules are provided with microscopic hooklets that can catch on the curved ridge cap of other kinds of barbules. The hooklets can slide along the barbules, thus providing a combination of flexibility and stiffness to the feather.* Based on: Storer TI, Usinger RL, Nybakken JW. 1968. Elements of zoology, 3rd ed. New York: McGraw-Hill Book Co., p. 415.

flight, including a special breathing system, special muscles, lightweight bones,[40] and above all, flight feathers. The so-called dino-fuz described previously does not qualify as flight feathers, although some evolutionists suggest that feathers evolved from a filamentous structure that first served as insulation. However, that is speculation, and new fossil discoveries could change all that. So far paleontologists have not discovered any real dinosaur with any flight feathers.[41] Evolutionists often suggest that feathers resulted from the modification of reptile scales of the evolutionary ancestor of birds, but this does not seem to be the case. On the basis of new findings,[42] the paleontologist Richard Cowen warns that "the proteins that make feathers in living birds are completely unlike the proteins that make up reptilian scales today."[43] Furthermore, flight feathers are highly specialized structures that are extremely light, strong, flexible, and complicated. They have a main shaft, lateral barbs, many smaller barbules on the barbs, and many hooklets on each barbule that act like Velcro (Figure 6.2). When barbs become separated, the bird can hook them back together by preening. But that is just a small part of a much more complex system of sensors and muscles that can adjust the precise movement of wings, and all of that requires a complex coordinating system in the brain.[44] A good explanation of the evolution of flying birds from dinosaurs or some unknown reptile ancestor is a long way away.

LESSONS FROM ARCHAEORAPTOR

On October 15, 1999, the National Geographic Society scheduled a major press conference at its Explorer's Hall in Washington, D.C. It announced a new fossil find on display called *Archaeoraptor*. The discovery, the Society claimed, was a "missing link" between dinosaurs and birds. The fossil had a bird's body, but the tail was definitely dinosaurlike. Some of the scientists present, who had studied the fossil, commented: "We're looking at the first dinosaur capable of flying. . . . It's kind of overwhelming." "We can finally say that some dinosaurs did survive, we call them birds."[45] Duly impressed, the public media responded with another wave of *dinomania*. The announcement preceded the publication of the November issue of *National Geographic* that featured the fossil find under the title of "Feathers for *T. rex?* New Birdlike Fossils Are Missing Links in Dinosaur Evolution." That article,[46] which depicted a flying model of *Archaeoraptor* and a young *T. rex* dinosaur covered with down, asserted that "we can now say that birds are theropods [dinosaurs] just as confidently as we say that humans are mammals" and that "everything from lunch boxes to museum exhibits will change to reflect this revelation." The article characterized *Archaeoraptor* as "a missing link between terrestrial dinosaurs and birds that could actually fly." Furthermore, "this mix of advanced and primitive features is exactly what scientists would expect to find in dinosaurs experimenting with flight." It was just the kind of find the paleontologists' camp needed to support their case that birds evolved from dinosaurs.

The euphoria accompanying the announcement did not last long. Within days some scientists began questioning the authenticity of the fossil. The BAND ornithologists were especially suspicious. Storrs Olson, in an open letter to Peter

Raven, the secretary of the Committee for Research and Exploration at the National Geographic Society, commented that "National Geographic has reached an all-time low for engaging in sensationalistic, unsubstantiated, tabloid journalism." He also pointed out that the baby *T. rex* "clad in feathers . . . is simply imaginary and has no place outside of science fiction." Furthermore, "truth and careful scientific weighing of evidence have been among the first casualties" in supporting the theropod origin of birds, "which is now fast becoming one of the grander scientific hoaxes of our age."[47]

Eventually it turned out that *Archaeoraptor* was a composite fossil consisting of many parts carefully glued together. The tail of a dinosaur had been tacked on to the body of a bird (see Figure 6.3 for identification). In addition, the legs were really just one single right leg, with its mold from the covering rock counterslab being used as the other leg. *Archaeoraptor* is now known as the "Piltdown bird," named after the famous Piltdown hoax, in which someone during the early part of the past century crudely fitted an apelike jaw to a human skull. For some 40 years, before more careful research revealed the deception, the fabrication held a respected position as a missing link in the evolution of humanity. The history of *Archaeoraptor* is just as sad. It originated from the famous Liaoning fossil beds in China, with extra parts glued on to enhance its value. Because it is illegal to take such fossils out of China, someone smuggled it to the United States, and it ended up at the yearly world-renowned gem, mineral, and fossil show in Tucson, Arizona.

Stephen Czerkas, director of a small museum in Blanding, Utah, was stunned when he saw the fossil, and immediately perceived its potential as an intermediate form between dinosaurs and birds. He paid the U.S.$80,000 asking price and, after returning to Blanding, sought to engage the renowned Philip J. Currie of the Royal Tyrell Museum of Paleontology in Alberta, Canada, in its study. Currie contacted the leaders at the National Geographic Society, which frequently publishes articles concerning evolution,[48] and they indicated they would support the project. They also imposed absolute secrecy on the study so as to enhance the effectiveness of a big bang type of publicity announcement about the amazing missing link. Xing Xu (of Beijing's Institute of Vertebrate Paleontology), Timothy Rowe (of the University of Texas), and others, joined the study team. Czerkas, Currie, and Xu have been fervent promoters of the paleontologist view that birds evolved from dinosaurs.

The scientists agreed that the contraband specimen would be returned to China. In addition, X-ray studies revealed that the fossil slab sample consisted of 88 separate parts.[49] Some of the investigators also noted that the dinosaur tailbones were not properly connected to the birdlike body and that

FIGURE 6.3 *Representation of the fossil* Archaeoraptor, *the faked fossil that fooled a number of scientists and was hailed as a missing link between dinosaurs and birds. The head is in the upper left corner of the rock slab. This fossil is a combination of mainly a bird fossil, top part, and the tail of a dinosaur below, (lowest arrow). The faintly appearing legs on each side of the tail in the lower half of the figure (two left and two right arrows) are actually just one leg that is also reflected in its cast on the counterslab and was used as a second leg on the opposite side. The fossil is only about a foot long.*
Photo by Lenore Roth. Interpretation from Chambers P. 2002. Bones of Contention: The Archaeopteryx Scandals. London: John Murray (Publishers) Ltd., p. 242.

the two legs were a slab and counterslab match of just one leg. The details of what happened during the study may never be known. Several red flags had surfaced, but they did not scuttle the project. While the debacle has been blamed in part on lack of communication, Louis M. Simons, a veteran investigative reporter who had been asked to look into the matter, found many discrepancies as he interviewed the participants. He notes that "few accept blame; everyone accuses someone else."[50] *National Geographic* would have liked near-simultaneous publication of the details of *Archaeoraptor* in a technical journal, but none was forthcoming. Both *Nature* and *Science* refused to print a technical report that admitted the composite nature of the specimen but still considered it to be one kind of organism.

In the meantime, *National Geographic,* with a deadline for its huge printing task, went ahead and published the infamous November issue without a supporting technical report, and it also proceeded with its extraordinary public announcement. Rumors that the fossil was a fraud persisted. Xing Xu, upon returning to China, was able to find the matching counterslab of *Archaeoraptor's* tail. It was a perfect match, and it was attached to the body of a dinosaur! He regretfully informed his colleagues in the United States that "we have to admit that *Archaeoraptor* is a faked specimen."[51] While some who had studied the specimen did not at first accept his report, all now seem to agree that it is a fraud. The embarrassment attracted the interest of the international press. The bird part of *Archaeoraptor* has been restudied along with a similar specimen, and it has received a different scientific name than the one given by *National Geographic.* It is now called *Yanornis martini*, and its describers propose that the legs, but not the tail, of *Archaeoraptor* belong to this new species.[52] The BAND ornithologists had won this round, but the paleontologists who have the media on their side have demonstrated a great deal of persistence. Others have expressed concern about "scientists being too afraid to voice their fears to their media paymasters."[53] The media keeps on providing feathers for *T. rex* although no feathers have been found with any *T. rex* fossils. Keith Thomson, professor and director of the Oxford University Museum, wryly summarizes the reasoning used to provide feathers for *T. rex* by giving the final score as "feathers 3, logic 0."[54]

It turns out that evolutionary theory still does not have an authenticated model for the origin of feathers, flight, or birds, and the battle between the paleontologists and BAND ornithologists continues as *theories instead of facts drive the science.* No one seems to have learned any lessons about being cautious. Since the *Archaeoraptor* disaster the National Geographic Society and Stephen Czerkas' museum in Utah have published books depicting feathered dinosaurs![55] Unfortunately bird evolution is not an isolated case. In the book *Icons of Evolution: Science or Myth? Why Much of What We Teach About Evolution Is Wrong,* biologist Jonathan Wells documents a variety of other examples.[56]

THE INSIDIOUS POTENCY OF PARADIGMS

Many factors favor the endurance of a paradigm, not the least of which is the persistence of the scientists promoting it. It is hard for anyone to give up what one wants to believe, and personal honor can be a strong factor. The renowned German physicist Max Planck once candidly observed that a "new scientific truth does not triumph by convincing its opponents and making them see the light, but rather because its opponents eventually die, and a new generation grows up that is familiar with it."[57] The principle sometimes gets frankly expressed as "science progresses one funeral at a time!"

Cynics claim that "history belongs to the victors," and that is too often the case. Once a paradigm wins the dominant position, those who support it are not likely to let that fact be forgotten. Ridicule of other paradigms can set a "climate of opinion" that strongly favors the dominant view, whether it happens to be true or not. One of the unfortunate results is that instead of probing thoroughly the deeper questions of their research, scientists stop searching[58] and start publishing when their data seems to agree with the accepted paradigm. This can keep the paradigm going and going, especially in the more speculative areas of science, in which we may have little data. It is not easy to revise a dominant paradigm, and when the public media and entertainment industry get involved, as is often the case with major scientific views, change becomes still more difficult. Paradigms have a way of taking on a life of their own, sometimes, as is the case for evolution, going far beyond the scientific community.

Dominant ideas and paradigms need not be based on facts in order to gain acceptance. Humanity too often goes off into unsubstantiated tangents, and science is not exempt. A few examples will illustrate:

1. The famed "Monkey Trial" took place in 1925 in the town of Dayton,

Tennessee. While derived from technicalities about teaching evolution in public schools, the trial actually turned out to be a world-famous public contest between evolution and creation. Popular opinion has held that the famed Chicago attorney, Clarence Darrow, who defended evolution, triumphed over William Jennings Bryan, a three-time United States presidential candidate, who argued in support of creation. That was the story I heard when I was in graduate school. Recent reevaluation of the trial by two prominent historians, Ronald Numbers of the University of Wisconsin and Edward Larson of the University of Georgia, reveals that evolution did not triumph.[59] At best for evolution the trial was a draw. On the one hand, Darrow had asked Bryan some probing questions that he did not answer well. On the other, many felt that Darrow's ridicule and arrogant attitude caused him to lose the case. He objected to any prayer in court, and the judge eventually cited him for contempt of court. Many newspaper reports at the end of the trial and other documents reflected serious concerns that evolution had lost. The current popular version that Darrow triumphed over Bryan largely reflects the position of the book *Only Yesterday*, which sold more than a million copies, and the very popular film and play *Inherit the Wind*. Both give a distorted view of the trial that greatly favors Darrow.[60] The broad acceptance of the idea that Darrow won is a novelty that crept in long after the trial ended.

2. You probably have heard about the outlandish concept of a flat earth and how Christopher Columbus dared to defy this false dogma being promoted by the church. Columbus went on to sail to North America and did so without falling off the edge of the earth! Such is the conventional "wisdom" reported in many textbooks and encyclopedias.[61] But it turns out that it is still another erroneous concept. A thorough research by Jeffery Burton Russell, professor of history at the University of California at Santa Barbara, gives a quite different picture. In the book *Inventing the Flat Earth: Columbus and Modern Historians*,[62] Russell explains how the falsehood became dogma. Hardly any church scholars believed in the flat earth during the first two millennia of Christianity—virtually all considered the earth as a sphere—but during the nineteenth century two widely distributed books succeeded in convincing the world otherwise. They were *History of the Conflict Between Religion and Science* and *A History of the Warfare of Science With Theology in Christendom*.[63] Both books promoted the superiority of science and accused

the church of propagating error. However, their authors were the ones guilty of falsehood as they presented their erroneous claim about the church teaching a flat earth. Fortunately, in the past few years textbooks and reference volumes have started correcting the misconception.

3. In 1860 at Oxford University in England a famous clash occurred between the Bishop of Oxford, Samuel Wilberforce, called "Soapy Sam," and Thomas Huxley, nicknamed Darwin's faithful "bulldog." One of the dominant anecdotes, told and retold by generations of evolutionists,[64] relates how Thomas Huxley quashed Wilberforce. Several versions of the incident exist. According to one, as Wilberforce expounded on the absence of fossil intermediates he importunately and unkindly turned to Huxley and asked him if it was on his grandmother or grandfather's side that he had descended from an ape. It drew a barrage of loud cheering and laughter from a then dominantly anti-Darwinian Oxford audience. Huxley immediately commented to a friend that the Lord had delivered the bishop into his hands. Later as he formally replied to the bishop's query Huxley indicated that he would rather descend from an ape than from a man who uses his influence to obscure the truth. His ridicule of the respected bishop drew a roar of protest, and one woman reportedly fainted while Huxley's few supporters cheered loudly.[65] Actually at the very best for Huxley the encounter was a draw. But the story has developed a great life of its own as it depicts a tremendous victory for Huxley.[66] The reality seems to be far from the current lore. A critical review of the incident by Oxford University historian J. R. Lucas[67] indicates that Huxley probably misrepresented the outcome of the encounter, and furthermore that Wilberforce's question about the line of ancestry from an ape was not at all directed to Huxley, but was a rhetorical question addressed to "anyone." However, through the years the story of Huxley's victory gained acceptance as Darwinian evolution became the dominant view, at least among scientists.

4. Many consider Margaret Mead to be the most famous cultural anthropologist of the twentieth century. In 1928 she published the legendary book *Coming of Age in Samoa*. Becoming an immediate success, it eventually sold millions of copies with translations into 16 languages. The book lauded the advantages of freedom from cultural mores as exemplified by the free sexual lifestyle in Samoa, especially among the young who grew up in an en-

vironment unencumbered by a family type of organization that stifles emotional life. Accordingly she also reported that in Samoa family values had a low priority.

In the United States Mead became a guru to many of the young and their parents during the turbulent 1960s. Her famous book had a broad influence, emphasizing the importance of culture, in contrast to heredity, in determining behavior. The theme touched the "nature-versus-nurture" controversy, which was a burning issue at the time and has been smoldering ever since. The sociobiology concept that we will discuss later[68] is on the nature (genes) side while Mead and many sociologists tend to be on the nurture (culture) side. Historians have called her and some of her colleagues absolute cultural determinists. Some credit her book with "almost single-handedly"[69] taking the heart out of the thriving eugenics movement of that time, which sought to improve humanity by restricting reproduction of individuals and groups considered genetically inferior. Now it appears that the book was largely a projection of Mead's fantasies, and moreover she may have been hoaxed into false conclusions. Some educated Samoans reacted with anger at the misrepresentation of their culture, while other locals indicated that if she ever dared return to Samoa they would tie her up and throw her to the sharks!

In the book *Margaret Mead and Samoa: The Making and Unmaking of an Anthropological Myth,*[70] Australian anthropologist Derek Freeman, who has studied Samoan culture for years, reports that many of Mead's assertions are "fundamentally in error, and some of them preposterously false."[71] His book, published by Harvard University Press, merited an announcement on the front page of the New York *Times* when released in 1983. Fortunately for Mead, it came off the press after her death. Freeman's study indicates that her evaluation of the sexual behavior of Samoans is largely false. Samoans have highly restrictive social standards, much higher than traditional Western ones. The society highly reveres marriage and virginity, and that was the case even before the coming of Christianity to the Samoan Islands.[72]

The reaction to Freeman's book was violent, some of it more reminiscent of political campaigning than scholarly activity. All kinds of views, pro and con, appeared in articles, books, book reviews, and reviews of book reviews. Some vilified Mead, others attacked Freeman, and still others wondered how such erroneous information could have brought such fame to Margaret Mead.

Our concern at this point is not whether nature, nurture, or free will determines behavior, but that it very much appears that Mead's invalid information caused or at least strongly influenced a major shift in worldview.

One can wonder about how many other erroneous concepts lurk in our libraries, textbooks, and classrooms. The four examples given above illustrate how we can easily accept ideas that may have little factual authentication. While we should be tolerant of various views, we should not be gullible. We should not accept uncritically intellectual fashions in science or elsewhere. The best way that I know of to avoid being taken in by erroneous popular ideas and paradigms is to be independent in one's thinking and do more thorough study, not confusing data with interpretations, and paying special attention to the best data.

THE SOCIOLOGY OF SCIENCE

When during World War II the United States government funded the Manhattan Project, some of the best scientists in the world became involved in producing the first atomic bomb—an example of government strongly influencing the direction of scientific inquiry. It has long been known that external factors such as public opinion and financial support[73] affect scientific investigation. In spite of this, the practice of science has claimed and has generally been considered to be objective and rational.[74] Unfortunately, too often such is not the case.

Science had its heyday following World War II, when the atomic bomb and the 1957 Russian *Sputnik* satellite success greatly enhanced respect for the endeavor. Research funds for scientific projects poured into universities at unprecedented rates, and it was not that hard to find funds for science research projects. I personally received a number of government research grants and worked on several other governmentally-funded science projects.

However, science has run into more difficult times since then. People no longer perceive its value to society as so necessary, and its objectivity and integrity face growing challenges. A number of sociologists have evaluated science, leaving some scientists wondering if sociologists should not keep to their own turf. The sociologists, however, claim the sociology of science as their turf. It is a sensitive issue that has generated its share of controversy and contention. Unfortunately, it is not difficult to pique the self-esteem of a scientific community that seems to have some difficulty remembering all the errors it has promulgated in the past. On the other hand, sociologists seem to forget that science sometimes deals with simple objective facts not easily subjected to sociological influences.

As studies on the sociology of science began to flourish, sociologist Bernard Barber published a seminal article on the topic in the journal *Science*.[75] Entitled "Resistance by Scientists to Scientific Discovery," it listed a number of factors that may affect the conclusions of science. They included: (a) previously held interpretations; (b) methodological concepts, such as being excessively partial or excessively hostile to mathematics; (c) the religion of the scientist as it influences science in various ways; (d) professional standing; (e) professional specialization; and (f) societies, groups, and "schools of thought." Examples of these various situations abound in the sociological and historical literature.[76] Scientists do not always welcome such views, since they question science's cherished image of being free of external influences.

The lamentable case of the Augustinian monk Gregor Mendel (1822-1884), who discovered the basic principles of heredity by breeding pea plants, well illustrates the influence of sociological factors in science. Mendel published his epic findings in a journal of the natural science society of Brünn. Contrary

Table 6.1

IDENTIFYING CHARACTERISTICS OF RELIABLE SCIENTIFIC INTERPRETATIONS

1. The interpretation fits the available data.

2. The idea is testable, especially by repeatable experiments and observation. It can be disproved.

3. The interpretation can predict unknown outcomes.

4. The concept is not enshrouded in controversy.

5. The conclusion is driven by the data of nature, not by theory or commercial advantage.

6. The associated claims made are well supported.

to what some accounts report, the journal circulated widely throughout Europe. But in spite of Mendel's astounding data, the authorities in his field completely ignored him.[77] It was not until years after his death that several biologists rediscovered and endorsed his seminal discoveries. Why did no one pay attention to him? It is a puzzling question for which we don't have good answers, but a number of suggestions reflect certain sociological influences in science. The fact that he was an unknown, isolated monk and not a member of the regular scientific community, was no doubt a significant factor. Scientists did not understand or appreciate his novel approach of mixing botany and mathematics. Competing ideas about hereditary factors drew attention away from Mendel, and it was the wrong time to get his revolutionary ideas accepted. Fortunately science moved past those barriers, and now Mendel is considered one of the most important persons in the history of science.

HOW TO TELL GOOD SCIENCE FROM BAD SCIENCE

One of the most important lessons we can learn is the realization that there is good science and there is bad science. The discovery of *Archaeoraptor* is an example of bad science, but the locating of the planet Neptune, based on the data of the irregular motion of Uranus, illustrates very good science. In our day and age, when science plays such an important role in our thinking, it is important to distinguish between its good and bad forms. Unfortunately, it is not easy, especially for the nonscientist. Incomplete data or false premises can fool even the best scientists. But a few clues (Table 6.1) can help any of us evaluate how trustworthy scientific interpretations may be.

1. Does the idea fit the facts? Does it engender a logical conclusion, especially when we consider a broad spectrum of data?

2. Is the claim testable? Especially, is it experimentally repeatable? Experimental science, such as results from a chemical experiment, is considered quite reliable. On the other hand, we have what we call historical science,[78] which is more speculative, and is regarded as less reliable. An example would be the study of a fossil that includes only part of one specimen, and we then try to infer from it what happened during a past that we cannot now observe. Some ideas are more easily tested than others. Both evolution and creation, that are considered past events, are not as easily testable as current observations. However, this does not mean that we cannot use present observation

to infer what may have taken place in the past. The important question is how well the inference fits the data. Some associate testability with the capability of being able to disprove the claim, concluding that if you cannot negate it, it is not really science.

3. Can the idea be used to predict unknown outcomes? An example, mentioned earlier,[79] was the energy level of the resonance of carbon turning out to be just about what Sir Fred Hoyle had predicted it would be. Predictability is science at its best.

4. Is the claim shrouded in controversy? If scientists are scrapping about it, the conflict suggests that alternative views could also be tenable.

5. Is the basis for the conclusion the data of nature, or is the outcome theory-driven? Be wary of the power of dominant paradigms and philosophical constructs—and especially be cautious if a particular theory has commercial or financial advantages to it. The research sponsored by the tobacco industry suggesting the harmlessness of smoking is a prime example of error induced by financial interest.

6. Are unsupported claims made? If so, again be wary. Unsubstantiated arguments cast suspicion on the integrity of the whole package. Especially common is the practice of confusing the correlation in the abundance of two factors with cause and effect. For instance, a study showed that cigarette smokers had lower college grades than nonsmokers. The correlation was taken seriously, and the obvious way for smokers to raise their grades was to quit smoking. But that conclusion could be very wrong. It could be that, instead, it is low grades that drive students to smoke. Or that sociable types who don't study as much also tend to smoke, thus producing the assumed correlation with low grades.[80] Just because two factors appear to be quantitatively connected does not mean that one causes the other. A high degree of correlation exists around the world between households that have telephones and those that have washing machines, yet we all know that the ownership of one does not cause the other. Conclusions based on correlated data without a careful study of cause-and-effect should not be trusted, yet both scientists and the public media frequently overlook this crucial factor. Many components of our complicated world can give the appearance of a cause-and-effect relationship that does not really exist.

In order to make maximum use of science, one has to evaluate laboriously what is being said and separate the good science from the bad science, and there is plenty of both.

CONCLUDING COMMENTS

The paradigm pattern in science and other studies indicates the strong influence of accepted ideas. This should put us on our guard and encourage us to dig deeper rather than just follow the prevailing "climate of opinion."

The long search for how birds could have evolved is not the kind of story that will convince anyone that data drives scientific interpretation. The many contradictory views that various groups of scientists have fervently pursued for more than a century and a half well illustrate how theories instead of data can be the motivating force in science. If science is the search for truth about nature that it proposes to be, why indulge in so much speculation accompanied by intellectual tribalism, instead of just letting the facts speak for themselves? Repeatedly, and more than many like to admit, scientists, like all the rest of humanity, believe in what they want to believe, filling in missing data with their own presuppositions. I am sure that some of my fellow scientists will find this assertion offensive, and I wish it were not so—but the sooner we realize this, the better it will be for science as a whole.

Too often science is more theory-driven than data-driven. Because of this, it is particularly important that we put forth special effort to try to separate good science, which leads to truth about nature, from bad science, which does not. Scientists are quite human, and it may be difficult to find one who, like all the rest of humanity, does not have an agenda. However, those scientists who give priority to data instead of theory will be more likely to discover what is really happening in nature.

All of this can be highly significant to the God question. In chapters 2 to 5 we presented many examples of data that indicate that a designer is necessary. Despite such evidence, scientists shy away from any such conclusion. The current dominant paradigm that science needs to explain everything without God prevails, even though that often entails unbridled conjecture to explain the facts encountered. Personal attitudes and the sociology of the scientific community too often determine what gets accepted as truth. Other factors than the data of nature frequently shape the conclusions of science.

---

[1] Cudmore LLL. 1977. The center of life. As quoted in: Fripp J, Fripp M, Fripp D. 2000.

Speaking of science: notable quotes on science, engineering, and the environment. Eagle Rock,Va.: LLH Technology Publishing, p. 37.

[2] Oreskes N. 1999. The rejection of continental drift: theory and method in American earth sciences. Oxford: Oxford University Press.

[3] Reading HG. 1987. Fashions and models in sedimentology: a personal perspective. Sedimentology 34:3-9.

[4] Kuhn TS. 1996. The structure of scientific revolutions. 3rd ed. Chicago: University of Chicago Press.

[5] For further views and insights into the argumentation, see: Lakatos I, Feyerabend P. 1999. For and against method. Motterlini M., ed. Chicago: University of Chicago Press; Popper K (1935). 2002. The logic of scientific discovery. London: Routledge; Ruse M., 1999. Mysteries of mysteries: is evolution a social construction? Cambridge: Harvard University Press. Lakatos favors science as somewhat objective, Feyerabend sees it as anarchy, Popper views it as rational, and Ruse gives many examples of external influences on the conclusions of science.

[6] Kuhn, p. x. [For publishing information, see note 4, above.]

[7] Ibid., p.151: See also: Cohen IB. 1985. Revolution in science. Cambridge: Harvard University Press. This book also refers to conversion experiences in science without implying religious significance to the word "religion" as commonly understood.

[8] See chapter 3.

[9] See chapter 5.

[10] Chambers P. 2002. Bones of contention: the Archaeopteryx scandals. London: John Murray, p. 103; Desmond AJ. 1979. Designing the dinosaur: Richard Owen's response to Robert Edmond Grant. ISIS 70:224-234.

[11] Darwin C. 1860. Letter to Asa Gray, June 8. In Darwin F, ed. 1903. More letters of Charles Darwin: a record of his work in a series of hitherto unpublished letters, vol. 1. New York: D. Appleton and Co., p. 153.

[12] Rupke NA. 1994. Richard Owen: Victorian naturalist. New Haven, Conn.: Yale University Press, p. 211.

[13] See chapter 5.

[14] Good general references for the Archaeopteryx portion of this section include: Chambers [see note 10]; Wells J. 2000. Icons of evolution: science or myth? Washington, D.C. Regnery Publishing, Inc., pp. 111-135. More technical references include Benton MJ. 2000. Vertebrate paleontology. 2nd ed. Oxford: Blackwell Science, pp. 260-276; Cowen R. 2000. History of Life. 3rd ed. Oxford: Blackwell Science, pp. 228-237; Ostrom JH. 1976. Archaeopteryx and the origin of birds. Biological Journal of the Linnean Society 8:91-182. I am especially indebted to Chambers' comprehensive reference for a number of the details of this section.

[15] Wagner JA. 1862. Reported in: Burkhardt F et al., eds. 1999. The correspondence of Charles Darwin, vol. 11, 1863. Cambridge: Cambridge University Press, p. 7.

[16] Falconer H. 1863. Letter to Charles Darwin, 3 January. In: Burkhardt, pp. 4, 5. [See note 15.]

[17] Ostrom. [See note 14.]

[18] Benton, pp. 263-265 [see note 14]; Walker AD. 1972. New light on the origin of birds and crocodiles. Nature 237:257-263.

[19] The cladistic analysis of characters is said to favor a theropod (dinosaur) origin of birds:

Benton, p. 265. [See note 14.] However, this does not fit with the sequence found in the fossil layers: Wells, pp. 119-122. [See note 14.]

[20] Chambers, pp. 192, 193. [See note 10.]

[21] From an interview with Paul Chambers, as reported in Chambers, p. 187. [See note 10.]

[22] For example: Feduccia A. 1999. 1,2,3 = 2,3,4: accommodating the cladogram. Proceedings of the National Academy of Sciences (USA) 96:4740-4742; Wagner GP, Gauthier JA. 1999. 1,2,3 = 2,3,4: a solution to the problem of the homology of the digits in the avian hand. Proceedings of the National Academy of Sciences (USA) 96:5111-5116.

[23] Dalton R. 2000. Feathers fly in Beijing. Nature 405:992.

[24] Benton, p. 267. [See note 14).

[25] Carroll RL. 1997. Patterns and processes of vertebrate evolution. Cambridge: Cambridge University Press, p. 9.

[26] Charig AJ et al. 1986. *Archaeopteryx* is not a forgery. Science 232:622-626.

[27] Clausen VE. 1986. Recent debate over *Archaeopteryx*. Origins 13:48-55.

[28] Chen P, Dong Z, Zhen S. 1998. An exceptionally well-preserved theropod dinosaur from the Yixian Formation of China. Nature 391:147-152.

[29] Qiang J et al. 1998. Two feathered dinosaurs from northeastern China. Nature 393:753-761.

[30] Chambers, pp. 229, 230. [See note 10.]

[31] Qiang. [See note 29.]

[32] Chambers, pp. 227-229. [See note 10.]

[33] Xu X, Zhou Z, Prum RO. 2001. Branched integumental structures in *Sinornithosaurus* and the origin of feathers. Nature 410:200-204.

[34] As reported by: Wang L. 2001. Dinosaur fossil yields feathery structures. Science News 159:149.

[35] Martin LD, Zhou Z, et al. 1998. *Confuciusornis sanctus* compared to *Archaeopteryx lithographica*. Naturwissenschaften 85:286-289.

[36] Xu X et al. 2003. Four-winged dinosaurs from China. Nature 421:335-340.

[37] For example: Martin LD [see note 35]; Prum RO, Brush AH. 2003. Which came first, the feather or the bird? Scientific American 288(3):84-93.

[38] The concept of parallel or convergent evolution, which suggests that separate independent evolutionary processes have produced the same structure, would allow for the independent evolution of feathers in both the dinosaurs and the evolutionary ancestors of *Archaeopteryx*. Some object, pointing out that feathers are such highly specialized structures that it is unlikely that their evolution occurred more than once. Both the BAND ornithologists and the paleontologists make free use of convergent evolution in their interpretations.

[39] For a review from the paleontologists' perspective, see: Norell MA, Xu X. 2005. Feathered dinosaurs. Annual Review of Earth and Planetary Sciences 33:277-299.

[40] For instance, see: Ruben JA et al. 1999. Pulmonary function and metabolic physiology of theropod dinosaurs. Science 283:514-516.

[41] A recent report by Mark Norell of the American Museum of Natural History (Norell M. 2005. The dragons of Liaoning: a trove of feathered dinosaurs and other astounding fossil finds in northern China shakes the roots of paleontology. Discover 26(6):58-63) does not provide any convincing evidence that real feathers have been found on dinosaurs.

[42] Brush AH. 1996. On the origin of feathers. Journal of Evolutionary Biology 9:131-142.

[43] Cowen, p. 205. [See note 14.]

[44] Thoresen AC. 1971. Designed for flight. In Utt RH, ed. Creation: nature's designs and Designer. Mountain View, Calif.: Pacific Press Pub. Assn., pp. 8-23.

[45] As quoted in: Chambers, p. 245. [See note 10.]

[46] Sloan CP. 1999. Feathers for *T. rex?* New birdlike fossils are missing links in dinosaur evolution. National Geographic 196(5):98-107.

[47] This letter and related correspondence is available on many Web pages, such as: Answers in Genesis, http://www.answersingenesis.org/ (viewed April 2005).

[48] For a recent example, see: Quammen D. 2004. Was Darwin wrong? No. The evidence for evolution is overwhelming. *National Geographic* 206(5): 2-35.

[49] Rowe T et al. 2001. The *Archaeoraptor* forgery. Nature 410:539, 540.

[50] Simons LM. 2000. *Archaeoraptor* fossil trail. *National Geographic* 198(4):128-132.

[51] As reported in: Simons. [See note 50.]

[52] Zhou Z, Clarke J, Zhang F. 2002. *Archaeoraptor's* better half. Nature 420:285.

[53] Chambers, p. 248. [See note 10.]

[54] Thomson KS. 2002. Dinosaurs, the media and Andy Warhol. American Scientist 90:222-224.

[55] Czerkas SJ, ed. 2002. Feathered dinosaurs and the origin of flight. Blanding, Utah: The Dinosaur Museum; Sloan C. 2000. Feathered dinosaurs. Washington, D.C.: National Geographic Society.

[56] Wells. [See note 14.]

[57] Planck M. 1949. Scientific autobiography and other papers. Gaynor F, trans. Westport, Conn.: Greenwood Press, Pub., pp. 33, 34.

[58] Branscomb LM. 1985. Integrity in science. American Scientist 73:421-423.

[59] Larson EJ. 1997. Summer for the gods: the Scopes trial and America's continuing debate over science and religion. Cambridge: Harvard University Press, pp. 206-208; Larson EJ. 2004. Evolution: the remarkable history of a scientific theory. New York: Modern Library, p. 217.

[60] For further comments, see: Ruse M. 2005. The evolution-creation struggle. Cambridge: Harvard University Press, pp. 164-167.

[61] Gould SJ. 1994. The persistently flat earth. Natural History 103(3):12, 14-19; Russell JB. 1991. Inventing the flat earth: Columbus and modern historians. New York: Praeger Publishers.

[62] Russell. [See note 61.]

[63] Draper JW. 1875. History of the conflict between religion and science, 5th ed. New York: D. Appleton and Company; White AD. 1896, 1960. A history of the warfare of science with theology in Christendom. 2 vols. New York: Dover Publications. Probably both Draper and White obtained the suggestion from William Whewell, who in 1837 published the book *History of the Inductive Sciences.*

[64] Ruse M. 2001. The evolution wars: a guide to the debates. New Brunswick, N. J.: Rutgers University Press, p. 60.

[65] For accounts of this incident, see Chambers, pp. 14-22 [see note 10]; Hellman H. 1998. Great feuds in science: ten of the liveliest disputes ever. New York: John Wiley and Sons, Inc., pp. 81-103.

[66] For example: Dampier WC. 1949. A history of science: and its relations with philosophy and religion. 4th ed. Cambridge: University Press, p. 279; Ruse. The evolution wars, pp. 59, 60 [see note 64]; Witham LA. 2002. Where Darwin meets the Bible: creationists and evo-

lutionists in America. Oxford: Oxford University Press, pp. 212-214.

[67] Lucas JR. 1979. Wilberforce and Huxley: a legendary encounter. The Historical Journal 22(2):313-330.

[68] See also chapter 7.

[69] Hellmann, p. 178. [See note 65.]

[70] Freeman D. 1983. Margaret Mead and Samoa: the making and unmaking of an anthropological myth. Cambridge: Harvard University Press.

[71] *Ibid.*, p. 288.

[72] Hellmann, pp. 177-192. [See note 65.]

[73] Merton RK. 1970. Science, technology and society in seventeenth-century England. New York: Howard Fertig.

[74] Segerstråle U. 2000. Science and science studies: enemies or allies? In: Segerstråle U. ed. Beyond the science wars: the missing discourse about science and society. Albany: State University of New York Press, pp. 1-40.

[75] Barber B. 1961. Resistance by scientists to scientific discovery. Science 134:596-602.

[76] As an introduction, see the seminal article: Shapin S. 1982. History of science and its sociological reconstructions. History of Science 20(3):157-211. More examples can be found in: Collins H, Pinch T. 1998. The golem: what you should know about science, 2nd ed. Cambridge: Cambridge University Press; Collins H, Pinch T. 1998. The golem at large: what you should know about technology. Cambridge: Cambridge University Press.

[77] Barber. [See note 75.]

[78] Documented further in chapter 8.

[79] See chapter 2.

[80] Huff D. 1954. How to lie with statistics. New York: W. W. Norton and Co., Inc., pp. 87-89.

Chapter Seven

Is Science Exclusive?

Literary intellectuals at one pole—at the other scientists . . . Between the two a gulf of mutual incomprehension.[1]

—Sir Charles Snow, author, scientist

AREAS SCIENCE NOW AVOIDS

Two centuries ago the famous French mathematician-cosmologist Pierre-Simon de Laplace wrote a famous book about celestial mechanics. In it he described his model of the origin of the solar system, in which the planets formed by the condensation of vaporous matter. Laplace, who had become a famous scholar, decided to make a presentation of his book to the emperor Napoleon. Someone informed the emperor in advance that the book did not mention God. As Laplace offered him the book, the emperor asked him why he had written a book about the universe and had not even once mentioned its Creator. Laplace bluntly replied that he "had no need of that particular hypothesis."[2] No need for God! While the various versions of the encounter differ in detail, the incident illustrates well the independent and exclusive scientific attitudes burgeoning at that time.

Theoretical physicist Stephen Hawking has reflected the same tendency as he proposes his entirely self-contained universe that "wouldn't need anything outside to wind up the clockwork and set it going. Instead, everything in the universe would be determined by the laws of science and by rolls of the dice within the universe. This may sound presumptuous, but it is what I and many other scientists believe."[3] In France the famous marine zoologist Félix Lacaze-Duthiers wrote over the door of his laboratory: "Science has neither religion nor politics."[4] Harvard physicist Philipp Frank comments that in science "every influence of moral, religious, or political considerations upon the acceptance of a theory is regarded as 'illegitimate' by the . . . 'community of scientists.'"[5] And Nobel laureate Christian de Duve, in discussing the troublesome problem of the spontaneous origin of life, indicates that "any hint of teleology [purpose] must be avoided."[6]

Recently the National Academy of Sciences and the American Association for the Advancement of Science have strongly objected to certain trends in secondary school science classes that encourage the discussion of alternatives to evolution. They find even the idea that there might be some kind of intelligent design in nature objectionable.[7] Not all scientists would agree, but the present general mind-set, or ethos, especially coming from the leaders of the scientific community, is that science should go it alone and exclude everything else. They especially want to avoid the specter of religious influence.

A degree of elitism encourages exclusiveness in science, and the two characteristics can foster each other. Quite a number of scientists feel that science is superior to all other methods of inquiry. Science's great success in several arenas has no doubt contributed to such an attitude, and a degree of pride is justifiable. Science is especially good at trying to answer the *how* kind of questions, such as how does gravity affect the motion of planets, but it does not do as well with the *why* question, such as why is there a universe in the first place. Legitimate questions do exist beyond the realm of science. "If you ask science to make an atomic bomb, it will tell you how. If you ask science if you should really make one, it will remain silent."[8] Anyone looking for truth and understanding is also entitled to ask the *why* kind of questions.

Harvard University's biologist Richard Lewontin also reflects some of science's exclusiveness in a perceptive comment whose candor is worthy of respect. "Our willingness to accept scientific claims that are against common sense is the key to an understanding of the real struggle between science and the supernatural. We take the side of science *in spite* of the patent absurdity of some of its constructs, *in spite* of its failure to fulfill many of its extravagant promises of health and life, *in spite* of the tolerance of the scientific community for unsubstantiated just-so stories, because we have a prior commitment, a commitment to materialism. It is not that the methods and institutions of science somehow compel us to accept a material explanation of the phenomenal world, but, on the contrary, that we are forced by our *a priori* adherence to material causes to create an apparatus of investigation and a set of concepts that produce material explanations, no matter how counterintuitive, no matter how mystifying to the uninitiated. Moreover, that materialism is absolute, for we cannot allow a Divine Foot in the door."[9] As far as God is concerned, science has now posted a "DO NOT ENTER" sign.

Evolution is one of the great players in the exclusive stance of science. It avoids the concept of God and all other nonmechanistic explanations of origins. The scientific community usually fervently defends evolution. And while science now feels quite free to exclude God, leading scientists seem shocked when anyone tries to set aside their evolutionary theory. When the Kansas State Board of Education decided to remove evolution and cosmology from the science curriculum, an editorial in *Science*, the leading science journal in the United States, characterized the move as a "cleansing atrocity" and "lunacy."[10]

The noted Columbia University geneticist Theodosius Dobzhansky, one of the leading architects of the modern evolutionary synthesis (Table 4.1), declared that "nothing in biology makes sense except in the light of evolution."[11] Such extreme pronouncements can imply that all current biological studies that don't include evolution, such as determining how fast a nerve impulse travels along a nerve, are apparently nonsensical! Furthermore, the meticulous works of Antony van Leeuwenhoek in describing microbes, and of William Harvey in discovering the circulation of blood, in the seventeenth century, before the acceptance of evolution, would become worthless under such a restriction. Geneticist Francisco Ayala, who served as president of the American Association for the Advancement of Science, expressed the same exclusivist tendency when he commented that "the theory of evolution needs to be taught in the schools because nothing in biology makes sense without it."[12]

The title of the book *The Triumph of Evolution and the Failure of Creationism*,[13] especially when the last half of the title was written backwards on the title page, to emphasize the desperate state of creationism, reflects such exclusiveness. While such an attitude is not unusual in human behavior, it is not helpful to serious scholarship. The author of the book is Niles Eldredge of the American Museum of Natural History, who is famous for being one of the architects of the evolutionary punctuated equilibrium concept. The late famed cosmologist Carl Sagan also asserted the eminence of science above everything else in his book *The Demon-haunted World: Science as a Candle in the Dark*.[14] Humility can sometimes be in short supply in the scientific community.

The examples given above illustrate an elitist scientific attitude that tends to isolate science from all other areas of inquiry. A few scientists feel so confident that they see virtually no limit to what science will eventually be able to do.[15] By postulating a mechanistic view of reality and near-infinite knowledge, we can reach a so-called omega point, where life becomes eternal and the resurrection of past life a reality. Science will provide us with immortality.[16] Confidence in the superiority of science is so great that at times it invades areas that it is unable to study, and then it tries to provide scientific answers for questions it cannot answer. Sociobiology offers an example.

SOCIOBIOLOGY–SCIENCE OUT OF CONTROL

Sociobiology seeks to investigate the evolution of social behavior. It tries to answer questions about how organisms behave as they do from an evolutionary perspective, and it gets into the thorny questions of what influences human actions. We should not confuse sociobiology with the sociology of science, although they do have some overlap. The former deals more with the biological causes of the actions of all kinds of organisms, while the latter deals with the behavior of the scientific community.

One of the problems that sociobiology addresses is: if, as Darwin proposed, evolutionary advancement takes place because the fittest survive over the less fit, how can you explain the evolution of altruistic behavior, when organisms are willing to sacrifice their lives for the good of others? This is suicide, and it has no survival value for the organism. Why should such traits ever evolve when the organism has no chance to pass them on to the next generation? A common example is the bee that stings you to protect others in the bee colony. Because it leaves vital parts of its body stuck in you, it dies soon thereafter. Evolutionists have several explanations for such behavior, including some suggesting that the whole bee colony evolves as kind of a single organism. Such organisms have genetic peculiarities that might favor this. Thus the bee colony itself, and not the individual bee, has survival value.

More problematic are many examples of self-sacrificing behavior among birds and mammals. Meerkats are a highly social kind of mongoose (Figure 7) that struggle for existence in the Kalahari Desert in southern Africa. They live in groups of three to 30 individuals in underground tunnels and are among the most cooperative animals known. A member of a group will

Figure 7 *Meerkats, also known as suricates; a type of burrowing mongoose.*
Courtesy of Corel Professional Photo Library.

babysit and cuddle the very young while the biological mother spends extended periods of time searching for food. Others will stand as sentinels on

exposed lookouts, where they are highly visible to predators. Their guard duty permits the other members of the group to go about their business of foraging for food in safety. If the sentinel spots a predator such as an eagle or a cobra, the meerkat will give an alarm call, further endangering itself by calling attention to where it is, but at the same time warning the others to scamper to safety. The sentinels risk their lives for the good of others. Why should such altruistic behavior ever evolve, since the altruistic ones would be less likely to survive? And when it comes to humans, why will a mother run into a burning house, putting her life at risk, to try to save her child?[17] Such self-sacrificing behavior is not what we would expect from an evolutionary process, in which the goal is survival and not altruism. Many have considered altruistic behavior to be a serious challenge to evolutionary theory.

Some evolutionists have proposed what they consider to be an answer for the puzzle: *kin selection*. In kin selection the important thing is not the preservation of the individual organism, but the continuation of one's particular kind of genes. By preserving closely related kin, one protects one's own kind of genes, since the next of kin tend to have the same kind. Siblings share the same parents, and cousins have the same grandparents, so by saving closely related relatives, one increases the chance of maintaining for posterity the special set of genes that one has. In other words, should an animal give its life to preserve the life of its close kin, this may help keep in existence its own kind of genes, even though the animal itself dies. The mathematics of the hereditary mechanism is such that it can be suggested that if you sacrifice your life to save three of your siblings or nine of your cousins, chances are you will be favoring the survival of your own gene pattern. The closer you are related to the ones you save, the fewer individuals you have to save in order to preserve your kind of genes. Many biologists regard kin selection as an evolutionary explanation for altruistic behavior. The profound implication of all this is that an altruistic act is not that at all—it is a selfish response to make sure one's own kind of genes get propagated by the relatives that survive. Darwin's concept of the selfish survival of the fittest becomes the reason for altruistic behavior.

The theory of kin selection came to the attention of the famed Harvard University entomologist Edward O. Wilson. He expanded on the concept and in 1975 presented it and related ideas in a volume that evoked one of the stormiest book reactions ever witnessed. Entitled *Sociobiology,*[18] the over-sized tome discusses the social behavior of a variety of animals, but without doubt it is a manifesto aimed at giving evolutionary reasons for human social behavior. The first chapter, entitled "The Morality of the Gene," implies that our emotions, such as love, hate, fear, and guilt, came about by natural selection. The last chapter, "Man: From Sociobiology to Sociology," clearly moved into the arena of human behavior. The emphasis was on genes controlling everything.

The next year Richard Dawkins promoted some of the same ideas in his famous book *The Selfish Gene.*[19] If an organism appears to behave altruistically, we can be assured, he argued, that its motive is fundamentally selfish. Organisms are largely under the control of their genes, and the principle of survival of the fittest promotes their own selfish survival to the detriment of other different genes.[20] In 1978 Wilson returned with the book *On Human Nature,* an expansion of the especially controversial final chapter of his *Sociobiology.* Here he claimed that altruistic acts bestowed even on nations do not result from any kind act, but from Darwinian survival of the fittest. Furthermore, he ventures into the sensitive area of religion: "The highest forms of religious practice, when examined more closely, can be seen to confer biological advantage."[21] Religion is not something we choose for its value or truth—we are religious because of the evolutionary survival advantage it provides.

All of this was more than could be endured.[22] From the moment of Wilson's *Sociobiology* publication scathing reactions produced an all-out war of words, personalities, books, and rare humor. The opposition came from surprising venues, including some formidable intellectual corners. The battle did not just involve the nature of humanity. It triggered many other surprising controversies. Critics declared sociobiology false, evil, fascist, and unscientific. Some sociologists saw an invasion of their turf by the biological sciences. One of the great issues was the fear that sociobiology would reestablish social Darwinism, in which society should enable superior humans to survive instead of inferior ones by limiting the latter's reproduction (eugenics). In contrast to the now-prevailing attitude that all human beings should receive equal treatment, sociobiology would encourage a return to belief in class superiority based on better genes. This gets into the nature-versus-nurture controversy of whether nature (genes) or nurture (environment) determines who we are.[23] Class distinction was acceptable in Darwin's Victorian England and reached ghastly inhumane levels during World War II when the Nazis used their gas chambers to eliminate millions of human beings they labeled as inferior. A half century later the Holocaust is still too fresh in people's minds to permit any general acceptance of genetic superiority.

Around Harvard University, activists, many of whom were on the faculty, began distributing pamphlets, holding meetings, and publishing articles against sociobiology. Wilson, who was to a certain extent misunderstood, became identified as a master race ideologue. The controversy spread to the public press, even appearing on the front cover of *Time*. The American Association for the Advancement of Science held a symposium in Washington, D.C., to discuss sociobiology. As Wilson prepared to give his talk, about 10 activists took over the microphone and accused him of racism and genocide. One poured a pitcher of ice water on his head, declaring, "Wilson, you are all wet!"[24] The presentation proceeded as scheduled, but was not as exciting as its hostile introduction.

The leading luminaries in the sociobiology controversy include Stephen J. Gould, a popular writer and, until his death the best-known promoter of evolution in the United States. He has strongly opposed sociobiology. Joining him was Richard Lewontin (a population geneticist, whom we referred to earlier). Both men happened to have worked in the same Harvard building as Wilson, and both have Jewish and Marxist affinities that would tend toward the egalitarian treatment of humans. Some scholars suggest that such a background may have influenced their rejection of sociobiology. Gould and Lewontin, along with many others, strongly object to what they consider the simplistic answers that sociobiology attempts to provide for complicated human behavior. On the other hand, the late John Maynard Smith at Sussex University in England, who specializes in theoretical biology, along with Richard Dawkins at Oxford, have lent significant support to sociobiology.

Attitudes toward religion among those involved in the controversy vary greatly. Dawkins actively opposes it; Gould[25] and Maynard Smith tend to separate religion from science; while Wilson, at times, claims to be a deist. A deist is one who believes in some kind of God who allows the universe to run on its own. Each of these specialists do not hesitate to criticize many things, including each other. Maynard Smith, who strongly supports Darwinism and is not in favor of Gould's deviance from that traditional view of evolution, comments that "the evolutionary biologists with whom I have discussed his [Gould's] work tend to see him as a man whose ideas are so confused as to be hardly worth bothering with, but as one who should not be publicly criticized because he is at least on our side against the creationists."[26] Gould reflects some of the same ill feelings, referring to Maynard Smith and Dawkins as "Darwinian fundamentalists."[27] In spite of internal scientific disputes, evolutionists tend to unite when facing the specter of creationism.

In the acrimonious sociobiology battle, Wilson felt betrayed by his colleagues, and wondered why Lewontin, who had offices in the same building, did not discuss his concerns privately instead of criticizing him in the public press.[28] We can at least commend Wilson for suggesting behavior akin to the biblical principle of going first to your offending brother before doing anything else.[29] However, his biblical suggestion makes one wonder about his loyalty to the evolutionary principle of competition and survival of the fittest as well as his willingness to face the consequences of the harsh Darwinian system he espouses.

One of the criticisms of sociobiology introduced by Lewontin was that research has shown that changes in gene frequency in human groups have been extremely slow while sociological transformations throughout history can be very rapid—hence, genetic changes could not be responsible for human sociology. Charles Lumsden and Wilson addressed this problem and others in another book titled, *Genes, Mind, and Culture*.[30] A proposed mathematical solution in the book did not meet with approval. Even Maynard Smith—who supported sociobiology—after extensive study, could not endorse the models given.[31]

A major problem with sociobiology is its claim to answer a large variety of questions on the basis of extremely limited data. Lewontin expresses his concerns in an interview: "If I am going to sit down and write a theory about how all of human culture is explained by biology, I have a lot of epistemological groundwork to learn, I mean, a fantastic amount. . . . These guys have just jumped feet first into a kind of naive and vulgar kind of biological explanation of the world, and the consequence is a failure. It is a failure as a system of explanation because they haven't done their homework. . . . It's cheap!"[32] Philosopher Michael Ruse at Florida State University expresses similar concerns about the work of the architects of sociobiology: "They did jump way ahead of their evidence, and then congratulate themselves on a hard empirical slog well done. And they were determined not to let a little counterevidence stand in their way. To be candid, they were determined not to let a massive amount of counterevidence stand in their way."[33] Ruse does point out that the critics have been unusually harsh.

Philosopher of science Philip Kitcher, at Columbia University, reflects further questions about sociobiology when he observes that "the ambitious claims that have attracted so much public attention rest on shoddy analysis and flimsy argument" and "the sociobiologists appear to descend to wild speculation precisely where they should be most cautious." Furthermore, he specifically compares Wilson's sociobiology to a ladder that "falls apart at each rung."[34] Three decades later, in a move that has baffled sociobiologists around the world, Wilson, although considered the "father of sociobiology," has repudiated kin selection as an explanation for altruism, at least in social insects such as bees.[35] He now favors a model of preliminary genetic flexibility and a single step leap into altruism. As expected, Hawkins and others disagree with this major revised stance.

Our special interest is that the sociobiology debate illustrates what happens when an exclusive, and sometimes elitist, scientific attitude fuels attempts to apply science to everything, moving freely into areas in which science has not provided significant evidence or any valid answers. There science can be a miserable failure.

In spite of its very weak scientific support, sociobiology is not completely dead. Such books as *The Triumph of Sociobiology*[36] try to rescue the concept, but reviewers have characterized the volume as "a disappointingly shallow analysis," "using the timeworn tactic of characterizing critics with the most extreme terms."[37] Sociobiology has made some improvements through the years as it has addressed some criticisms, and it is still popular with some biologists, but it comes far short of authenticating most of its claims, and many appear to be definitely in error. For instance, consider one of the fascinating icons of sociobiology, the meerkats which we mentioned earlier. They live in groups that usually include genetically unrelated "immigrants," visitors to the dominant family of the group. The unrelated meerkats also participate as sentinels for the group and as babysitters for the new offspring. Since they are unrelated, their altruistic behavior cannot result from the kin selection principle of sociobiology.[38] Such data challenges evolution's explanation for altruism in these kinds of organisms as a way of protecting one's own kind of genes.

The battles have subsided, and a new similar concept called *evolutionary psychology* has replaced traditional sociobiology as a way of studying humanity. While evolutionary psychology still emphasizes genes as responsible for almost everything, including religion,[39] it at least focuses more on what causes the mind to function as it does. A significant number of new books promote the idea.[40] Among them is Robert Wright's *The Moral Animal,* whose listing on the New York *Times* bestseller list for two years says something about the popularity of evolutionary psychology. Wright speaks of us humans as "a species with conscience and sympathy and even love, all grounded ultimately in genetic self-interest." [41] Opposing views, emphasizing limitations, appear in such books as *Alas, Poor Darwin: Arguments Against Evolutionary Psychology* [42] edited by sociologist of science Hilary Rose and neurobiologist Steven Rose. Their volume includes a chapter by Stephen J. Gould, who raises questions about traditional Darwinism and its inadequacy in explaining cultural changes. While Gould has aggressively endorsed evolution, he has not supported the simple traditional scenario.

DO WE HAVE THE POWER TO CHOOSE?

All of us are aware that we can choose to give money to the Salvation Army, paint a house purple, steal a car, or kick a dying dog. We can decide to do such things because we have free will. Most humans believe that we have freedom to make decisions—but some called determinists do not.[43] They reject the idea that there is any such thing as free will. Instead, our actions result entirely from purely mechanical factors, such as our genes or our environment. This gets us into the blazing conflict underlying the sociobiology and evolutionary psychology debate. Are we just machines controlled by our genes and environment, and thus not responsible for our actions, or do we have the power to choose (such as right from wrong) and thus become accountable for our actions? Without free will, there can be no responsibility or blame. Related to this are questions of whether absolute moral values, good and evil, etc., actually exist.

Courts of justice over the world basically assume free will and hold individuals responsible for their actions. If you choose to "commit the crime," you are expected to "do the time" in jail. However, is it not possible that genes control our activities? Evolutionary psychology, which is becoming a significant component of recent behavioral discussions, would suggest so. I behave a certain way because it is in my genes. The acme of such thinking came out recently in the book *A Natural History of Rape: Biological Bases of Sexual Coercion.*[44] According to the authors, rape is an evolutionary adaptation that permits men unsuccessful in marriage to propagate their genes. They support their argument by using examples of what they consider forced sex among animals. That argument seems rather strained, but demonstrates how, in trying to explain everything within an exclusive naturalistic mode, one has to resort to some rather loose analogies. It also illustrates a growing crescendo of excuses for aberrant behavior that seems to have permeated society during the past few decades.

Researchers sometimes refer to the God gene or the spiritual gene. Some use it to infer that humanity's ubiquitous religious tendencies are gene controlled. However, the fact that some scientists and others change their views from belief in God to atheism and vice versa while their genes remain the same suggests that the cause of spirituality is not primarily gene controlled. We have free will.

One can argue that genes are responsible for certain behavioral patterns, and occasionally that is the case. For instance, it appears that alcoholism has a genetic component, but this does not mean that if one has alcoholic tendencies one has no choice but to become an alcoholic. Millions of successful Alcoholics Anonymous members testify that this is not the case—they have chosen and used their willpower not to be alcoholics. Other more regrettable hereditary abnormalities also limit the power of choice, but they are exceptions. Our interest here is about normal human beings and how they decide to use their willpower.

It is not just our freedom of choice that the assumed power of the genes has challenged. As sociobiology would suggest, our feelings of love and concern for others are not really that. They are just selfish motives that only appear sentimentally altruistic. All our actions are just the influence of those selfish genes. The conclusion is that we are not really good and generous or concerned about others—we are just selfish. The philosopher Michael Ghiselin of the California Academy of Sciences gives us an example of how pervasive such thinking can be as he comments: "No hint of genuine charity ameliorates our vision of society, once sentimentalism has been laid aside. What passes for cooperation turns out to be a mixture of opportunism and exploitation. The impulses that lead one animal to sacrifice himself for another turn out to have their ultimate rationale in gaining advantage over a third; and acts 'for the good' of one society turn out to be performed to the detriment of the rest. Where it is in his own interest, every organism may reasonably be expected to aid his fellows. Where he has no alternative, he submits to the yoke of communal servitude. Yet given a full chance to act in his own interest, nothing but expediency will restrain him from brutalizing, from maiming, from murdering—his brother, his mate, his parent, or his child. Scratch an 'altruist,' and watch a 'hypocrite' bleed."[45] Are we really just the helpless victims of circumstances? Can we not, with nobility of character and firm decisions, rise above evil and be good?

Evolutionists use several explanations for the presence of free will. Wilson and Dawkins recognize its existence, but explain it as something programmed by genes that can sometimes overcome their power and dictates. As expected, such muddled argumentation has received much criticism. Can one have both determined and undetermined results from determining genes? Why try to combine such separate realms as genetics and free will? Can free will really be free if it is determined by genetics? Some evolutionists simply deny the existence of free will. William Provine, the historian of biology at Cornell University, simply states that "free will is the most destructive idea we have ever invented."[46] However, almost all humans believe that normal individuals have the freedom to choose, and thus we are responsible for our actions.

The question of the existence of free will is a fundamental issue that dramatically influences our worldview. Are we simply meaningless mechanical entities, with evolutionary psychology legitimizing all kinds of aberrant behavior? Or, on the other hand, do we truly have free will and are thus responsible for our actions? Life feels as if the latter is the case. To this we can add our normal innate sense of right and wrong, of moral rectitude and immorality, of justice and unfairness, and of kindness and selfishness. Such attributes, which most admit to experiencing, all point to a reality beyond a gene-limited evolutionary psychology, and also beyond ordinary scientific interpretations. *Reality seems to be much more than that which a restricted materialistic (mechanistic, naturalistic) scientific interpretation allows.* Furthermore, it raises the weighty question about whether there is a God that created all these perceptions that give meaning and purpose to existence as well as any responsibility we might have to such a Being. The degree of responsibility can depend on what kind of deity you postulate. *In a biblical context the Christian's response to a beneficent and forgiving God is not laden with burdens.*

It is true that some scientists such as Gould and the well-known scientist-writer Aldous Huxley, who have opted for a meaningless universe, speak of the "maximal freedom" and "liberation" that such a conclusion provides.[47] However, it is of interest that most scientists who do not believe in God, free will, or other special features of the mind, do not behave as simply animals, making sure their selfish genes get passed on to as many offspring as possible. Such scientists are almost always fair and honest, and have a sense of moral values. They are decent human beings, and as such witness to the fact that reality has aspects that go beyond their simple materialistic scientific explanations. *Our freedom of choice and sense of moral values are strong evidence of a reality above what science can explain.* As a result of such attributes our existence has meaning, and that meaning extends well beyond the gene level.

A RECENT SIDESHOW: THE SCIENCE WARS

"It has thus become increasingly apparent that physical 'reality,' no less than social 'reality,' is at bottom a social and linguistic construct; that scientific 'knowledge,' far from being objective, reflects and encodes the dominant ideologies and power relations of the culture that produced it; that the truth claims of science are inherently theory-laden and self-referential."[48] The preceding quotation sounds really impressive and is sympathetic to a cultural interpretation of science, but that is not at all why its author composed it. It was written to fool sociologists into publishing something they did not know much about—and it worked! The quotation comes from the pen of Alan Sokal, a theoretical physicist at New York University, who prepared an impressive article under the erudite title "Transgressing the Boundaries: Toward a Transformative Hermeneutics of Quantum Gravity."The article has a conciliatory tone and is heavily documented and embellished with many quotations from leading thought specialists. It also includes a number of errors that would be obvious to specialists in the field of physics. Sokal represented himself as a political cultural leftist to the editors of *Social Text*, a leading journal of cultural studies. He asked them to publish the article, and they did.At the same time, in a different journal, *Lingua Franca*, he announced that the article was a hoax designed to show how one's political stance determines what gets published regardless of accuracy. The editors of *Social Text*, who should have had the article checked for scientific errors, felt that Sokal had deceived them. The story of the hoax made the front page of the New York *Times*, and the public media had a field day deprecating scholarly pursuits. But that was not at all Sokal's original intent.[49]

What motivated him was what has become known as the "science wars." It is a continuation of a century-old battle between the "two cultures," that is, with the humanities that deal with cultural studies on one side and with science concerned with the study of nature on the other. In the past decade the science wars have been a conflagration between extreme postmodernism along with social constructivism on one side, and science on the other. Science emphasizes facts and reason.The postmodernism movement denies objective knowledge and espouses no universal value standards. Constructivism suggests that the conclusions of science, as well as all other human studies, are socially determined, and therefore, science is no better than studies in the humanities. Many regard even mathematics and logic as social constructs. Science is just one among many belief systems. Scientific "facts" themselves are just the social constructs of the scientists.This novel approach to science has opened a whole new area of investigation for the constructivists, and they have pursued the opportunity with fervor. Kuhn's view[50] of science as pursuing paradigms that change from time to time has helped undermine the view that science was a steady, well-reasoned path to truth. Constructivists have labeled science as a mere political power game. Unfortunately, science has often been its own worst enemy. Its too frequent exclusiveness and arrogance has helped fuel the fires of the conflict.

Some scientists were not pleased to see others outside of their club evaluating their work and tarnishing the immaculate perception of science they held so dear. Others worried about the loss of objectivity in society as a whole if science were relegated just to a package of ordinary opinions. Books and conferences by scientists started addressing the issue. A major influence in the controversy has been a volume published in 1994 titled *Higher Superstition: The Academic Left and Its Quarrels With Science.*[51] The "academic left" in the title refers to the constructivists and postmodernists that have been attacking science. Authored by a biologist, Paul R. Gross, and a mathematician, Norman Levitt, it is a polemic that devastates a significant portion of the argumentation being used against science, and it speaks of the "peculiar amalgam of ignorance and hostility"[52] of the critics of science. The authors give a large number of examples of errors made by those that have been criticizing science but do not even understand it. Some of the argumentation follows the same kinds of logic that constructivists and postmodernists have been using against science, but turned against them. The Sokal hoax, which occurred two years later, is just another argument that scientists use to emphasize the superiority of science. On the other hand, constructivists point out that the hoax was an isolated incident. So the battle rages on.[53]

The science wars underline the deep and persistent dissatisfaction many have with an elitist science. It also illustrates the shabbiness and arrogance of some of humanity's intellectual skirmishes. While science has significant strengths and appears to have won this recent fracas, we have no reason to think that the conflict between it and the rest of culture has been resolved. The reasons for the controversy are complex, but it seems obvious that science's self-sufficiency and exclusiveness will not escape attack from several perspectives. Furthermore, until secular science can produce more satisfactory answers to our deeper questions, such as the nature of our consciousness and our reason for existence, exclusive science will continue to face attack.

CONCLUDING COMMENTS

Where does this all lead? Is there a light at the end of the tunnel? Science now tends to exclude those areas of reality not on its materialistic menu. It shows an elitism when it moves into areas such as sociobiology and tries to answer questions beyond its area of expertise as though they were science. Secular science attributes human behavior factors such as altruism and religion to mechanistic factors such as genes. Then the academic left enters the fracas and accuses science of being just a social construct. The picture is a complicated one, but I believe that some important conclusions have begun to emerge. Through all this we have some dependable scientific data to guide our thinking.

The goal is to find what is true, or, in other words, what is reality or actuality. The postmodern pattern of thinking of some sociologists that suggests that everything is relative and that there are no absolutes is not a solution. That kind of thinking leads more toward skepticism than to the truth we are looking for. Besides, it is difficult to take seriously a premise such as postmodernism, which suggests that nothing is objectively true. That would mean that the premise of postmodernism is also not objective truth.[54] *The best solution is to draw the best conclusions we can on the basis of the best data available, and to be open to all possibilities and revisions as new information becomes available.* The various factions could all profit from recognizing that there is value beyond their particular turf.

Science has been too exclusive, avoiding some important areas of inquiry while allowing certain dominating paradigms to determine what it considers to be true. Sometimes this has gotten science into trouble, as was the case when it ignored deaths caused by childbed fever germs or denied the possibility of major physical catastrophes.[55] On the other hand, we need to remind ourselves that science has a lot of good in it. When I read philosophical, sociological, psychological, and varied theological opinions, the lack of data and abundance of conjecture, often disappoint me. My training as a scientist may bias my view, but I am always glad to get back to science, in which one can find some plain hard facts of nature to start out with. This is especially the case in the physical sciences, such as physics and chemistry, and there we find some of the strongest evidence for God. Biology is more complex, making firm conclusions harder to come by. Psychology and sociology are even more difficult, because these systems are extremely complicated and difficult to analyze. There we are dealing with the human mind, something that is not that well understood. However, these fields are all worthy of careful investigation and respect. In all these areas there is good and bad, and we need to sort out carefully the one from the other.

Science has a number of problems, one of which is that scientists are too focused on its success—and some scientists will not hesitate to let you know how successful it has been. The problem especially intensifies when scientists purport that science can explain almost everything. While some of this is normal human behavior and we should all understand this, still we must never forget that we should not interpret the success of science in some areas as a universal superiority and a license to be exclusive. The sociobiology battle teaches us that in some fields science simply cannot make acceptable contributions. As a result, science needs to learn to give due respect to those areas of reality beyond its expertise. An example is human free will. Science rests on cause and effect. Free will, which most agree we have, is not cause and effect. If it were, it would not be free. Thus free will is an example of one of those realities beyond science that science needs to defer to.

In summary, science is not as bad as some sociologists think it is, and it is not as good as many scientists assume. Unfortunately, science tends to be too exclusive and elitist. Too often scientists envision science as an impregnable castle rising high above the plain of ignorance. In reality, it is more like an important house among other houses, such as history, art, and religion, all with their strengths and weaknesses. All the houses are important in the search for truth. The problem with science is that too many scientists in the science house have pulled the drapes shut and can no longer see the church that is right next door.

[1] Snow CP. 1959, 1963. The two cultures: and a second look. New York: Mentor, pp. 11, 12.

[2] As reported: in Dampier WC 1949. A history of science and its relation with philosophy and religion. 4th ed. New York: Macmillan Co., p. 181. Translated by me from a French quotation.

[3] Hawking S. 2001. The universe in a nutshell. New York: Bantam Books, p. 85.

[4] Quoted in: Nordenskiöld E. 1928. The history of biology: a survey. Eyre LB, trans. New York: Tudor Publishing Co., p. 426.

[5] Quoted in: Barber B. 1961. Resistance by scientists to scientific discovery. Science 134:596-602

[6] de Duve C. 1995. The beginnings of life on earth. American Scientist 83:428-437.

[7] For a recent action by the board of the American Association for the Advancement of Science, see: Frazier K. 2003. AAAS board urges opposing "intelligent design" theory in science classes. Skeptical Inquirer 27(2):5.

[8] Chauvin R. 1989. Dieu des fourmis Dieu des étoiles. Paris: France Loisirs, p. 214. English translation, mine.

[9] Lewontin R. 1997. Billions and billions of demons. New York Review of Books 44(1):28-32.

[10] Hanson RB, Bloom FE. 1999. Fending off furtive strategists. Science 285:1847.

[11] Dobzhansky T. 1973. Nothing in biology makes sense except in the light of evolution. The American Biology Teacher 35:125-129.

[12] Ayala FJ. 2004. Teaching science in the schools. American Scientist 92:298.

[13] Eldredge N. 2000. The triumph of evolution and the failure of creationism. New York: W. H. Freeman and Co.

[14] Sagan, C. 1996. The demon-haunted world: science as a candle in the dark. New York: Random House.

[15] Barrow JD, Tipler FJ. 1986. The anthropic cosmological principle. Oxford: Oxford University Press, pp. 613-682.

[16] Tipler FJ. 1994. The physics of immortality: modern cosmology, God and the resurrection of the dead. New York: Doubleday.

[17] To explain such behavior, some have proposed the concept of *reciprocal altruism*, in which you help individuals in crisis so that they can assist you when you are in crisis. The problem with the idea of gradually establishing such group-dependent behavior in a population is that it can't function until already established. See: Wilson EO. 1975. Sociobiology: the new synthesis. Cambridge: Harvard University Press, pp. 120, 121. In a way, this is another example of interdependent parts that cannot function until all essential subsystems are present.

[18] Wilson, Sociobiology. [For publishing information, see note 17, above.]

[19] Dawkins R. 1976, 1989. The selfish gene, new edition. Oxford: Oxford University Press.

[20] For an evaluation of Dawkins' view, see: McGrath A. 2005. Dawkins' god: genes, memes, and the meaning of life. Malden, Mass.: Blackwell Publishing.

[21] Wilson EO. 1978. On human nature. Cambridge: Harvard University Press, p. 188.

[22] Three good references for understanding the conflict are: Brown A. 1999. The Darwin wars: the scientific battle for the soul of man. London: Touchstone; Ruse M. 2000. The evolution wars: a guide to the debates. New Brunswick, N. J.: Rutgers University Press, pp. 203-230; Segerstråle U. 2000. Defenders of the truth: the battle for science in the sociobiology debate and beyond. Oxford: Oxford University Press. This last reference is comprehensive.

[23] Discussed in chapter 6.

[24] Segerstråle. Defenders of the truth, p. 23 [see note 22]; Wilson EO. 1994. Naturalist. Washington, D.C.: Island Press/Shearwater Books, p. 307.

[25] Gould SJ. 2002. Rocks of ages: science and religion in the fullness of life. New York: Ballantine Books. Evidence suggests that Gould may not have always been as supportive of religion as reflected here.

[26] Maynard Smith J. 1995. Genes, memes, and minds. New York Review of Books 42(19):46-48.

[27] As quoted in: Ruse, The evolution wars, pp. 231, 232. [See note 22.]

[28] Segerstråle, Defenders of the truth, pp. 29, 30 [see note 22]; Shermer M. 2001. The evolution wars. Skeptic 8(4):67-74; Wilson. Naturalist, p. 338 [see note 24].

[29] Matthew 18:15-17.

[30] Lumsden CJ, Wilson EO. 1981. Genes, mind, and culture: the coevolutionary process. Cambridge: Harvard University Press.

[31] Maynard Smith J, Warren N. 1982. Models of cultural and genetic change. Evolution 36:620-627; Segerstråle, Defenders of the truth, pp. 162-164. [See note 22.]

[32] Interview reported in: Segerstråle. Defenders of the truth, pp. 165, 166. [See note 22.]

[33] Ruse. The evolution wars, p. 224. [See note 22.]

[34] Kitcher P. 1985. Vaulting ambition: sociobiology and the quest for human nature. Cambridge: MIT Press, pp. ix, 9, 333.

[35] Wilson EO 2008. One giant leap: how insects achieved altruism and colonial life. BioScience 58(1):17-25,

[36] Alcock J. 2001. The triumph of sociobiology. Oxford: Oxford University Press.

[37] Beckwith J. 2001. Triumphalism in science. American Scientist 89:471, 472.

[38] Bednekoff PA. 1997. Mutualism among safe, selfish sentinels: a dynamic game. The American Naturalist 150:373-392; Clutton-Brock TH et al. 2001. Effects of helpers on juvenile development and survival in meerkats. Science 293:2446-2449; Clutton-Brock TH et al. 1999. Selfish sentinels in cooperative mammals. Science 284:1640-1644.

[39] For two recent and unimpressive attempts, see: Hamer DH. 2004. The God gene: how faith is hardwired into our genes. New York: Doubleday; Newberg A, d'Aquili EG, Rause V. 2002. Why God won't go away: brain science and the biology of belief. New York: Ballantine Books.

[40] For instance: Gander EM. 2003. On our minds: how evolutionary psychology is reshaping the nature-versus-nurture debate. Baltimore: Johns Hopkins University Press.

[41] Wright R. 1994. The moral animal: evolutionary psychology and everyday life. New York: Vintage Books, p. 378.

[42] Rose H, Rose S, eds. 2000. Alas, poor Darwin: arguments against evolutionary psychology. New York: Harmony Books.

[43] Wegner DM. 2002. The illusion of conscious will. Cambridge: Bradford Books.

[44] Thornhill R, Palmer CT. 2000. A natural history of rape: biological bases of sexual coercion. Cambridge: MIT Press.

[45] Ghiselin MT. 1974. The economy of nature and the evolution of sex. Los Angeles: University of California Press, p. 247.

[46] Provine, WB. 2001. From a lecture I attended, given at the Riverside campus of the University of California, 5 April.

[47] Gould SJ. 1989. Wonderful life: the Burgess shale and the nature of history. New York: W.W. Norton and Co., p. 323; Huxley A. 1937. Ends and means. New York: Harper and Brothers, p. 316.

[48] Sokal AD. 1996. Transgressing the boundaries: toward a transformative hermeneutics of quantum gravity. Social Text 46/47; 14(1, 2):217-252.

[49] For accounts of this curious incident, see: Editors of Lingua Franca. 2000. The Sokal hoax: the sham that shook the academy. Lincoln, Neb.: University of Nebraska Press; Segerstråle U. 2000. Science and science studies: enemies or allies? In: Segerstråle U, ed. Beyond the science wars: the missing discourse about science and society. Albany, N.Y.: State University of New York Press, pp. 1-40.

[50] Discussed in chapter 6.

[51] Gross PR, Levitt N. 1994, 1998. Higher superstition: the academic left and its quarrels with science. Baltimore: Johns Hopkins University Press.

[52] Ibid., p. 34.

[53] For further information about this fascinating struggle, see the four references immediately above and: Brown JR. 2001. Who rules in science: an opinionated guide to the wars. Cambridge: Harvard University Press; Collins H, Pinch T. 1998. The golem at large: what you should know about technology. Cambridge: Cambridge University Press; Collins H, Pinch T. 1993, 1998. The golem: what you should know about science, 2nd ed. Cambridge: Cambridge University Press; Gross PR, Levitt N, Lewis MW, eds. 1996. The flight from science and reason. New York: New York Academy of Sciences; Koertge N, ed. 1998. A house built on sand: exposing postmodernist myths about science. Oxford: Oxford University Press; Sokal A, Bricmont J. 1998. Fashionable nonsense: postmodern intellectuals' abuse of science. New York: Picador USA.

[54] For a discussion of this conundrum, see: Forman P. 1995. Truth and objectivity, part 1: irony; part 2: trust. Science 269:565-567, 707-710.

[55] See chapters 3 and 5.

Chapter Eight

Putting It Together

The meaning of life consists in the fact that it makes no sense to say that life has no meaning.[1]

—*Niels Bohr, physicist*

THE GOOD PART OF SCIENCE

Two young girls faced the tragedy of being unable to fight off the germs that lurk all around us. They were like the famous "bubble boy" who survived for 12 years by living in a plastic "bubble." Many children with this condition don't get to celebrate their first birthday. They have a defective gene that impairs the function of the white blood cells, which fight off infection. Fortunately for the two young girls, the wonders of genetic engineering came to the rescue. Researchers removed some of their cells, genetically altered them to provide the right gene, and re-implanted them in the girls. In time the cells grew, providing the resistance needed. Another scientific triumph! Such procedures are not simple, and this type of gene therapy has had its problems. Sometimes the virus used to transfer the gene can cause complications, but scientists are not giving up. New approaches include trying to alter the viruses, direct transfers of genes, and repairing the genes by using the proofreading and editing systems of cells that we mentioned earlier.[2]

Employing genetic engineering, scientists have been able to alter the DNA of a number of organisms. Genetically modified microbes can produce vaccines; hormones, such as insulin (which controls sugar metabolism); and interferon (which improves resistance to virus infections). We have been able to develop huge pigs and mice, and cows that give more milk. Researchers have also worked with plants. New golden rice synthesizes the precursor to vitamin A, fruits keep their freshness longer, and cotton plants now have a toxin borrowed from a microbe that makes them resistant to the dreaded boll weevil. Of course, many fear that some of these new kinds of organisms might cause a universal biological disaster by rampant infections or uncontrollable reproduction. It is a deep concern that cannot be easily dismissed, and it illustrates the potential power of science.

When history records the great accomplishments of the twenty-first century, it will no doubt include the mapping of the more than 3 billion DNA bases found in the human genetic formula. Researchers have found some 30,000 genes in human beings, and the genes perform all kinds of different functions. For instance, at least eight of them are associated with our biological clock, which regulates our hormones, temperature, and sleeping patterns. Cloning of mammals is another impressive accomplishment. However, we are cloning only the physical body of the organisms. Thus far science has done little about duplicating our mysterious minds.

The impressive accomplishments of science do not limit themselves to genetic engineering. One has only to mention such terms as *computer, Hubble telescope,* or *Mars rover* to realize that science has been one of the most successful human enterprises. We need not spend more time on this. In many areas science is eminently successful.

In the previous two chapters we gave examples of problems in science such as following closed paradigms and being very exclusive. As we look at the total picture we also need to keep in perspective the good aspects of science, such as its many fascinating and useful discoveries. The successes of science are legendary, and it is getting hard to find anyone who does not think that on the whole science is a good thing.

WHERE IS GOD, AND WHY IS THERE SO MUCH SUFFERING?

Once I attended a large secularists' convention during which a speaker asked that those in the audience who were willing would pray to God that he would grow six inches during the 20-minute talk he would present.[3] Naturally, it didn't happen. It was a bit like the so-called Dial-a-Prayer for Atheists—you dial the number, but no one answers! Secular scientists frequently raise two questions about God: Where is He? and How could God, especially the beneficent deity of the Bible, allow so much suffering in nature? These are real and serious concerns especially pertinent to the God question.

While we observe lots of evidence that points to an intelligent designer God, sometimes when we discuss these matters questions arise as to who designed the designer, and what was He doing before He started creating? Augustine reportedly had an answer to the latter query. Before creation, God was preparing hell for people who ask such questions! The question about who designed the Designer is somewhat invalid, simply because if someone did design the Designer, then the Designer is not the real designer of everything, and someone had to design the designer of the designer, etc., ad infinitum. The question can imply that if we do not know who designed the designer or where God came from, our information is sketchy, and as a result there may be no designer at all. On the other hand, we can ask where the universe came from. In the context of complicating concepts such as the relationship between time and space, as illustrated by Einstein's ideas about relativity,[4] our common questions about the nature and timing of ultimate beginnings may actually be meaningless.

The question about why there is anything rather than nothing is a very real one. Neither science nor theology has provided any good answers to the questions of ultimate origins. However, we are all sure that something does exist. Our ignorance of why there is anything at all should engender a healthy dose of humility as we consider how inadequate our knowledge is.

The questions of where God or the universe came from are real, but are not at all the same questions as to whether God or the universe exists. Just because I do not know the origins of God or the universe does not mean that they do not exist! I am very willing to accept the existence of many things, even though I do not know how they came into being. If a huge crocodile is chasing me, I am willing to concede its existence long before I know anything about its past history. Likewise in nature we can see evidence for a Designer, even though we may not know how, why, or from where the Designer came into being.

We don't know where God is. In spite of this serious shortcoming, those who believe that He exists are still in the vast majority. While people may have varied definitions of God, a 1996 Gallup poll indicates that 96 percent of adults in the United States believe in God,[5] and religion is a nearly universal phenomenon around the world. In the query about God's existence, we must keep in mind that the absence of evidence is not the same as the evidence of absence. Although we may not see God, there is an abundance of convincing evidence that He does exist. We don't have to view Him in order to believe in His reality. Suppose in a clearing in a deep forest I find a well-ordered and well-manicured garden, with no weeds and neat rows of flowers and vegetables. While I may not spot the gardener, the evidence is so compelling that I am sure that he or she exists. Likewise, if I inspect the charred timbers, burnt roof, and melted belongings of a house, I can be sure that a fire gutted it even though I do not observe any flames at the moment. Evidence can be so compelling that it leaves little doubt.

One can legitimately ask, If there is a God, why doesn't He make Himself more visible? We don't have much information about this, but an attractive suggestion is that He, in the context of a warfare between good and evil, isolates Himself in order to protect our freedom of choice. Otherwise He might compromise that freedom and violate His fairness should He dominate too much and thus manipulate decisions. As a crude analogy, should a father sit in the kitchen day in and day out to make sure that the children do not get into the cookie jar, they will have little freedom to choose whether to eat any cookies. Furthermore, the children may not have a chance to learn integrity and practice strength of character by staying out of the cookie jar simply because it is the right thing to do. We may be able to learn the great lessons of life more readily if we are more on our own than if we are constantly supervised. Such an argument may not carry much weight if you have a purely mechanistic worldview and you don't believe in any kind of deity, but for others the concept can be very important. If God needs to give us the freedom to accept or reject Him, He may stay out of the picture. Or there could be a number of other reasons. During battle the soldiers do not always understand the war plan.

Then there is the question of suffering. How could an all-powerful and kind God, especially the deity described in the Bible, create a world exhibiting so much pain and suffering? A number of scientists and others feel that the presence of moral evil, fear, pain, and natural calamities such as earthquakes that kill thousands at a time, challenges the concept of a good and intelligent Creator-God. To these problems we can add sharks that eat human beings, babies with cancer, and terrible parasites, such as tapeworms. While the universe has much compelling evidence of intelligent design, all is not well.

Philosophers, theologians, and other thinkers have written much about the problem of suffering in the presence of a good Creator-God.[6] I will list a few solutions, but they are only suggestions:

1. While it would be nice to have no pain or fear, without them our lives could be disastrous. Pain and fear of consequences seem to be necessary to keep us from hurting ourselves, such as, for example, burning off our hands when working around a fire or great heat.

2. Moral evil, such as injustice, should not be blamed on God when we have freedom of choice and we ourselves can cause evil. We should not condemn Him for our wrong choices any more than we should blame the architect of a house whose tenants burn it down. The question of freedom is vital here, as it is for the question of the existence of God mentioned above. True freedom of choice requires that moral evil be allowed. Instead of human beings, God could have created only creatures, somewhat like apes, without the freedom of making moral choices, thus excluding the possibility of good or evil, but such an existence appears unchallenging and really boring. Fortunately, we can make moral choices, but we also have to face their consequences.

3. Some suggest that suffering helps develop a virtuous character. They sometimes defend the idea that we remember acquired virtues better than innate ones. The suffering we experience helps us to better remember the effects of evil.

4. Others explain the evil of natural calamities by postulating a God who distances Himself from His creation, thus letting nature take its course. While the concept may have some truth, it does not seem to fit what we would expect from the kind of God who made such a very complex universe.

5. A Creator God could perform all kinds of miracles all the time to prevent suffering. However, it may well be that if God manipulates nature too much and introduces too many miracles, we would not grasp the concept of cause and effect. Calamities may serve to remind us that there is rationality, i.e., cause and effect, in the universe. If the universe were not basically orderly, it is doubtful that meaningful logical thinking would be possible.

6. The suffering we see in organisms, such as infectious diseases, cancer, and even carnivorous preying, may be the result of minor biological variation, especially the usually harmful mutations, and not of God's specific de-

sign or intent. They can also serve to remind us that we live in a rational universe, in which cause and effect are normal.

We don't have answers to all the questions we might have about the suffering we see in nature. There is much that we simply don't know, but the concepts we have listed above do provide some plausible explanations.

SOME CAUTIONS ABOUT SCIENCE

An apocryphal story tells about a biologist who became famous for being able to train fleas. He would order the fleas to jump, and they would obediently do so. One day, in order to demonstrate to some of his friends how thoroughly he had trained his fleas, he started pulling the legs off one of his trained fleas one at a time and then asked it to jump. Each time the well-trained flea kept leaping. He continued until the flea had only one leg left, and when ordered, the flea dutifully jumped. Finally the scientist removed the final leg and asked the flea to jump, but nothing happened. Turning to his friends, the biologist remarked that through the years he had learned that if you take all the legs off a flea it can no longer hear! That is one interpretation. Of course, another interpretation is that the flea did not jump because it had no legs. The story illustrates the difference between data and interpretation. That the flea did not jump when it had no legs is a fact—that is data. That it could not hear is an interpretation. One of the great confusions we have in science is that far too often we make no difference between data and interpretation. An interpretation can be just an opinion. In order to find out what is really going on, one has to distinguish between the two.

Scientists have long been aware of this problem, and, as mentioned earlier, they use the term *historical science*[7] to designate those aspects of science that tend to be more on the subjective or interpretive side. These are areas in which authentication is more difficult. For example, they do not allow you to perform an experiment repeatedly so as to check your results. It turns out that many of these more speculative corners of science deal with past events, and they are usually more difficult to test. Cosmology, paleontology, evolution, creation, and physical anthropology fall more on the historical side. On the other hand, we have experimental science, such as physics, chemistry, and such aspects of biology as genetic engineering, in which we can easily and repeatedly test something in the laboratory. One needs to be especially careful to sort out data from interpretation when dealing with historical science.

The fact that paradigms dominate science is very pertinent to our overall evaluation of the God question. Paradigms imply a sociological component to science, one that challenges the purity, objectivity, and openness that some scientists like to claim for their discipline. However, when instead of exhibiting individual independent thinking, the scientific community shifts as a whole from strong loyalty to one paradigm to strong loyalty to another, as was the case for moving continents, it is hard not to believe that the conclusions of science involve strong sociological aspects. Many interpret changes in paradigms as progress, but the fact that sometimes the shift returns science to an old rejected paradigm, challenges that concept. This was the case for the earlier examples we gave of the spontaneous generation of life and of geological catastrophes.[8] While in these cases the readopted paradigm does differ in some details from the old rejected one, the underlying principle remains the same in both the old and new versions, hence science at times reverts back to rejected interpretations. As additional scientific information accumulates there is little question that science progresses in a general way toward truth, but there can be many side trips, some of them very long ones, down erroneous paradigm paths.

After intensively studying the question of origins for decades, and with all due respect for all the scientific effort put forth to demonstrate evolution, it seems to me that the idea that organisms originated by themselves and evolved from simple to complex faces insurmountable scientific problems. Although many accept evolution, the data supporting macroevolution is especially hard to find, while the data challenging it is very significant.[9] Furthermore, a number of scientists have been raising serious questions about evolution and writing books questioning the concept.[10] Huston Smith, the distinguished professor of philosophy at Syracuse University, reflects some of the same concerns. Speaking of evolution, he states that "our personal assessment is that on no other scientific theory does the modern mind rest so much confidence on so little proportional evidence."[11]

We get a little sense of the captivating powers of a paradigm when we see how confident some evolutionists are in spite of the paucity of evidence. Douglas Futuyma of the University of Michigan and SUNYSB has written the most widely used textbook on evolution in the United States. In it he states that "evolutionary biologists today do not concern themselves with trying to demonstrate the reality of evolution. That is simply no longer an issue, and hasn't been for more than a century."[12] When science exhibits such a confident attitude, especially in the face of such significant contrary data, it has moved from searching for truth into advocating dogma. *Evolution is a symptom of an overconfident secular science.*

As we have noted, science tends to isolate itself. Thomas Huxley once declared that no man could be "both a true son of the church and a loyal soldier of science."[13] Such an attitude reflects problematic exclusivity in science.[14] Scientists frequently state that science and religion are separate realms. We can separate out all kinds of different areas of information, such as literature, economics, and psychology, but purposefully ignoring some of them, as science too often does for religion, can only eventually end up as just a minor distraction along the broad highway to finding what is true. Our search for real truth—reality or ultimate truth, as some call it—needs to include as much information as possible, especially when asking broad questions, such as the origin of everything. The more possibilities we look at, the more likely we are to encounter correct explanations.

Unfortunately, science's disposition toward exclusiveness and isolation is unusually strong. As a result, science sometimes finds itself attempting explanations, such as that of life originating from information in atoms, or explaining human behavior through sociobiology, that are beyond its capabilities.[15] Most scientists are quite aware of science's power, and it is not something that they are likely to give up. It all contributes to a sense of superiority that tends to barricade science from other realms of inquiry that are also a part of reality. Too much success has actually hindered science from finding other aspects of truth. Scientists are entitled to specialize in science, but they can get in trouble when they don't recognize that one of the disadvantages of such specialization is that it restricts the broader outlook. You may think about little else than your own narrow field.

Some wonder whether science is being less than honest when it arbitrarily excludes God, yet at the same time claims to have the truth about questions of origins. While occasional intentional deception does occur in science, and while it is something that we would be unwise to ignore totally, it is very rare and is probably not a significant factor in the conflict about the God question.

And we needn't look too far to find a lot of dishonest mischief executed under the banner of religion or God. The main problem is not deliberate deception, but what is called self-deception, in which scientists honestly think they are right and others are wrong. They believe that they can exclude God because, after all, don't most scientists try to explain most everything without Him? For instance, self-deception seems evident when scientists believe that certain organisms lived hundreds of millions of years before they can find them in the fossil record[16] simply because they are sure they evolved from other kinds, and they know that would take a lot of time.

While scientists usually think they are right, history teaches us that science has often been wrong in the past. Self-deception is not just a problem of science—it is a failing for all—but science is especially vulnerable because of its usual success. It can more easily run off into erroneous tangents thinking it is right. Scientists need to pay more attention to the data of science and less to being in agreement with other scientists.

SECULARISM IN SCIENCE

At present, science usually claims a strict naturalistic stance, and does not allow God into the picture. Such scientific gurus as Stephen Gould characterize the idea of an intelligent designer as a "fallacy" that is "historically moth-eaten."[17] Several other notable scientists make a special point that the apparent appearance of design in nature is illusionary, or that the concept should be avoided. Julian Huxley, the grandson of Thomas Huxley, comments that "organisms are built as if purposefully designed," but that "the purpose is only an apparent one."[18] Richard Dawkins, in his book *The Blind Watchmaker*, observes that "biology is the study of complicated things that give the appearance of having been designed for a purpose."[19] He then spends the rest of the book trying to show how that is not the case. Nobel laureate Francis Crick warns that "biologists must constantly keep in mind that what they see was not designed, but rather evolved."[20] It is hard not to conclude that a secular agenda is at work here (and we cited more such examples at the beginning of the previous chapter). All of this indicates that in science as now practiced we are dealing with a closed secular materialistic philosophy and not an open scientific search for the real explanations about nature by following the data wherever it may lead. The fact that a half million scientists interpret nature without God while only a handful include Him leads to a tremendous bias against Him in the scientific literature. Any evidence for God is systematically overlooked. God should receive His "day in court" in the scientific arena, especially if science is truly looking for truth.

While the idea of some kind of creation is receiving much more attention now from scientists than in the past, many do not welcome it, and some leaders of science despise the concept. This is, after all, the new scientific age, in which God does not exist or is irrelevant. While most scientists are intelligent, kindly, and responsible, secular aggressiveness is not dead. Some scientists never seem to tire of complaining about how the church abused Galileo for his unorthodox but correct belief that the earth rotates around the sun. Galileo has become kind of an icon of how science was right and the church was wrong, and that can reflect on belief in God. It would be a very brave scientist who would now dare invoke any kind of deity who is active in nature, although the data of science very much points to this necessity to explain the precise contrivances and complexities we find.[21] In advanced educational institutions those scientists who believe in God remain quiet about it. Peer pressure, the dislike of ridicule, and fear of dismissal can keep the 40 percent of scientists who believe in a God who answers their prayers[22] from publishing about Him. University of Washington sociologist Rodney Stark points out that "there's been 200 years of marketing that if you want to be a scientific person you've got to keep your mind free of the fetters of religion."[23] If a chemist designs a complex organic molecule, that is science. But if God does the same thing, it isn't science!

Two centuries of excluding God have left an insidious secular intellectual matrix in science that pervades its theories, interpretations, and even its vocabulary. Hubert Yockey, a molecular biologist of the Berkeley campus of the University of California, has criticized science's confident but limited outlook and derides the use of *"oxymorons"* such as *"chemical evolution, prebiotic soup, . . .* [and] *self-organization"*[24] that prejudice the mind about how life originated.

Presently science asks the question How did life evolve? not Did life evolve? But doing so bypasses the crucial God question. A strong secular component in science biases the conclusions being drawn. It turns out that *as presently practiced, science is the odd combination of the study of nature and a sec-*

ular philosophy that rules out God. You can exclude God by definition, but that does not work very well if He exists!

It is unfortunate that the self-censorship against God is so strong in contemporary science. When leading evolutionary biologists such as Richard Dawkins write a book titled *The God Delusion*,[25] the message is clear: scientism, which is excessive confidence in science, is very much alive. Scientists who fervently believe in God can sometimes face a heart-wrenching dilemma, as they have to maintain a secular stance and essentially pretend they are atheists, in order to be accepted by the scientific community and in order to publish in scientific journals.[26] Some believing scientists have lost their academic position because of bias against them. When scientists investigate those areas of science that involve the God question, they can find their intellectual integrity challenged as they have to live the secret life of an undercover agent. Hopefully, as more evidence for God becomes accepted, such scientists will be able to express their beliefs more freely and help liberate science from the secular prison it has created for itself.

One can rightfully ask if science doesn't have a right to define itself as a secular enterprise. It certainly has—but if it does so, it should address only secular issues. That can be extremely difficult to do, because unfortunately knowledge does not easily fall into distinct compartments. For instance, when science tries to answer everything in a secular context, it is inadvertently making the strong *theological* statement that God does not exist, and that strays into religious issues. Intellectual seclusion into isolated disciplines such as art, religion, or science does not work when you are wondering where all things came from.

If science desires to define itself as strictly secular, it must avoid all areas that might raise the God question, and refrain from making pronouncements about the beginning of almost everything without sufficient evidence. Science should frankly declare that it is atheistic and closed to any conclusion that God exists. However, earlier we pointed out how the National Association of Biology Teachers was unwilling to take such a strong stance.[27] Evolutionists often assert that creation is not science because there exists no scientific way to evaluate a miracle such as creation, but that argument tends to lose its validity when scientists turn about-face and write such books as *Scientists Confront Creationism*[28] and try to evaluate creation by using science. Can they have it both ways? The definition of science, as presently practiced, is nebulous.

From a different perspective, some surmise that scientists are a band of atheists. The reality is more complicated. There are all kinds of scientists out there, and only a very few are charlatans or deliberately hostile to religion. We need to keep in mind that part of the reason many scientists do not mention God is that often their experiments, hypotheses, and theories have no direct relationship to the God question. Scientists like to deal with what they can observe in nature. It is their specialty, and they are most comfortable in that realm. A lot of science, as, for example, the chemical changes that take place when cement hardens, can be studied without involving any questions about God. The consistent laws of nature permit much science that does not require invoking any direct reference to Him. However, it does not mean that He does not exist, but rather that God is not as simple as some of our science. The God question comes more into focus when we raise harder questions, such as How did the laws of nature come into such a correlated pattern as to make our universe possible? or How did life originate?

A significant number of scientists associate God with evolution. With this kind of approach you can have both a semisecular scientific stance and a God to solve evolution's most difficult problems, such as the origin of life or the Cambrian explosion. Exponents of such an approach have proposed a variety of ideas.[29] However, you won't find any of them promoted in standard scientific journals and textbooks. Such ideas are not compatible with the current secular idealism of science. Furthermore, in the context of the major problems that evolution faces, if you have a God who is active in nature solving these problems, you have little need for the general theory of evolution anyway! Once you really let God into the picture the whole horizon changes, and many scientists resist this. To include God tends to reduce the autonomy of science.

Other scientists elect to live in two different worlds (specifically, two different philosophical realms of reality)—one that includes God and one that excludes Him—at the same time! While it might be convenient, it is not a way to find all truth. Truth cannot contradict itself. Either there is a God or there isn't one.

In summary, the current secular stance of science creates a serious bias and does not reflect the beliefs of many scientists. To introduce the idea of

God is, in the minds of those who dominate the field, considered unscientific. Such a stance restricts science and compromises its claim to search for all truth. For instance, if God exists, science can never find Him as long as it excludes Him from its explanatory menu. Here science no longer respects academic freedom and has lost its credentials. *In science, let the data of nature speak for itself, including the possibility that there is a God.* In my opinion this would be a more open and better scientific approach.

THE SCIENTIFIC EVIDENCE FOR GOD

A lot of scientific data points to the necessity for some kind of perceptive intellect to have planned the universe around us. Some may feel that we are dealing here with historical science, which is not as objective as experimental science, but that is not the case. Most of this data, like the forces of physics and complex biochemistry, is of the hard observational, experimental, and repeatable kind of science. Here we have the great advantage of dealing with facts, not fiction. We have already discussed much of this evidence,[30] and we will not repeat it here except to recapitulate a few highlights. Table 8.1 summarizes them.

1. Why should matter have organized itself with laws that permit the interaction of subatomic particles, such as quarks, neutrons, and protons, within very precise parameters that facilitate the formation of at least 100 kinds of elements? These versatile elements have the capability to combine with each other in unique ways, thus providing for the matter of the universe and the molecules and chemical changes necessary for life, and they can provide light so that we can see. Matter does not need to exist, and it certainly does not demand such elaborate laws controlling it in order to exist. It could just be a blob of chaotic goo. The laws and orderliness of matter as seen in atoms and their parts suggests that they were devised for a purposeful universe. For instance, the mass of a proton has to be precise within one part out of a thousand in order for us to have the elements that comprise the universe.

2. The realm of action and the very precise values of the constants of the four basic forces of physics certainly could not have just come about by chance, although some scientists try to suggest exactly that. Without these exact characteristics we would not have a habitable universe. If the value of the electromagnetic force or of gravity varied by only the minutest amount,

it would be catastrophic for our sun. Our sun has faithfully provided us with just the right amount of light and heat for a very long time. We are not only just the right distance from it, but if the basic forces of physics changed only slightly, the sun and all the rest of the universe would collapse in an instant. Furthermore, the preferred position of the all-important element carbon (which makes life possible) in the scheme of element formation, also looks very much like a purposeful design that makes life possible.

3. The origin of life is the most baffling problem organic evolution faces. Science has not been able to provide any plausible scenarios as to how life could have emerged by itself. The various speculations offered do not explain the formation of the multitude of special protein molecules needed, the origin of the complex information of DNA, the marvels of ribosomes, the elaborate biochemical pathways, proofreading, and editing systems, and existence and source of a genetic code. The problem only worsens when you look at all the other parts of the typical cell. And, if you do have life, all of this has to be able to reproduce itself so as to make more similar organisms. How could all of this happen all by itself? It surely looks as though some kind of very intelligent designer must be involved.

4. When we come to advanced living organisms, more problems accumulate for a mechanistic interpretation. Just one average human brain has 100 billion nerve cells connected by 248,000 miles (400,000 kilometers) of nerve fibers, involving 100 trillion connections. As is the case for computer chips, you have to have the right connections for proper function. When we study the advanced eye, it does not look as though it could have evolved. The eye has many complex systems, such as the integrated light-sensitive biochemistry of the retina and the auto-exposure and auto-focus features, which consist of many components that would not work and would not have evolutionary survival value until all the necessary parts were present. Color vision is another example of irreducible complexity, because the ability to separate out various colors in the retina would not help provide color vision without a brain mechanism to analyze the different colors. Specific receptors and analyzers need to be present and function properly in order to provide a system with inherent survival value.

5. While time is an important factor in increasing the chance of improbable evolutionary events, it turns out that when quantitatively evalu-

ated, the eons of time proposed for the age of the earth and the universe are totally inadequate. Calculations indicate that all the oceans of the earth would take an average 10^{23} years to produce one specific protein molecule from amino acids already present. Hence, the 5-billion-year age for the earth is at least 10,000 billion times too short a time. Furthermore, even the simplest form of life that we know of would require at least hundreds of different kinds of protein molecules. DNA is much more complex than the proteins —and then you need fats (lipids), carbohydrates, etc..

6. Little evolution appears to have taken place during the first five sixths of evolutionary time. Then when you examine the fossil record it turns out that most fossil animal phyla appear suddenly in a Cambrian explosion that lasts for less than 2 percent of all evolutionary time. The usual sudden emergence of most of the major plant and animal groups does not suggest that evolution ever occurred. If evolution had really taken place, we would expect a solid continuity of all kinds of fossil intermediates of various forms trying to evolve, but evolutionists suggest only a few examples of usually closely related organisms. The reproduction rates of advanced organisms are way too slow for evolution to have taken place. Such difficulties demand the existence of a Creator.

7. Some aspects of our minds point to a reality above the normal mechanistic confines of science. Science has done very poorly with such issues, indicating they operate far beyond the simple cause-and-effect system of science. Such factors imply a transcendent God to account for them. One of these mysteries is our consciousness, the feeling and self-awareness that we exist. Matter does not seem to have this characteristic. Another is our power of choice or free will. If it is really free, as most agree, it is beyond the normal cause and effect of science. Also consider our sense of good and evil, sometimes reflected in our recognition of justice and injustice. We object to unfairness and the mistreatment of the weak and poor, something that sharply contrasts with the evolutionary concept of competition and survival of mainly the fittest. As human beings we have ideals above such ruthless behavior. On the other hand, if we simply evolved, self-centered behavior and desires would be precisely what should survive. Where did all the higher characteristics of our mind come from? There seems to be a meaningfulness and a goodness in humanity above what science finds in matter, and evolution does not account for this.

Either there is a God who designed nature or there isn't one. When one looks at all the hard data presented above, ranging from the precision of the forces of matter and the complexity of life (especially the wonders of our brains and our minds), one has to acknowledge an abundance of significant evidence that is extremely difficult to explain if one does not believe in a God. *The scientific data forces the concept of a Designer.*

CAN SCIENTISTS IGNORE THE SCIENTIFIC EVIDENCE FOR GOD?

Science often provides data that scientists do not accept. Examples that we have looked at earlier include such cases as Semmelweis and the germs that cause childbed fever; Mendel and the principles of heredity; Wegener and his idea that the continents move; and Bretz and catastrophic geological interpretations. They all illustrate how the scientific community can hold on to erroneous conclusions despite contrary data. Abundant and convincing evidence indicates that a designer God is necessary, but the paradox is, why don't scientists acknowledge this?

At present, scientists have essentially shut the door to any consideration of God in science. As mentioned earlier, that was not at all the case when intellectual giants such as Kepler, Boyle, Pascal, Galileo, Linné, and Newton laid down the foundations of modern science. They saw themselves as discovering the principles and laws that God had created. The present secular ethos does not reflect the beliefs of science's pioneers, and neither does it represent the beliefs of many present-day scientists. The somewhat facetious statement that many scientists believe in God but only on weekends when they go to church has a ring of realism to it! Recall that a study reveals 40 percent of scientists believe in a God who answers their prayers, 45 percent do not, and 15 percent are not sure.[31] Presently God is not fashionable in science. We can probably best explain the secular stance of science as an attitudinal or sociological phenomenon, and furthermore several scholars have suggested that at times evolution can take the form of a religion.[32] *The fact that science has excluded God from science for a century and a half without being able to provide any satisfactory answers to the main questions of origins should be a matter of deep concern.*

We like to think that our newest ideas are the best, and that the past was wrong, and thus we can feel quite superior if we can show that the past was very wrong. But sometimes the past was right and old discarded paradigms can again gain acceptance as true. The twentieth-century philosopher of

225

science Imre Lakatos does not seem to be so sure about the superiority of the present over the past when he wryly comments, "Wastepaper baskets were containers used in the seventeenth century for the disposal of some first versions of manuscripts which self criticism—or private criticism of learned friends—ruled out on the first reading. In our age of publication explosion, most people have no time to read their manuscripts, and the function of wastepaper baskets has now been taken over by scientific journals."[33] We should not just follow the current "climate of opinion," especially since we have no reason to believe that what we consider to be true today will be regarded as true in the future, as new ideas and information emerge. If history is any indication, many of our ideas will be ridiculed in the future.

Humanity's major modes of thinking have at times changed dramatically. Alchemy and witch hunting have had their centuries of dominance. Thankfully, they are gone. In antiquity intellectual leaders such as Socrates, Plato, and Aristotle placed a great deal of emphasis on the thought process itself, how we arrive at truth, the importance of reason, and the subordinate significance of the senses. Then in the Western world during the Middle Ages a different set of priorities in intellectual pursuits began to emerge. The pattern of thought of that period, known as scholasticism, paid special attention to logic, grammar, rhetoric, the relation of faith to reason, and respect for authority, especially Aristotle's. Now we have a still different set of priorities, with scientific ideas engendering a high degree of acceptance. Some sociologists caution, however, that science is primarily a subjective enterprise molded by the whims of those who participate in it. Regardless of whether or not they might be right, we live in an age of science, and it is the bias of our present intellectual matrix. I would like to suggest that through all this maze of human ideas, which come and go, there still exists firm data to help keep us on the track toward truth, and I find the scientific data that point toward God both abundant and compelling. Fortunately we have some solid anchor points.

The question is not just a battle between some kind of evolution and some kind of creation—that discussion is only a symptom of the deeper question of whether naturalistic (mechanistic, materialistic) science alone can provide a satisfactory worldview. This raises the weighty question of whether science has led us down an erroneous pathway as it has excluded

God. Without doubt I believe that is the case. The current scientific mind-set has placed itself into an intellectual straitjacket that does not allow God in the picture, and a lot of scientists insist on staying there in spite of compelling evidence to the contrary. But acknowledging what has taken place in science forces us to deal with still another significant question: Why did it happen? The question of the behavior of scientists—or of any other group of human beings, for that matter—is far too complex to permit any final answer, but a few suggestions definitely appear significant.

1. One reason, referred to earlier, is that science involves the study of facts and explanations about nature, and the scientist feels more at home with that than thinking about God. While it is a valid explanation, it can be only a minor reason for science rejecting God, because scientists entertain all kinds of speculative ideas.

While science dismisses the relevance of God, it at the same time accepts a host of really wild ideas that it should evaluate first. Their existence points to a serious bias in the current scientific mindset. We have already looked at examples of some of the speculative ideas that science toys with. They include the singularity at the beginning of the big bang, during which many believe that the laws of science did not apply; multiple universes, for which we have no valid evidence; a non sequitur anthropic cosmological principle; information in atoms that might create life; or assuming the evolution of organisms long before we can find them in the fossil record. Science takes all kinds of imaginary ideas seriously, and its tolerance for fantastic "just so stories"[34] is sometimes almost beyond belief. However, when it comes to God, at present the discipline will not allow Him in its picture. *Scientists may feel more at home with the data of nature, but since they do a great deal of speculation and theorizing beyond that data, they should also be willing to consider the possibility that God exists.*

2. A second suggestion comes from the much-respected twentieth-century science philosopher Michael Polanyi, who attributes the secularism of science to an overreaction to the constraints of medieval thinking. During medieval times people would consider God to be the cause of almost anything. According to some ideas, He created mice to teach us to put food away, and He brought bedbugs into being to keep us from sleeping too much. Polanyi states: "This is where I see the trouble, where a deep-seated distur-

bance between science and all other culture appears to lie. I believe that this disturbance was inherent originally in the liberating impact of modern science on medieval thought and has only later turned pathological.

"Science rebelled against authority. It rejected deduction [reasoning based on premises] from first causes in favor of empirical [sense perception] generalizations. Its ultimate goal was a mechanistic theory of the universe."[35] The pendulum of science has swung too far into severe secularism. As indicated earlier,[36] we find some evidence of a recent trend away from a purely secular science, but only time will tell if it is real or just a variation in background noise.

3. More than a few scientists feel that to allow God into the picture is the equivalent of giving up rationality. An unpredictable God does not fit with the cause-and-effect principle of science. However, this argument loses much of its significance when put in the context of the well-accepted thesis mentioned earlier[37] that science developed in the Western world because of the rational kind of God of the Judeo-Christian tradition. The fear of irrationality is valid only if you postulate an irrational deity.

4. Some scientists fear that to let God into the picture would encourage a religious-political fundamentalist type of takeover of society, something they regard as dangerous to science. The persistent debate about teaching creation along with evolution in the public schools of the United States particularly concerns them.

5. Intellectual pride in science may be another factor. Scientists have reason to be proud of science's advances, but authoritarianism can be highly contagious in a climate of success. We love power, but dictators, CEOs, intellectual leaders, and all those favored with prestige and power can have difficulty managing it. The famous statement by the British historian Lord Acton, "Power tends to corrupt and absolute power corrupts absolutely,"[38] is too often true. It is not just a special problem of scientists—it is something every one struggles with. In science, when you introduce into the picture a God that created nature, scientists can feel that they are losing control of their intellectual edifice and power. However, *the accomplishments of science are not so great that we can ignore God, especially when science leaves us with so many unanswered questions.*

The pride and aversion to God that we now often see in science stands in stark contrast to the humility, devotion, and respect for God shown by

Table 8.1

SCIENTIFIC EVIDENCE FOR GOD

CATEGORY	DESCRIPTION
1. MATTER	Why is matter organized into subatomic particles that follow laws permitting them to form more than 100 elements that provide the matter for the universe as well as the atoms, molecules, and chemical changes necessary for life? Furthermore, this matter produces light so we can see. Matter could just be chaotic, without laws. The laws suggest intelligent planning. Why is the mass of these subatomic particles often exactly what is needed to a precision of just one part out of 1,000?
2. FORCES	The very precise value and realm of action of the four basic forces in physics are just right to permit a universe that is suitable for life to exist. The strength of gravity as it relates to that of the electromagnetic force has to be extremely precise or the sun would not faithfully provide the earth with just the right amount of heat we need. Such precision looks very much like design by God.
3. LIFE	The simplest living organisms are so intricate and complex that it does not seem possible that they could have originated without intelligent planning. Complexities include DNA, proteins, ribosomes, biochemical pathways, a genetic code, and the ability to reproduce all this, including a proofreading and editing system when duplicating DNA.
4. ORGANS	In all organisms we find many systems with irreducible complexity. These have interdependent parts that cannot function until all the necessary parts are present. Examples would be the auto-focus and auto-exposure mechanism of the eye, as well as our intricate brains, etc. The useless individual parts of these systems have no inherent evolutionary survival value, hence would require planning by a designer.
5. TIME	The proposed very long ages for the earth and the universe are way too brief to accommodate the improbable events envisioned for evolution. Calculations indicate that the 5-billion-year age of the earth is thousands of billions of times too short for the average time required to produce a single specific protein molecule by chance. God seems absolutely necessary.
6. FOSSILS	During most of evolutionary time virtually no evolution occurs, then suddenly toward the end, and during less than 2 percent of that evolutionary time, most of the fossil animal phyla appear in what is called the Cambrian explosion. Furthermore, we don't find any significant ancestors to those phyla just before that. Many other major groups also appear suddenly, as if they had been created. Evolutionists propose a few suggested intermediates, but if evolution had taken place, the fossil record should be full of all kinds of intermediates trying to evolve.
7. MIND	The mind has characteristics that science has great difficulty analyzing, and as such they point to a reality beyond the naturalistic level and toward a transcendent God. Our freedom of choice, if really free, as most agree, is above the normal cause-and-effect principles of science. Other factors include our consciousness (namely, the feeling that we exist) and our perception that reality has meaning. We also have a sense of morality, as well as love and concern for others. You will not find these higher characteristics of the mind in ordinary matter.

the geniuses who established the foundations of modern science. We noted this for Newton,[39] and the same applies to Johannes Kepler as he writes in a prayerful context: "If I have been allured into brashness by the wonderful beauty of thy works, or if I have loved my own glory among men, while advancing in work destined for thy glory, gently and mercifully pardon me: and finally, deign graciously to cause that these demonstrations may lead to thy glory and to the salvation of souls, and nowhere be an obstacle to that. Amen."[40] Not many scientists can claim to be greater than Kepler or Newton. Such intellectual giants exemplify how science and God can work together.

6. Factors such as personal ego and freedom can stand in the way of recognizing God, especially a deity to whom one may feel responsible. As mentioned in the previous chapter, leading science writers such as Gould and Huxley refer to the "maximum freedom" and "liberation" provided by a worldview without God.

7. Another reason science now excludes God is simply because that is the contemporary "scientific spirit," the current scientific fashion or paradigm of our age. If you are a scientist, that is the way you are expected to behave. In addition, self-appointed guardians of science will not hesitate to notify you if you stray from that path. Regardless of what the data of nature might say, if you are going to call yourself a scientist, you had better not allow the idea of a God into the picture. Kansas State University biologist Scott Todd comments in the journal *Nature*: "Even if all data point to an intelligent designer, such an hypothesis is excluded from science because it is not naturalistic."[41] This kind of science is an attitude and a subjective secular philosophy that refuses to allow one to follow the data of nature wherever it leads. Such a narrow view of science would exclude Newton and Kepler from the cadre of scientists because they included God in some of their conclusions about nature, but to infer that Kepler and Newton were not scientists is heresy. Furthermore, as noted in the last part of chapter 1, a number of modern scientists also give serious consideration to a God active in nature.

The natural desire for approval, social survival, and academic advancement can lead many scientists to conform to the secular pattern of science. One gets a little view of the closed box that scientists now find themselves in from an observation by the theoretical physicist Tony Rothman: "When confronted with the order and beauty of the universe and the strange coincidences of nature, it's very tempting to take the leap of faith from science into religion. I am sure many physicists want to. I only wish they would admit it."[42] Although many scientists believe in God, to bring Him into the scientific picture is, at present, simply not the "cool" thing to do. To appear professional one must avoid the specter of religion. Conformity prevails.

All the suggestions given above are significant, but I suspect that the last three are most important. *Science excludes God mainly because of personal and sociological factors related to the behavior of scientists, not because of the scientific data itself.*

For three centuries modern science included God in its explanatory menu. Now, in spite of the fact that a lot of data point to His existence, science shuts Him out. In my opinion, *science made its greatest philosophical error a century and a half ago when it rejected God as an explanatory factor in nature and tried to explain everything in a naturalistic (materialistic, mechanistic) way.* Had science not done so, it would not now be facing the insurmountable problems and improbabilities that challenge current interpretations (Table 8.1). *God has a place in science.*

A SYNTHESIS

Does life have any meaning? Is humanity's existence for nothing? Are we just accidental flukes of nature? The secular British philosopher Bertrand Russell has penned one of the more meaningful descriptions of meaninglessness: "But even more purposeless, more void of meaning, is the world which science presents for our belief. Amid such a world, if anywhere, our ideals henceforward must find a home. That man is the product of causes which had no prevision of the end they were achieving; that his origin, his growth, his hopes and fears, his loves and his beliefs, are but the outcome of accidental collocations of atoms; that no fire, no heroism, no intensity of thought and feeling, can preserve an individual life beyond the grave; that all the labors of the ages, all the devotion, all the inspiration, all the noonday brightness of human genius, are destined to extinction in the vast death of the solar system, and that the whole temple of man's achievement must inevitably be buried beneath the debris of a universe in ruins—all these things, if not quite beyond dispute, are yet so nearly certain, that no philosophy which hopes to reject them can hope to stand. Only within the scaffolding of these truths, only on the firm foundation of unyielding despair, can the soul's habitation henceforth be safely built."[43]

Sounds pretty grim! Fortunately, the scientific data that points to God (Table 8.1) challenges Russell's "firm foundation of unyielding despair." Beyond that, it is hard to make the case that life is meaningless or that what we do has no purpose. Alfred North Whitehead, the eminent twentieth-century philosopher of Cambridge and Harvard fame, challenges purposelessness as he quips: "Scientists who spend their life with the purpose of proving that it is purposeless constitute an interesting subject of study."[44] That there is a reality beyond science Huston Smith clearly points out when he observes that "in envisioning the way things are, there is no better place to begin than with modern science. Equally, there is no worse place to end."[45]

The secular stance of modern science is especially irrelevant to some of the deepest issues of life, such as our reason for existence, our consciousness, our moral values, our will to do good or bad, and our love and concern for others. To this we can add other mysteries, such as our curiosity, creativity, and ability to understand. They are aptitudes science has not found in simple matter and usually ignores, but we all realize they are part of reality and part of what especially makes life meaningful. As Hubert Yockey illustrates, human beings are not just matter: "If all life is only material, then the crimes of Hitler, Stalin, and Mao Tse-tung are of no consequence. If humans are only matter, it is no worse to burn a ton of humans than to burn a ton of coal."[46] Francis Collins, director of the National Human Genome Research Institute, who had much to do with the recent mapping of the human genetic pattern (our 3 billion base DNA formula), believes that "a higher power must also play some role in what we are and what we become." He also wonders if genetics and molecular biology can "really account for the universal intrinsic knowledge of right and wrong common to all human cultures in all eras" and "for the unselfish form of love that the Greeks called *agape*."[47]

If naturalistic science had come up with plausible models for the origin of matter, life, and our minds, then one might seriously consider the possibility that God does not exist. However, secular science's essential silence on these salient aspects of reality implies the need for a masterful designer. Since it appears that we are the result of design, we have very good reasons to believe that our lives are not meaningless and purposeless and that when we die, it is not all over. The scientific data that points to God also suggests that there is light at the end of the tunnel of life.

I cannot believe that we just happened here by accident, and I cannot accept that God would create us for nothing. However, we all have the freedom to decide whether or not our life has any significance, whether humanity's existence has any purpose, or whether there is a God. It is so sad that in spite of all the data that points to Him many scientists decide that life has no meaning. They tend to miss out on all the richness, significance, satisfaction, and hope that one can get from a life directed to the highest ideals of goodness and concern for others.[48] All are ideals that you will not find anywhere in the harshness of evolution's competition and survival of the fittest, nor in simple mechanistic interpretations of nature.

As I examine nature it seems to me that there has to be a God who created the extremely precise and very complex things we find. This would include our complex brains and the intellectual power they have to reason and understand as well as our consciousness and our conscience. It would be very peculiar to have a God create such thinking beings and not leave some kind of communication from Him, so I search for that communication. To me, the Bible seems to be the best candidate, not just because of its meaningfulness and candor, but because the rational cause-and-effect kind of God found therein coincides with the rational cause and effect that science has discovered in the universe. Such a conclusion fits nicely with the broadly accepted thesis we discussed earlier: that modern science developed in the Western world because of the rational logic of the Judeo-Christian tradition inspired by the kind of God described in the Bible.[49] One can look at other major religions, such as Hinduism, Buddhism, Confucianism, or Shintoism, and encounter mysticism, no divine being, many gods, sometimes deities in conflict with each other, but not the one consistent God of the Bible. That God is congruent with the rationality we find in the universe and with science—particularly, the laws of science that function all about us.

One can object that one still has to invoke "irrational miracles" by a God who is active in nature in order to accommodate mysteries such as the origin of life. But that may not be the case. We don't know how God works. He may operate largely through laws that we don't understand yet. What may at first seem irrational to us may not be so when better understood.

Furthermore, such "miracles" seem to be scarce enough that for us the usual rationality of reality remains even though a few miracles do occur.

Does it require faith to believe in God? Yes. But in view of all the data that points toward a designer, *it requires much less faith to believe in God than to believe that all the precision, complexities, and meaningfulness we find in the universe just happened by chance.* Furthermore, there must be some significance to the fact that the Bible, of which billions of copies have been printed, and which has a distribution many times that of any other book, is humanity's most accepted guide for life. Although written by dozens of authors on three continents during a span of 1,500 years, its internal consistency is remarkable. To me, combining science and the Bible provides the best answers to my deepest questions.

One can always claim that an extremely fortuitous set of circumstances brought us into being just by accident. However, in view of the many improbabilities that kind of thinking entails, it does not appear to be a reasonable solution. A mastermind seems necessary. Too many major problems remain unresolved when we exclude God. Nature suggests a Being of design and purpose, and that our existence has actual meaning. At present, science with its restricted outlook does not embrace such a view. But to build a sound perspective, you should be willing to evaluate alternatives, not exclude them. *Science should return more toward the openness it had when the pioneers of modern science allowed God into the explanatory picture.*

CONCLUDING COMMENTS

During modern science's first three centuries God was part of its interpretations. Now the ideas of scientists have changed, and they rule Him out. However, many recent scientific discoveries show a degree of precision and complexity in nature virtually impossible to explain on the basis of random natural changes. Especially notable are the fine-tuning of the forces of physics that have the just-right constants to permit a habitable universe, and the numerous and extremely integrated complexities of biological systems. A number of other factors also seem to require an elaborate formulation far beyond what can be explained by natural occurrences (Table 8.1). All such discoveries point to some kind of complex designing by an intelligent planner, a Being that we would regard as God.

Science has discovered God. Scientific data indicates that He is necessary. Hopefully, more and more scientists will allow Him back into scientific interpretations.

---

[1] As quoted in: Horvitz LA. 2000. The quotable scientist: words of wisdom from Charles Darwin, Alfred Einstein, Richard Feynman, Galileo, Marie Curie, and more. New York: Mc-Graw-Hill, p. 151.

[2] See chapter 3.

[3] Talk by Gary Posner, Nov. 9, 2001, Center for Inquiry Convention, Atlanta.

[4] See chapter 2.

[5] For example: Shermer M. 2000. How we believe: the search for God in an age of science. New York: W. H. Freeman and Co., p. 21.

[6] For example: Emberger G. 1994. Theological and scientific explanations for the origin and purpose of natural evil. Perspectives on Science and Christian Faith 46(3):150-158; Hick J. 1977. Evil and the God of Love, 2nd ed. London: Macmillan Press, Ltd.; Lewis CS. 1957. The problem of pain. New York: Macmillan Co.; Wilder-Smith AE. 1991. Is this a God of love? Wilder-Smith P, trans. Costa Mesa, Calif.: TWFT Publishers.

[7] See chapter 6. For a dissenting view, see: Cleland CE. 2001. Historical science, experimental science, and the scientific method. Geology 29(11):987-990. For an authoritative introduction, see: Simpson GG. 1963. Historical science. In: Albritton CC, Jr., ed. The fabric of geology. Reading, Mass.: Addison-Wesley Pub. Co., Inc., pp. 24-48.

[8] See chapters 3, 5.

[9] See chapters 3-5.

[10] For some examples illustrating this, see: Behe MJ. 1996. Darwin's black box: the biochemical challenge to evolution. New York: Touchstone; Crick F. 1981. Life itself: its origin and nature. New York: Simon and Schuster; Denton M. 1985. Evolution: a theory in crisis. Bethesda, Md.: Alder and Alder; Ho M-W, Saunders P, eds. 1984. Beyond neo-Darwinism: an introduction to the new evolutionary paradigm. Orlando, Fla.: Academic Press; Løvtrup S. 1987. Darwinism: the refutation of a myth. London: Croom Helm; Ridley M. 1985. The problems of evolution. Oxford: Oxford University Press; Shapiro R. 1986. Origins: a skeptic's guide to the creation of life on earth. New York: Summit Books; Taylor GR. 1983. The great evolution mystery. New York: Harper and Rowe; Wells J. 2000. Icons of evolution: science or myth? Why much of what we teach about evolution is wrong. Washington, D.C.: Regnery Publishing, Inc.

[11] Smith H. 1976. Forgotten truth: the primordial tradition. New York: Harper Colophon Books, p. 132.

[12] Futuyma DJ. 1998. Evolutionary biology. 3rd ed. Sunderland, Mass.: Sinauer Associates, Inc., p. 28.

[13] Huxley, TH. 1871 (1893). Darwiniana: essays. New York: D. Appleton and Co., p. 149.

[14] See also first part of chapter 7 for earlier discussion.

[15] See chapters 3 and 7.

[16] See the discussion in chapter 5.

[17] Gould SJ. 1985 (1998). Mind and supermind. In: Leslie J, ed. Modern cosmology and philosophy. 2nd ed. Amherst, N.Y.: Prometheus Books, pp. 187-194.

[18] Huxley J. 1953. Evolution in action. New York: Mentor Books, p. 13.

[19] Dawkins R. 1986. The blind watchmaker: why the evidence of evolution reveals a universe without design. New York: W. W. Norton and Co., Inc., p. 1.

[20] Crick F. 1988. What mad pursuit: a personal view of scientific discovery. New York: Basic Books, Inc., Pub., p. 138.

[21] See chapters 2-5.

[22] See chapter 1.

[23] As quoted in: Larson EJ, Witham L. 1999. Scientists and religion in America. Scientific American 281(3): 88-93.

[24] Yockey HP. 1992. Information theory and molecular biology. Cambridge: Cambridge University Press, p. 288.

[25] Dawkins R. 2006. The God delusion. Boston: Houghton-Mifflin Co.

[26] There are a few rare exceptions. Of recent interest is: Meyer SC. 2004. The origin of biological information and the higher taxonomic categories. Proceedings of the Biological Society of Washington 117(2):213-239. This article, which advocates intelligent design, caused a furor since it appeared in a peer-reviewed scientific journal. Such reactions substantiate the current resistance of the scientific community toward the God concept.

[27] See chapter 1.

[28] Godfrey LR, ed. 1983. Scientists confront creationism. New York: W.W. Norton and Co.

[29] For discussion and evaluation, see: Roth AA. 1998. Origins: linking science and scripture. Hagerstown, Md.: Review and Herald Pub. Assn., pp. 339-354.

[30] See especially chapters 2-5.

[31] See chapter 1.

[32] For example: Midgley M. 1985. Evolution as a religion: strange hopes and stranger fears. London: Methuen and Co., Ltd.; Ruse M. 2003. Is evolution a secular religion? Science 299:1523, 1524.

[33] Quoted in 1987 in Palaios 2:445. Lakatos believes that in general, science progresses through time.

[34] The expression "just so stories" occasionally appears in the scientific literature to refer to fanciful concepts not considered to have good authentication. The expression comes from Rudyard Kipling's book *Just So Stories* for children. One account relates that the elephant developed its trunk because a crocodile pulled for a long time on the elephant's nose. See: Kipling R. 1907. Just so stories. Garden City, N.Y.: Doubleday, Doran, and Co., Inc.

[35] Green M, ed. 1969. Knowing and being: essays by Michael Polanyi. Chicago: University of Chicago Press, p. 41.

[36] See chapter 1.

[37] See chapter 1.

[38] Lord Acton (John Emerich Edward Dahlberg, First Baron Acton). 1887. As quoted in: Partington A, ed. 1992. The Oxford dictionary of quotations, 4th ed. Oxford: Oxford University Press, p. 1.

[39] See chapter 1.

[40] As quoted in: Gingerich O. 2004. Dare a scientist believe in design? Bulletin of the Boston Theological Institute No. 3.2:4, 5.

[41] Todd SC. 1999. A view from Kansas on that evolution debate. Nature 401:423.

[42] Rothman T. 1987. A "what you see is what you beget" theory. Discover 8(5):90-99.

[43] Russell B. 1929. Mysticism and logic. New York: W.W. Norton and Co., Inc., pp. 47, 48.

[44] As quoted in: Du Noüy L. 1947. Human destiny. New York: Longmans, Green, and Co., Inc., p. 43.

[45] Smith Forgotten truth, p. 1. [For publishing information see note 11, above.]

[46] Yockey HP. 1986. Materialist origin of life scenarios and creationism. Creation/Evolution 17:43-45.

[47] Collins FS, Weiss L, Hudson K. 2001. Heredity and humanity. The New Republic 224(26):27-29.

[48] I am speaking here of concerns far beyond the limited concern for your closest relatives, as suggested by the kin selection concept of sociobiology.

[49] See chapter 1.

GLOSSARY OF SPECIAL TERMS

Agnostic: One who believes that the answers to ultimate questions such as God's existence, the origin of the universe, etc., are unknown.

Amino acid: Simple organic molecule with a nitrogen-bearing amino group. Amino acids combine to form proteins. Living organisms have 20 different kinds of amino acids.

Anthropic cosmological principle: The concept that intelligent life can find itself only where conditions can accommodate it. Scientists have proposed several versions of the concept.

Atheist: One who believes that God does not exist.

Base (DNA, RNA): Also called nucleotide base. It is a ringlike molecule that contains nitrogen and serves as the main part of nucleotides. These bases form the units of the genetic code. The five different kinds found on DNA and RNA are: adenine, guanine, cytosine, uracil (only in RNA), and thymine. See nucleotide.

Big bang: The special explosive singularity that supposedly occurred at the beginning of the universe, changing it from a minute speck to an expanding cosmos.

Biochemical pathway: The series of sequential steps followed in a biochemical process as enzymes gradually change a molecule to produce a needed end product.

Cambrian: The lowest division (period) of the Phanerozoic portion of the geologic column. It is the lowest unit with abundant fossils.

Cambrian explosion: A term used to describe the fact that as one ascends through the geologic layers, suddenly the majority of the fossil animal phyla appear fully formed in the Cambrian. The term refers to what evolutionists consider to be an "explosive" phenomenon of rapid evolution.

Catastrophism: The theory that phenomena outside our present experience of nature (major catastrophes) have greatly modified earth's crust by violent, sudden, but short-lived event(s) more or less worldwide.

Chemical evolution: The chemical changes postulated to have taken place on the primitive earth that produced the first form of life.

Chromosome: The threadlike compressed form of DNA that forms during cell division.

Cladistics: Classification of a select group of organisms according to similarities, especially unique ones.

Cladogram: A branching diagram illustrating the similarities and differences within a group of organisms based on cladistics. Many scientists consider a cladogram to represent evolutionary changes.

Class (classification): See classification of organisms.

Classification of organisms: Biologists often use the following hierarchical system for classifying organisms. Each category below the first is a subdivision of the one above.

Kingdom

Phylum (animals) or Division (plants)

Class

Order

Family

Genus

Species

Climate of opinion: The prevailing opinion or viewpoint in a societal group.

Codon: A basic unit of the genetic code. Each codon consists of three nucleotide bases and codes for one kind of amino acid.

Complexity: The relationship of parts that are interconnected in some way with each other. In this book we use the term especially to designate parts that depend on each other in order to function properly.

Cone (eye): Light-sensitive cell (photoreceptor) of the retina of vertebrates that is sensitive to different colors of light. Cones enable the eye to detect color and provide acute vision in bright light.

Consciousness: The personal awareness we have that we exist.

Counterslab (paleontology): A slab of rock that was in contact with another slab that contains a fossil and that reflects the image of the fossil.

Creation: The term has many meanings. As used in this book, it refers to the specific act of God bringing something into existence, such as the universe, life, consciousness, etc. For some more specific uses, see recent creation; progressive creation.

Deism: Belief in some kind of God who may be impersonal and who is not presently active in nature.

Deist: One who believes in deism.

Design: The concept that something has been purposefully created or structured, in contrast to happening just by accident or by chance.

Disconformity: A significant gap in the sedimentary geologic layers in which the layers above and below the gap are parallel to each other and usually display no or only minor erosion of the underlayer.

DNA: Common abbreviation for deoxyribonucleic acid, which forms the long chain-like molecules that code the genetic information of an organism. DNA molecules can have millions of nucleotides attached to each other. See nucleotide.

Electron: Small subatomic particle found outside of the nucleus of atoms that carries a negative electrical charge.

Elitism: Consciousness or feeling of being the best or being superior to a larger group.

Enzyme: Protein molecules in living organisms that promote changes in other molecules without themselves being altered or destroyed.

Eugenics: The science of improving the human race, or breeds of animals, by controlling or eliminating the reproduction of individuals that have undesirable characteristics.

Evolution: Gradual development from simple to complex. The term generally designates the development of life from simple organisms to the most advanced ones; see macroevolution and microevolution. Scientists also use the term for the origin of life (see chemical evolution) and for the gradual development of the universe, etc. Commonly the term implies that no God is involved, but see theistic evolution.

Fact-free science: Scientific conclusions based on conjecture instead of facts or data.

Family (classification): See classification of organisms.

Free will: The power to act according to one's own choices.

Gene: The basic unit of heredity that controls a given characteristic. Also, the sequence of nucleotide bases on DNA that encodes for a protein, or the transcription of that information.

Genetic code: The 64 combinations of three nucleotide bases found on DNA (see codon) that determine which of the 20 amino acids found in living organisms will appear at a specific position on a protein molecule.

Genus (classification): See classification of organisms.

Geologic column: The vertical or chronological sequence of rock layers, usually represented in a column format, with the lowest and oldest layers at the bottom, going on up to the youngest at the top. The column can represent a local area or the general combined vertical sequence of all the earth's rock layers.

God: The Supreme Being who is Creator and Sustainer of the universe. People have many other understandings of God. Some think of Him as the laws of nature, or as nature itself. Others conceive of several different kinds of gods.

God question: As used in this book, this refers specifically to the question of whether or not God exists.

Historical science: The kind of science that is less objective and more difficult to test. It often involves past events that cannot be repeated, hence the "historical" qualifier. Historical science contrasts with experimental science, in which one can repeat a test.

Intelligent design: The concept that the universe exhibits objectively discernible design.

Interdependent parts: Parts of complex systems, such as those found in atoms or eyes, in which the subunits depend on each other in order to function properly. See irreducible complexity.

Invertebrates: Animals who do not have a backbone (vertebral column). Examples are: sponges, worms, starfish, jellyfish, snails, and squids.

Irreducible complexity: Complexity in which the various components are all necessary for proper function. See interdependent parts.

Isomer: One of two or more molecules that have the same kind and number of atoms, but the spatial arrangement of the atoms is different.

Kin selection: The proposition that by sacrificing one's own life to save the lives of several close kin, one is able to preserve one's own kind of genes because kin tend to have similar genes.

Kingdom (classification): See classification of organisms.

Macroevolution: The proposed large evolutionary changes in organisms assumed to have taken place between the higher classification levels, such as between families, orders, classes, phyla, etc. See microevolution.

Materialistic view: The philosophical view that matter is all that there is to reality. It is very similar to mechanistic view and naturalistic view.

Mechanistic view: The philosophical view that all of reality consists of matter and motion. There is no God. It is very similar to materialistic view and naturalistic view.

Messenger RNA: The RNA that transfers the information from the DNA in the nucleus of a cell to the ribosomes.

Microevolution: Minor inherited changes in organisms around the species level of classification. See macroevolution.

Middle Ages: A time of weak communication and coordination of intellectual activity in Europe in the centuries before the period of the revival of learning. The revival of learning, known as the Renaissance, took place in the fourteenth to sixteenth centuries. Modern science followed.

Modern science: The science of the past five centuries, characterized by objectivity, experimentation, and mathematics. More recently it has also displayed a naturalistic (materialistic) philosophy.

Mutation: A more or less permanent change in a cell's DNA formula. This includes changes of nucleotide bases, shifts in gene position, removal or duplication of genes, and transfer of foreign sequences into the cell.

Natural selection: The process whereby the fittest organisms survive over the less fit because of the competition between the organisms or adaptation to the environment. See survival of the fittest.

Naturalistic evolution: Evolution that excludes God in contrast to theistic evolution, which allows for a God where needed.

Naturalistic view: The philosophical view that allows for only natural phenomena, thus excluding the supernatural as part of reality. Recognizing no God, it is very similar to materialistic view and mechanistic view.

Nature versus nurture: An expression used to designate the conflict about whether nature (genes) or nurture (cultural environment) are more important in shaping indiviuals and society.

Neocatastrophism: A term used to designate the new kind of catastrophism, which suggests several major catastrophes during long geologic ages, in contrast to classical catastrophism, which considers the biblical Noachian flood to be a major event.

Neutron: One of the main subatomic particles found in the nucleus of atoms. Slightly larger than a proton, it has no electrical charge.

Nucleotide: A basic unit of the long DNA and RNA molecules. A nucleotide consists of a base, a phosphate, and a sugar molecule.

Nucleotide base: See base (DNA, RNA); nucleotide.

Optical isomers: Isomers that are mirror images of each other and that rotate light in opposite directions. See isomers.

Order (classification): See classification of organisms.

Organic soup: The postulated brothlike fluid on the early earth that contained various organic compounds that eventually produced the first life.

Paleontologist: One who specializes in the study of fossils.

Paraconformity: A significant gap in the sedimentary geologic layers in which the layers both above and below the gap are parallel to each other and the gap is represented by a dominantly flat contact or is not visible.

Paradigm: A generally accepted idea that for a time provides an area for investigation and suggests solutions to a community of practitioners.

Phanerozoic: That portion of the geologic column above the Precambrian. Its lowest major unit is the Cambrian. In contrast to the Precambrian, the Phanerozoic has abundant fossils of large organisms.

Photoreceptor: A part of a cell, a cell, or an organ that detects light. In the case of the vertebrate eye, the rods and cones are the cells that detect light.

Phylum (classification): See classification of organisms.

Precambrian: That portion of the geologic column below the Phanerozoic. It lies just below the Cambrian, the lowest major unit of the Phanerozoic. The Precambrian, in contrast to the Phanerozoic, has few fossils, and those present consist mostly of microscopic organisms.

Progressive creation: The idea that God created more and more advanced kinds of organisms during eons of time.

Protein: Large organic molecules composed of sometimes hundreds of amino acids. Living organisms harbor hundreds to many thousands of different kinds of proteins.

Proton: One of the main subatomic particles found in the nucleus of atoms. Slightly smaller than a neutron, it carries a positive electric charge.

Punctuated equilibrium: An evolutionary model that postulates that species usually exist for long periods of time without modification, but occasionally are "punctuated" with brief periods of rapid change.

Quantum theory: Also called quantum mechanics. The theory is especially significant at the atomic level and includes concepts that energy comes in discrete units and that some atomic and subatomic interactions are only statistically predictable.

Quarks: Proposed small subatomic particles that form larger subatomic particles, such as neutrons and protons.

Rational: The characteristic of being based on reason, being sensible and sane—i.e., not foolish or absurd.

Recent creation: The idea that God created life a few thousand years ago and rapidly in a six-day period, as indicated in the Bible.

Redshift: The shift of the spectral light lines from distant galaxies toward the red end of the light spectrum. Astronomers interpret it as indicating movement of the galaxy away from the point of observation.

Relativity: Theory in physics that recognizes the universal character of light and the relative relationship of space and time, etc., on the motion of the observer.

Religion: Belief in a superior personal being or beings entitled to obedience and worship. While many other definitions exist, the one given here is the usual understanding and the one employed in this book. Religion is also sometimes understood as something one is devoted to, such as principles of morality, or even a secular idea, such as science.

Renaissance: Historical period in Europe during the fifteenth and sixteenth centuries, when, following the Middle Ages, there occurred a revival in art and literature. The Reformation and modern science accompanied and followed it.

Resonance (quantum mechanics): Combination of factors (such as energy levels and targets) that favor a particular nuclear reaction.

Ribosome: Complex particles in cells composed of various proteins and RNA. They assemble amino acids into proteins according to the formula coming from the DNA.

RNA: Common abbreviation for ribonucleic acid. Long chain of nucleic acids similar to DNA, but containing ribose sugar and slightly different bases. See DNA, nucleotide, and base.

Rod: Elongated photoreceptor cell in the retina of vertebrates sensitive to dim light, but not to various colors of light. See cones.

Science: The study of facts and interpretations about nature. Some rule out the possibility of a God active in nature from the conclusions of science, but a thesis of this book is that such an exclusion is restrictive and can interfere with the discovery of truth about nature.

Secular: Something not concerned with religion or religious beliefs.

Sociobiology: Study of the evolution of social behavior in animals, including humans.

Species (classification): Similar organisms that actually or potentially interbreed. See classification of organisms.

Spontaneous generation: The concept that living forms arise from nonliving matter.

Subatomic particle: The subunit building blocks of atoms, such as electrons, protons, neutrons, quarks, etc.

Supernova: A star that suddenly blows up, exhibiting a great and temporary brilliance.

Survival of the fittest: The concept that those organisms that are superior or most adapted to their environment will survive over inferior ones during periods of stress or competition. See natural selection.

Theistic evolution: Evolution that includes God's activities, especially for helping with the more difficult problems, such as the origin of life and the Cambrian explosion.

Transfer RNA: Short sequence of RNA that attaches a specific kind of amino acid at the right place as the ribosomes assemble proteins.

Truth: That which actually is; reality; freedom from error. Sometimes people will use the term *ultimate reality* to describe absolute truth in contrast to what is personally believed or accepted as truth, but which may be in error. In this book, unless indicated otherwise, we use the term *truth* in the sense of ultimate reality.

Uniformitarianism: The concept that geologic processes in the past did not differ in rate or kind from what we now observe on the earth. Sometimes expressed as "the present is the key to the past." See catastrophism.

Vertebrates: Animals with a vertebral column or backbone. They include fish, amphibians, reptiles, birds, and mammals.

Willpower: The control of behavior based on deliberate purpose or rational thinking in contrast to impulsive behavior or behavior triggered by genetic or other agencies outside of a person's control.

INDEX

Science Confirms the Bible Record

ORIGIN BY DESIGN

In this revised edition Harold Coffin, Robert H. Brown, and L. James Gibson present new advances in plate tectonics, turbidity currents, and recent geological catastrophes, resulting in an impressive catalog of evidence for creation, a short chronology, and a titanic deluge that once reshaped our planet. Hardcover, 480 pages.

EVIDENCES FOR CREATION

George Javor explains how genes, germs, and galaxies all show the fingerprints of God. Delving deep into neurons, proteins, and bacteria, he dissects the cell to reveal the self-replicating, fully automated microscopic factories that maintain the endless cascade of life. Paper, 144 pages.

INCREDIBLE CREATURES THAT DEFY EVOLUTION
Volumes 1-3, DVD

Dr. Jobe Martin takes you to the fascinating world of animals to reveal sophisticated and complex designs that shake the traditional foundations of evolutionary theory. DVD. Volumes 1-3.

EVIDENCES I
The Record and the Flood

Award-winning presentation of the scientific evidence supporting the biblical account of the Flood. Uses beautiful on-location photography and animation. DVD, 45 minutes.

EVIDENCES II
The Tale of a Trilobite

Evidences II interprets the fossil record from the perspective of Creation, showing how the complexity and abundance of fossils suggest that th biblical story rests on a solid foundation. VHS, 40 minutes.

Educational, Spiritual, and Amazing Films

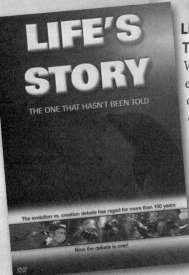

Life's Story DVD
The One That Hasn't Been Told

What does modern DNA research now prove? Simply that evolution is impossible. In a wildlife program unlike any other seen before, you will journey to discover the story of life itself and examine the long-held beliefs that have been the foundation of natural election for more than 150 years. One of the most visually stunning and informative wildlife productions available today. DVD, 56 minutes.

Life's Story 2 DVD
The Reason for the Journey

A factual and visual feast from beginning to end, this is a journey that unravels some of the most amazing mysteries of the world. See unusual, rare, and endangered species, and witness animal behavior never before caught on tape. DVD, running time approximately 100 minutes.